Also by Jack Dunphy

JOHN FURY
FRIENDS AND VAGUE LOVERS
NIGHTMOVERS
AN HONEST WOMAN
FIRST WINE

"Dear Genius..."

"*Dear Genius...*"

A Memoir of My Life with Truman Capote

Jack Dunphy

McGRAW-HILL BOOK COMPANY

New York   St. Louis   San Francisco   Auckland   Bogotá
Hamburg   London   Madrid   Mexico   Milan
Montreal   New Delhi   Panama   Paris   São Paulo   Singapore
Sydney   Tokyo   Toronto

1 2 3 4 5 6 7 8 9 D O H D O H 8 7

ISBN 0-07-018317-1

Library of Congress Cataloging-in-Publication Data

Dunphy, Jack.
    Dear genius.
    1. Capote, Truman, 1924–   —Biography.
2. Dunphy, Jack—Friends and associates.   3. Authors,
American—20th century—Biography.   I. Title.
PS3505.A59Z63   1987   813'.54 [B]   87-4121
ISBN 0-07-018317-1

As for me
I could leave the world
with today in my eyes.

A Christmas Memory

"Dear Genius..."

Something Steve Wick said the other day while interviewing me for Newsday *gave me heart. Steve said he saw me three books from now, say in about five years, writing about a priest. "And the priest," says Steve, "will be you." This gave me heart because I don't see myself writing anything. I would like to write about Truman and myself (myself as a priest?), and what Steve said began to stew in my head. The story would begin now. The sun, having ridden in glory, has already sunk out of sight, though it is not yet five o'clock. Grey-blue clouds streak a Halloween sky. Dead leaves twitch, each in its own way, like hanged men, from the stiff, sapless branches of trees. Cars race home in a hurry to beat the dark. Geese, their orderly processions broken by shots from the guns of hunters, fly from things now, instead of towards them, as they did when they first flew over Sagaponack in their ever-changing but ever-orderly V formations.*

Chapter 1

Father Synge, having decided to quit the priesthood, did not feel his decision would affect anyone very profoundly but himself. He was wrong. He was thirty years old and wanted to get away from the constant smell of men. He did not think he would be considering apostatizing himself had his father still been alive. His mother did not care. Religion meant nothing to her. Father Synge rather envied her in this. "Harry," she used to say to the father, "don't trouble yourself about the hereafter. This is *it.*"

Father Synge used to think his mother would follow them to church someday, but she never had. "That's your father's doing," she said when he told her he wanted to be a priest. Her opinion mattered. Even now he felt he might be trying to enter into dialogue with her in carrying out his intention to leave St. Roses.

First Avenue being what it is, a roaring river of multicolored metal, teeming motors, a reek of gas, screech of tires, bicycles, motorcycles, trucks, cars, skaters, joggers—Father Synge stilted himself mentally, and as nearly as he was able physically, as he crossed the intersections. He quite forgot what he had done to himself back in his room at the rectory. No longer did he feel he had cut himself off from the world and was bleeding. It was as if in fighting the traffic, he had expunged from memory the boy he had been, the boy who had walked over his mother's astonished face to study God.

Out of a saloon across from a high rise on Forty-ninth

Street there emerged a short, sturdy figure of a little man whose face was familiar to Father Synge, as it was to most of the other fairly numerous passersby. The celebrity, preoccupied with climbing down a single concrete step as if it was a descent from Mount Etna, did not at first take in Father Synge, who alone came to his assistance. "Need any help?" As he spoke the light of a photographer's flashbulb exploded in their faces.

Father Synge had often taken his evening walk on First Avenue but he had not before experienced being photographed in so public a way. What was far more startling to him than being photographed was that his decision to quit the priesthood, dismissed during his stroll, came back to him as the photographer's light flashed on and off, so that he felt inundated, changed, as if his decision had waited until now to make its full effect.

"Let's cross the street together."

The man's arm slipped under Father Synge's jacket and around his waist and clutched the belt of his pants.

"All right."

"You...shouldn't allow yourself to get into this condition," Father Synge found himself saying as they crossed Forty-ninth Street together. "You're lucky there's no traffic to speak of now. Usually it's a racetrack."

Father Synge tried to free himself from the man's embrace, but to no avail. So he supposed he was meant to see him home.

"Oh yes, the traffic's very bad. The drivers are very naughty."

Father Synge looked at him to see if he was kidding or not, but it was plain that he wasn't.

"Very naughty sometimes."

"I don't see how you got so drunk," Father Synge said to him.

"Oh! It was very easy."

Again Father Synge attempted to extricate himself. At the same time he squelched the disciplinarian rising in him: Say three Hail Marys and go home to bed. No, that was finito. He had been riding a hypothesis long enough, lashing out at poor devils in the guise of helping them, when all the time he was helping himself, giving himself a job, a raison d'être. *Oh my God I am heartily sorry....*But all that was over, too. Still he went on...*for having offended thee.* No, it is you who have offended me by not giving me a sign of your existence. What's wrong with me asking that? Blaise Pascal did as much.

The little man struggling to walk straight beside him seemed to have metamorphosed into a child.

"Don't worry, Father. Remember, tomorrow's another day. I suppose you don't know who said that? Scarlett O'Hara said that in *Gone with the Wind.*"

People came from the apartment house—a palace of a place—to help him after he let go of Father Synge. A wheeled chair was brought out and the man fell into it, protesting: "What's this all about, for God's sake?"

But the next morning their pictures were in the paper together and there was hell to pay at the rectory.

"John, what in the name of Christ were you doing barhopping with a guy like that?"

"A guy like what?"

"Why, a guy like that, John. You know. Gay. Besides..."

"Besides what?"

"Well, he says so himself that he's nearly everything odd. Go work in a shelter if you want to lift people up. Dorothy Day's dead. The Second Ecumenical Council is held in low repute by the powers that be. The winds of change have very definitely stopped blowing. So settle down. Enroll yourself in a course somewhere. Notre Dame's taking all sorts of dopes. The best way you can be your brother's keeper is to work within the confines of a parish like ours. And don't laugh."

"I was helping him across the street."

"John, you were pictured coming out of the Rajah's Bar together!"

At lunch five priests assembled. They were the pastor, Father Colfaxen, who already had spoken to Father Synge, then Father Devine and Father Schenck, two very old priests who were dying on their feet, the youngest, Father Benito Scarpia, who at twenty-five looked as if he was never meant to die—like a cactus plant, except that he was very dark and juicy, always in a sweat—and lastly, Father Synge himself.

"Ooh la la!" Father Scarpia murmured to his own obvious delight as Father Synge entered the dining room.

Father Colfaxen rubbed his hairy red hands together as if he next meant to spit into them before taking up a pick.

"Now let's not make a ballgame of this thing, Benito," he said to the younger priest, "else I'll send you to Rome to that infamous cellar in the Piazza Navona where your namesake sent better men than us to die."

"Ooh la la!" was Father Scarpia's pop-eyed response to that harangue.

Fathers Devine and Schenck handled their food as if they were meant to build things with it and did not seem to hear any of this badinage.

The food was awful and the cook came into the dining room with a belligerent air to see that they ate all of it.

"Is everything all right?" she hollered. "Father Devine, I'm speaking to you. Father Schenck, is everything all right?"

"I wonder at you, Mrs. Wallop," was Father Devine's reply.

"I do too, Mrs. Wallop," adjoined Father Schenck, and the two old priests returned their attention to their plates.

"Father Scarpia!" the contentious cook yelled, "you've done good by yourself as usual."

"I have, Mrs. Wallop?"

"Sure you have!" And with that Mrs. Wallop left them alone, but not before crying out over her shoulder in her contrary way that Father Synge's mother was on the telephone.

"On the phone?" Both old priests came to at that. "On the phone?" they asked one another. "Why, for how long, for heaven's sake, has his poor mother been on the phone?"

"John," Mrs. Synge cried out over the telephone to her only son, "I'll bet that old bitch of a housekeeper only just told you I was on the line. Did she? Sure she did. What's wrong with her, anyway? Well, I know what's wrong with her. She's

man-hungry. Priests should be old. To have a woman like
that around young men like you and that wild Scarpia is
just putting her too much to the test. A test she has failed,
by the way. Her dreams must be terrible. John, I wouldn't
have your life if you paid me. I put on a good face and say
how proud of you I am, but I'm not. Nobody has to go to
Harvard to become a priest. Look at Colfaxen. Colfaxen's
straight out of Hell's Kitchen. John, you're going to do something someday disgraceful enough for them to put you out.
That I could not live with. Get out while the going's good,
John. What's this I see in the paper about you bar-hopping
on First Avenue? *John, come see me.*"

"I want to."

"Well, get over here!"

Father Synge's mother lived in Brooklyn in stuffy Brooklyn
Heights. She was delighted by the whole thing, his picture
in the paper, everything. But she had no idea of what was
on his mind, what he felt he had come to Brooklyn to talk to
her about: quitting.

She heaved about in her brown leather chair by the window looking out on Willow Street, belching and passing wind
as was her way since as long as Father Synge could remember.

"I was ever so proud. I could have dropped, of course, but
I didn't let on about that to anybody but myself. You aroused
envy in the old and curiosity about you in the young. It's
about time, don't you think? Don't you think your bright-
ness and good looks began to pay off? I do. I think it's about
time you came out of the woodwork."

A devotee of the gossip columns was Nora Synge, and
there was nothing else on the inflammatory side of the news
that she did not devour. TV football for its bodies, broadcast
news for disaster, soap operas for their endlessly whining
dialogue and gobbledegook sexuality.

"Cavorting while converting is nothing new. Priests in
high places are as old as the church. What do they say about
the picture at the rectory?"

"Oh! Why, everything."

"Too bad about them. Seeing him again?"

"I hadn't thought."

She stirred, but it was at nothing he had said. There was a fire out on the street, on Willow Street, and Father Synge feared people were about to burn up in it while he sat there doing nothing. A pity, since he felt he was meant to do so much. He had not before experienced so forceful a sense of urgency. He stood up. He tried opening a window.

"Sit down, John. You don't have to worry, they don't leave anything burn down in this part of Brooklyn. You're as your father was before you, concerned over the plight of others. Well, he was alone here, a loner on Willow Street in Brooklyn Heights. Look for yourself. Go out, John, go out. You'll be the only one beside the firemen. We don't mix, we don't meddle, we're well off and mean to stay that way, on Willow Street."

It was true. She was always right. There was not a soul out on the street but himself. The firemen stared at him from little windows in their engine. False alarm? He would not have dared ask. Then he remembered he was still a priest, at least in appearance, and could get away with things like that, expect a response in most cases if not all, especially in New York.

"False alarm?"

"Yes, Father. But we're used to them. Good night, Father."

There was something holy in that response, in that adieu there was a blessing. Like a boy, the fireman has said *"we're used to them."* Amongst other things, they were used to floors sagging beneath them, to the smell of burning flesh (their own sometimes). They were used to children thrown at them through smoke, to saints pushing others first while their own legs burned away under them. Forced as they were to a heroism that often betrayed them to death, a necessary camaraderie developed between them, so human, so male. How could he tell them (as of course he should have done), those bearded, baby faces, that he was no longer a priest, thus taking one more thing away from some of them, a last underpinning of an already scarred and battered faith that might help them someday, voodoo them up out of a burning building, be the difference between being a cripple and going on to fight more fires, present themselves at more false alarms?

Chapter 2

"John, will you please tell me why you're ass-dragging around here ever since your picture was in the paper?"

Father Synge had always liked his superior's office. Bookshelves were all around, but as they were only waist-high, they weren't overpowering. The walls were covered by a red burgundy-colored material that Father Synge fancied was damask. It was a strawberry-colored room and Father Colfaxen was a strawberry-colored man, with a big red-haired chest and chapped-looking red hands. People who did not know him felt he was a bishop, but people who did knew he'd never be one. He was too kind and considerate, too thoughtful of others, and more ambitious for them by far than he had ever been for himself, though he denied this vehemently. He was too too. Too careless of his clothes, too careful of his books. He was often too late for appointments but never (as far as he was concerned) too long at the Met Museum. And he cursed too much for a priest. He never could get over his early days and didn't seem to want to.

"Don't look at me as if you don't understand me, John. Don't join the army of hypocrites who can't see the man for his office and prefer not to. Is it sex, John? Is it your faith? Is it crisis number three hundred and eighty-five you're going through? Or is it crisis number four hundred? You're too young to have reached the five hundreds, John. The devil's at everybody's elbow, not only yours. Come, my boy. Spill it. Digame, Juanito."

Accessibility being a synonym for priestliness to him, Father Colfaxen did not budge when his study door altogether opened, since it was never altogether closed, and a pretty, dark girl appeared and talked rapidly to him in Spanish. He gave her all his attention without seeming to have forgotten Father Synge once.

"I cannot marry my boy, Padre, as you say I must. He won't have me—not yet, anyway. He says he will send for me when he gets a job."

"Good, good."

"You don't believe he will send for me."

"I'm not sure."

"I am because I love him."

"I don't want you to be left with his child."

"Our child, Padre."

"Marry. Marry, marry, marry. Then we'll see."

"You do not talk with us but at us, Father Colfaxen."

"True."

"Yes, and you are worse than any of the rest because you agree with everything one says, Father Colfaxen," the determined girl said.

"Get him to marry you. Promise, Maria."

"If you do not see me again, you'll know that I have left you and your church forever."

Maria went out. The priests were alone together, everything between them as unresolved as ever.

"Why should she see me again? I'm no answer. I just want to make life easier for her, knowing that I can't. Let's go to the Met, John. Let's sneak out the back door over Mrs. Wallop's big feet and go stare at something humbling. Let's look at Pisarro's Paris, the Seine. Why, I bet you haven't even read him."

"Who?"

"The guy you went out with the other night, John. Is that what's the matter with you? Sulking because people are making game of you? No, it's more than that. I can see it is."

Chapter 3

"Now, Mary, I want you to seize this," one old woman said to another that day at the Metropolitan Museum of Art. "Two priests studying a nude."

"It's not a nude, it's the Blessed Mother."

"Don't tell me the Blessed Mother had thick lips and a dark skin, Mary."

"Gauguin," said Father Colfaxen, "interests me more than any other painter of recent times. Why, John? Why do you think that is? It's probably the medievalist in me wanting to bring him to heel for leaving his wife and kids behind and tearing off to paint in Tahiti. Suppose he had conformed, John? He would have been good. Oh yes, but he would not have been Gauguin. How's the writing, John?"

"Writing, Father? Oh! You mean *my* writing. I'm conforming."

"There's a lot to be said for conforming, John. Why? Doesn't it agree with you?"

"Not really. Well, maybe it does. After all, when have I ever done anything else but conform?"

"It doesn't seem to be exactly your nature to conform, John. But go on."

"Go on about what? To telling you that I think religion's bunk?"

Father Colfaxen stepped forward to get a closer look at Pisarro, his favorite painter of Paris, his favorite city, and of the Seine, his favorite river.

"Well, John," he said, turning an ironical gaze on his young, unhappy friend, "that's some conforming you're doing. Congratulations."

"Congratulations, my eye! I wish you meant it. I really do. I wish you were somebody other than who you are. Or, at least, someone willing to show me more of what you are."

"You're not leaving us, John. You're going into the thing deeper."

"I know I am. I mean I feel I am, hope I am...now."

"I hope you see your way to work within the framework already set up for you, John. That leaves out Tahiti, that means staying home and conforming. Everything Gauguin should have done, but didn't. Instead he became Gauguin."

Father Synge followed his superior out into Fifth Avenue. He did not feel he had seen much of the works of art displayed inside, or rather he felt he had taken little in. Two old ladies trailing them from picture to picture, from Monet to Manet, had interested him most—almost to the point where he felt he was unconsciously performing for them, avoiding looking at what they would have him avoid or else doing just the opposite, which was still more or less as they would have it, in a contrary sort of way—but of this he said nothing to his superior.

Fifth Avenue was a blaze of colors, the wind was up, and the flags flying. People sat drinking beneath the red, white, and blue awning of the Stanhope Hotel across the street, but in the hotel itself lights had been turned on. The Met's steps were crowded with young people. In front of them, down on the pavement, an army of food vendors hastened to satisfy the hungry and thirsty. A performer in white greasepaint packed his trappings, his real face working thoughtfully behind his red sickle smile. The day was done, thought Father Colfaxen. Night was falling. He inhaled the air of his native city and thought of all the lives he might have lived as he took in those around him, most of them young. Young and serious. The best of their kind. Of course he had missed a lot. Of course he had.

"Of course I did," he said.

"Did what, Father?" a smiling Father Synge wanted to know, caught in the breeze as all the young on the steps seemed to be to Father Colfaxen, caught up and riding in the evening breeze over the scraping of dead leaves from the park.

A blaze, not a breeze, and of envy, not of hope, swept through the elder, more powerfully built man. I'll be dead before he ever makes up his mind what he means to do with himself, Father Colfaxen thought, looking away from the younger priest, whose years, he felt, could not have weighed on him, since they did not amount to anything anyway; nor his troubles either, for that matter, since they were as nothing as well.

"What's on your mind, John?" he asked, trying desperately not to sound belligerent and almost succeeding, though it was all one to John Synge, he could see, so that he himself felt left out of things, divorced utterly from the young people on the steps. Then he remembered Maria and her baby—"our child, Padre"—and he felt wanted again.

"What do you think those two old women who were following us about inside wanted, John? Do you think they are somewhere still watching us? I don't dare look."

Father Synge stared about him with interest. It was not often he got the chance to play open spectator in a crowd. Here, he felt no one would pester them. No priest-flies. The crowd began to move as he observed it, some couples hugging as they descended the steps. It was the breaking up of a lovely congregation, Father Synge felt. None here nurtured sore prejudices yet. It was in essence biological, really. They were nice because they wanted one another. Growths of hate, of hurts, of festering ambitions, of hopes unfulfilled, of money lost or never got, worries over a place to live, over prides to keep up—such had yet to be visited on these young people. Not all were happy. Here and there one could see early signs of toppled illusions, flamboyancy, flagrancy, a disposition to unbutton before uncaring eyes.

Father Colfaxen would never have sat down on the steps if he had thought they meant to quarrel.

"Sit down, John. Take a load off your feet."

Father Synge did so, but it seemed to make him more restless than ever.

"John," said Father Colfaxen, "you remind me of Jacob wrestling all night with the angel in Delacroix's painting in the church of St. Sulpice in Paris."

"Yes, I've seen it in reproduction in one of Kenneth Clark's books. I like the way Jacob continues on his journey at the back of the picture, into the rising sun and the dust of the road, refreshed and vigorous after their fight."

"You must go see it, John."

"What, and leave my charge?"

"Your 'charge,' John? You mean the guy you picked up the other night? Of the two of you, who is the angel? In any case, it's a losing battle, John. He'll only drag you down with him. Go to Paris. Go somewhere. No, go to Paris. You know how I went?"

"No, tell me, Father."

"My poor father, a ditch digger amongst other things, left me the money. John, go borrow the money from your mother and go to Paris."

"You can't get rid of me. You're afraid for me. Don't be, Father, because I have no fear for myself."

Father Colfaxen's great red face became redder.

"Don't be a fool, John. Never relinquish the sense of things to be feared. That is not being afraid, not exactly, anyway, if at all. The wickedness of the world is all around us and in us, John, in us because we are of the world and worldly. Vigilance is not cowardice, John. It is a sense of the enemy. An enemy not necessarily lying in ambush for us, either, John, as the saying goes, but sometimes something we cuddle as it eats us alive. Remember Jacob and continue on your journey, John. Don't stop in the middle of it because of a chance meeting with a guy on First Avenue."

"I don't think it was chance. I think it was fate, or what have you. I think I can help him."

"Oh, Jesus."

"I think he can help me, then."

"He can by you fleeing him, running away from him. Leave him to his friend. They're reputed to be close."

"Yes, but they're not. I can tell they're not."

"John, stay out of the stews. You know nothing about life. You have nothing of your mother in you. You're all your father, God rest him, from head to foot, as innocent, as gullible. Don't try to act worldly and come between two characters speeding on their way to perdition."

"You're better than to say such things as that."

"I'm not. Flattery will get you nowhere. I'm a Ninth Avenue fellow still in my heart, as my ditch digger father was, and I believe heart and soul in all of it, up and down the line. In my own way I'm as hard-headed and rigid as those filthy sonsabitchin' Fundamentalist bastards. I believe the world was made in three days too."

"You don't. You can't. Father, you hurt me when you say such things as that. You don't mean it, of course. You're angry. I don't see why. I'm only trying to help him, Father Colfaxen."

Chapter 4

When I first saw them together, I was grateful as usual that someone had seen Truman home. I had no idea that I was dealing with a priest, since Father Synge was in mufti, and said nothing. He was one of an army who had helped Truman home in the years since we had moved into the building on Forty-ninth Street where we occupied an apartment on the twenty-second floor, and I thought no more of him for awhile than I did of all the other self-appointed Good Samaritans. They were nearly always women, lumpy-shaped good-doers, whereas Father Synge was a man and good looking. A young man. My voice was cold when I thanked him.

I tried to act patrician and as though I had been to some swell school. I wanted desperately to appear to be able to handle this sort of thing. Even if I had not overdone it, which of course I did, it would still have been fake. It was all done to make us appear to be all right, really. We were, too. Now that we were together, and home, it did not matter what Truman had taken, or said, or done. Whatever it was, it was past.

"Jack...!" He had a way of calling me when we met after a parting no matter how short, that called up the past. It was as though Truman never got over me. "Jack...!"

It brought something back to me the night I took him away from Father Synge, though what it was I did not know until later in bed beside him, hoping he would not wake up and reach for a pill...

SICILY

...a little town near Taormina up off the beautiful road to
Catania. Orange trees, lemon trees, but mostly orange trees.
Blood oranges. It is night and I'm standing alongside the
bandstand. The musicians are playing things from operas
of Bellini, Donizetti, Verdi in a charming thump-thump sort
of way. Truman is looking down on all of us in the square
from a balcony of one of the surrounding houses. There
are colored electric lights strung across the square, some
of the bulbs half-hidden by tree leaves. People are eating
gelati, dining al fresco. Sunburned farmers in gleaming
white shirts stroll around with their brown hands buried in
their pockets. The instruments of the musicians shine, some
silver, some gold. Truman calls to me to come join him.
"Jack...! Jack...!" He still has the same way of calling to
me, as if I'm still new to him, as if he has yet to get over me.
I love him.

Chapter 5

Father Colfaxen stood at his study window and looked out
on an alley. He looked up for sky, there was no sky to be
seen except for a speck, a tiny, sooty speck marked by snow
drops. The story of my life, Colfaxen remarked. The white
against the black. Religion has been that to me. The gleam
in the dark. The leap at the end of the road. And I'm willing
to swallow all the rest of it, all the bunk, for that little light
that has lit my life.

Father Colfaxen turned back to the empty room, yet he
did not feel he was alone, his doors being unlocked and
never closed all the way.

A slim male form stood still against the red wall. "Padre?"

"Yes, Juan. Now what? I thought Maria had told me you
were off to look for a job."

"You don't trust me, Father."

"I'm worried, Juan. You worry me. Maria is already pregnant."

"It will be easier to get a job if I say I am single."

"It won't be, but no matter. When are you leaving her?"

"The way you put it, Padre."

"How else should I 'put it'?"

"Padre, I can't see my way clear because of you. I can do nothing if I do not see my way clear. I will be defeated before I even start out."

"Then why go?"

"We must eat, Maria and me. Then the little one. I feel cursed by the little one, Padre. I did not want it."

"Then go, Juan. Go. You'll get something."

"I can't, Padre. You have made it so I can't. I must marry Maria first, I guess. Then take her with me."

Father Colfaxen, who had been so sure of this, did not feel at all sure now. He felt no sense of victory, only of defeat, really. He felt the boy had given in to him, not because he was Stephan Colfaxen who had made his way in the world, but because he represented establishment to the Mexican—here in the country by the skin of his teeth.

However that may have been, Juan appeared to be all the better for his decision. "Maria is here. All set, Padre," he said, grinning a flash of white teeth. "Do it now, the ceremony. OK?"

"OK," said Father Colfaxen, and he married them.

"Leave the door open as you go out," he said, by way of good-bye to them, after the ceremony.

After the marriage of Juan and Maria, Father Colfaxen called Ann Bushnell, now Sister Secret. "Well, Ann, I've married my Mexicans and got rid of them."

"You haven't," was Sister Secret's testy reply. "You only think you have."

"I've pushed them into it, then. Better marriage than burning, you know."

"Not today, it's not always better, if it ever was, and I have my doubts about that. You've mishandled the whole thing. I wonder why. It could only be because the girl got pregnant."

"That's right. You hit it as usual, Ann. The girl was pregnant and the boy was going to Mexico to an uncle in Tasco who would give him a job."

"I never heard of a Mexican going back for work."

"He has an uncle who owns a little hotel in Tasco who will give him a job. A job, not two. In other words, the uncle doesn't want Maria—especially not Maria with a baby on the way."

"They'll be back. Then what?"

"Ann, sometimes I don't believe you pray."

"I haven't got time to go into that now, Stephan. We had a fire up the street and the place is jumping. God knows where I'll sleep tonight."

After talking to Sister Secret, Father Colfaxen felt he'd done wrong in pushing Juan and Maria together. He dreaded ever seeing them again. He was glad Father Scarpia was sick so that he could take five-thirty mass for him. He was so wrapped up in his thoughts that he forgot where he was, and found himself acting for all the world as though he was down in his old parish on Forty-fourth Street where the diocese had sent him as a young man because "you'll know how to take care of the Micks, Stephan." Then he felt he knew everybody, and that everybody knew him. "Mick" parishes in New York City were depleted these days. They had gone, but the world had come in. Father Colfaxen remembered where he was when he saw an Indian woman enter the church and kneel with what to him used to be astonishing reverence, though he was used to it now, somewhat. Every once in awhile there was a black. Unheard of in the old days.

A familiar face joined the scarce congregation. It was amazing how young John Synge could be without his collar and black clothes. John did not have it in him to handle such a case as that article in the building down on Forty-ninth Street, nor his friend either. If anything, the friend sounded worse than the troubled celebrity. Most alarming, John had told Father Colfaxen himself that he had picked the guy up on First Avenue the very night he had chosen to quit the priesthood, throw in his love, put on bright clothes, and cease to mourn Jesus Christ.

Chapter 6

Almost from the first Father Synge gave me the impression that he suspected I was hiding Truman from him. I had enough to do keeping my head up without being accused of kidnapping.

Father Synge had all the things that might have made me feel cheap and upstart alongside him. Schooling, good clothes, an easy past life, and his mother's money to spend should he see fit to do so.

Salvationists surrounded Truman like Indians dancing around a man tied to a stake.

My pride in us made me wary of anyone offering to salvage him from a fate that I found it hard to admit even to myself that he had fallen into. He could always straighten himself out. I'd had hints, suggestions, signs from him through the years that kept me from ever being astonished by anything Truman did, had done, or was likely to do. He was nothing if not resilient.

Everything in our life together supported me in my belief that no matter how tough the going got, we two would see it through together. When we used to drive into New York from Sagaponack and had reached the summit of the bridge leading to the Midtown Tunnel, Truman would shout, *"Thar she blows!"* to the spires of Manhattan to which he had aspired from the sticks of Alabama. It was like a war cry, a cry of certain victory.

Lots of times our pride in one another made us close our eyes to particular actions and never to mention them to each other, or to anybody else ever. But that did not mean we forgot them. What we hoped was that one or the other would overcome the shame, bad luck, dumb choice—whatever it was. Of course these actions could be funny, but not so funny that we wanted them repeated, either as anecdotes or as things likely to happen again.

As, for example, the time at a bullfight in Barcelona when Truman jumped into the seats behind us because he was sure the bull was about to leap the barrier and trample him.

I didn't mind. I could not have cared less. I loathed bull-fights from that moment on—the filthy deviling of a hand-some creature whose bravery is answered by butchery. Better for Truman to run away from the bloody show for good and all than come back and resume his seat as if nothing out of the way had happened in the first place. But he did not run away. He came back and suffered. He probably sat trembling. I don't know. Certainly he said nothing about how he felt about bullfights. It wouldn't have suited his image of himself to state they were cruel, that it was a dirty boy's game. He couldn't have seen its beauty, he was much too scared of it to see that. Or its tragedy, the dying bull standing, bleeding to death, breathing but otherwise still, breathing his noble last but refusing to fall. Truman didn't see that because, basically, it all was a bore to him.

He saw other bullfights. Sure he did. He saw them because he felt it was expected of him—something else grown-ups did that he did not understand, not really, any more than he ever got to understand the grown-up world, its houses, its boring dinner parties, except to admire and try to emulate it, before he saw its people were no better, and perhaps in some cases worse, than Perry and Dick, the multiple murderers he wrote about in his book *In Cold Blood.*

Chapter 7

"You would have thought with having written a book like *In Cold Blood* he would have been aware of the pitfalls of overindulgence."

"His friend tells me that even in their halcyon days together Truman knew, though he might not actually have had, a doctor in nearly every foreign town they lived in."

"'Halcyon days,' John? I must say your conversation grows more esoteric each day. I haven't heard that word since I last read...why, *Antony and Cleopatra.*"

"So you read *Antony and Cleopatra,* do you, Father?"

"Yes, and I'd go see it if only the Shakespeare Company did it. They're doing worse and worse things. Not at all like when they did *Nicholas Nickleby.*"

"So you saw *Nicholas Nickleby,* did you?"

"Yes, I did. I...wore a turtleneck sweater. They still spotted me. Catholics, I mean, John. There's no escaping them."

"Not even at *Nicholas Nickleby?*"

"Yes, I was surprised too. But there they were. Greatly outnumbered by the other persuasion."

"I don't like you running around. I want you to stay the old-fashioned parish priest."

"I am the old-fashioned parish priest, John. I'll never say die, nor will my parishioners let me. Look at this. A letter from Juan and Maria, saying they don't want the baby, that the very thought of it has caused dissension between them, and that they will be better off by themselves. Besides, the uncle can't afford Maria. She's coming back to fight it all out with me. I'll tell you one thing, John. I'd sooner die than agree to an abortion, all kidding aside."

"Not even if they don't want the child?"

"Don't get me riled, John. Answer the phone. I'm out for the day. You know where to find me."

"The Met?"

"Did I say that? Phone, John."

The pastor of St. Roses left his office and Father Synge answered his telephone for him.

"I knew he wouldn't be there. The coward. Off to the Met, the old devil. Just because I put him in a quandary about what I'm to do with two fighting couples I've put up here from a tenement fire. John, be a love and get your mother to take them in."

"My mother, Sister? Are you mad?"

"Hopeful, John. Try her, anyway. I saw your picture in the *News.* Don't tell me the boy's gone wild. Have you, John? Whatever you do, don't drink except to excess. The only way to do anything. Call your mother."

"I never heard of such a thing," was Mrs. Synge's response to Sister Secret's plea. "You just let me talk to that so-called Sister Secret. Ann Bushnell's what she is, and always will be. If she's a sister, then so am I. Sisters of wickedness the two of us used to be until she got the calling. What's she mean, take in victims? I'm the victim and Ann Bushnell is my persecutor and always was. My mailbox is never clear of her begging. I hope she remembers Matt Malloy with his arms around her like they were glued? Well, I do. It would all have been different had Matt looked at me. But he didn't.

"Mother..."

There was a pause. She was a terrible bore, but she could surprise you. "Mother? What about it?"

"And you're as bad, with your goodikins act when all the time you want to pull out as I want you to. It's bad for your health. You're not like your father. Not at all like. You're more me. How about that guy in the paper? I hope there's no funny stuff going on between you. You know his rep. At least I do. Hey, in a way, I'm all for him. There's the sweetest man in the world in that man there. But John, don't run off with him."

"How about the people, Mother?"

Another pause.

"All right, John. Just for the devilment of it. Besides, it just breaks my heart sometimes..."

"What, Mother? What breaks your heart?"

"The mess people get themselves into, if you must know, John, from their own doing. Look at yourself."

Father Scarpia came into the office. Father Synge put down the phone softly, hoping that he didn't look pale and haggard. At least not haggard. It was nice to be good looking. Father Scarpia was ugly as sin and equally boring. "What's the matter, John? You look awful."

"I do? Haggard?"

"Like you won the lottery. You know, crazy."

"Oh well, just so long as I don't look haggard."

"John, Father Colfaxen's failing. I want to talk to you about him. All sorts of things. He just sent two kids off to Mexico. Mexico, John. For work. Everybody comes here for work from Mexico, John. Even you know that."

"Why do even *I* know it?"

"Well, even if you were born with a silver spoon in your mouth, you know it, you're aware of it, John. The economics. Or are you? John, let's get a petition up to have Colfaxen certified. He's off the wall, John. Sweet and all, but wall material."

"Benito, sometimes I think you're as bad as your name, Benito Scarpia."

"My father was a terrible Fascist, John. You know that. Look at your own mother's politics."

"Yeah, terrible."

"And my mother loved opera. What did she care that Scarpia was a villain's name? She loved all the characters. And my father."

"Benito's a nice name, really; it's not its fault that it was Mussolini's."

"John, can I tell you something?"

"Sure, but..."

"But what, John? Can I or not? Have you a minute or not? You're the busiest unbusy person I know, John. You know what else?"

"What?"

"I envy you. I envy you your vocation, the way you believe in God, the Father, the Assumption, Pentecost, the Real Presence. I could go on, John."

"Spare yourself."

"John, I don't have a vocation."

"You do."

"I don't, John. Not like you. You never think of genitals. You might be gay, for all I know."

"Gay, and not think of male genitals? I don't get it."

"John, women are definitely not your problem."

"No, I'm gay, I guess."

"Well, you know, lots were, and are, and will be, John. Did you ever think of that? Did you ever think that funny things cross all our minds, even a perfectly straight male like myself, John?"

"I'm sure. Like what?"

"Like...I don't know. Deep, John. I don't think I'd ever run off with a nun now. First of all, they're so homely. But you never know, do you? That's why I'd like to be really busy. Colfaxen's all right, but he has no idea of business, of administration. And that's what it's all about, really. You can bet your ass they're not reading Thomas à Kempis down at Fiftieth Street and Madison Avenue right at this minute, John. No, nor did with Spellman, or especially not with Spellman."

"When...did they, you think?"

"Read à Kempis? Gee, John, how would I know? The only reason I bring him up at all is there's his book on Colfaxen's desk.

"Wherefore, O Lord God, I even esteem it a great mercy, not to have much of that which outwardly and in the opinion of men seems worthy of glory and applause."

À Kempis's words seemed to Father Synge the very heart of his pastor, the secret heart, not one Father Colfaxen was likely to brazenly set forth before the world.

Chapter 8

It was November. I went up First Avenue to St. Roses and confessed for the first time in years. What brought this about, as far as I know, was a general feeling of diminishment. I felt things were being taken from me, and I felt I was losing myself in the process. Of course it was all very slow and not nearly so fast as I'm telling it. I had been going to church on and off for years, beginning in Switzerland in the sixties, in the mountains, where we had, and I still have, a little three-room apartment in a chalet, and where I heard the news of the death of my wife, Peach. Then our dogs died, two of them; one, Kelly, we'd had for years. So we were both pretty sad, though there wasn't much you could say about it. Truman took trips down the mountain to Italy to see his friends the Agnellis, and I was left with the Alps and my memories.

The church was down in the village, bound together by faith and wood—no nails. God does not seem so remote in the heights as down in the plain. It was years since I had been to mass and seen people taking communion, so I was a little in awe of them.

November seems to be my time for decision. I met Truman in November. I quit drinking in November, but that was after the time I'm talking about now, the November I resolved to go up to St. Roses. The priest who answered the rectory door to me was Father Synge, the last bird I wanted to talk to, to say nothing of confessing to him. Maybe he felt the same way about me, because he told me to come back in an hour. I don't think he thought I ever would. When I did he was in the church across the street expecting to hear I'd committed murder at least. It was soon apparent that he wasn't thinking of anything I said, but of Truman, and could not wait to finish with me and get on to that subject.

"I'm not the best thing for him, you know, Father."

"You're not? Then…"

"Why don't I get out? I'd never do that."

"Do you drink, yourself?"

"Yes I do."

"What do other people think about his excessive drinking?"

"They don't know what to make of it. They hide their liquor. He's losing friends because of it."

"And making new ones—like me."

I considered that a pretty grabby thing to say, but I was used to people claiming they were friends of Truman's as soon as they met him.

"What are you thinking?"

"Of how you can't talk to a priest."

"Well, that's your upbringing. Things have changed. Priests are different today."

I did not think so. Power is so poisonous, even the power of a mother over a child. People in power rot before your eyes. They love having a say over you. Father Synge was to tell me why he was making so much of Truman. It only proved to me how right I was in suspecting him of opportunism. He told me he had been on the verge of leaving the church the night he helped Truman home from Rajah's Bar.

"Suddenly I was being given a reason for staying, a reason that I unhesitatingly accepted, though I didn't quite realize I had at the time."

"Don't tell me you're putting all this weight on Truman?"

"Oh, he won't mind. A man in his position expects people to want something from him."

So I was right about him. I knew it. Truman would know it. He always knew when people were depending on him to give them something that they could only give themselves, provided they had anything in the first place, which was rare enough. Besides, my knees were killing me. "If you will excuse me, Father..." He let me go, but reluctantly. I don't think I will ever go into the box again.

Chapter 9

When Truman put himself into Roosevelt Hospital under an assumed name, we were both happy and hopeful about it, and when a young doctor came in and asked Truman was he Owen Wister, author of *The Virginian,* all three of us laughed. But as hospitals are a particular bête noire of mine, I was anxious to leave and soon did.

Outside on Ninth Avenue I found a taxi waiting for me as if by command. I did not give our address, but that of a liquor store nearby where we lived. In the store, rough-dealing as all such places are, I found myself talking to such an extent to the proprietress that I soon suspected she was anxious to get rid of me.

I showered when I got home and put on a long white bathrobe, not mine but it felt good and matched my sense of well-being and expectancy. The November heaviness of the air had lifted, and the view from the windows of the apartment was so clear you could see all the way down the East River to a piece of Brooklyn Bridge. Maggie nestled beside me, Diotima scrunched up in back of me on the top of the sofa. I had a drink, and another. I felt I had been excited getting here, walking Maggie, showering. I almost felt I was doing something underhanded. The robe felt good too, wherever it had come from. Tant pis!

While I was mixing a third gin and Perrier, the uncalled-for unlovely vision of the liquor store owner came to me, about as unwelcome an apparition as could have been wished on me in my euphoria. I blotted her out by watching a tug go upriver in the dark.

Why had she come back to me in the first place? I recalled how she had wanted to get rid of me, and how I had gone on talking to her in my excitement of being able to buy a bottle and settle down to drink without Truman.

Without Truman.

Was it true that I wanted him away then, that I'd assisted at his incarceration, his burial-alive? Just so I could knock them back without being reminded what a pain in the ass people who drink too much and can't help it anymore can be to a person who feels he doesn't drink too much and can help it?

I put down the glass, put away the bottle of gin, and haven't had an alcoholic drink since. I never wore the long white terry cloth robe again either.

Truman was nice about it when I told him. That is, he didn't say anything. Not a word. We never chopped things to pieces conversationally between us: what was done was done. We would think about it, of course, but privately, as one prays and works.

In the end it doesn't matter why I did it. Freedom, so despised and feared by all of us, really, was given to me. The drinking hour was returned to me to do with it what I would. When I told Father Synge about it, he looked blank for seconds, then he told me he was sorry for me.

"Why, Father?"

"Well, I wasn't aware of the extent of your problem."

We neither of us gave the best of ourselves to each other, either because we could not or because we did not want to. Not at first, anyway. He made me feel guilty about Truman, which I already was. He made me feel I was not doing enough for him; I could not have agreed more. Had I known Father Synge's hang-ups at the time, his seriously questioning his whole life-style, his doubts of a vocation, I might have tried to dialogue with him more than I did. But priests don't talk about themselves except from the altar, which is play-acting mostly. Priests act as if they are in God's pocket and only pop out at you when bells ring.

Chapter 10

Truman called me constantly from Roosevelt, and I visited him every evening. Even then he was beginning to assume a bored look, totally resigned and unbelieving. There seemed to be no stupidity he could not undergo. As in all hospitals he went to afterwards, there was this mystique of taking blood, of wheeling him all over the place, doing the same things to him that had been done sometimes only a few months ago or even a week before, all under the name of tests.

What they could not test, take away, touch, play with, proselytize, or in any way ever change was the brain, the sensibilities, his way of looking at things, his charm. Only Truman could do that. This I hoped would never happen.

Abhoring confinement as he did he broke free of me in the taxi coming home from Roosevelt. I did not blame him. He came home hours afterwards, but he looked all right. He said he had been to a movie.

"How was it?"

"Lousy."

They usually were, but he liked going to them all the same. He looked at me as if he felt I was scrutinizing him too closely, when it was really the other way around. This was because it was time for my annual trip to Switzerland.

It did not seem to me that he could afford to be too alert anymore. It hurt him too much. It wasn't worth it. The brain, his sensibilities that he had sharpened to receive as well as trap everything, were enemies now, and best thwarted by numbing; else, I used to sometimes think, he felt he would go mad.

Sad he would be. He seemed content with that. He never made faces when he cried. A tear would appear on his cheek, sometimes two. That's all. But his appearance would be elegiac enough to break your heart. Times like that he appeared to be his own monument. As December drew near every move I made was a threat to him.

"Where are you going?"

"Out for a walk, Truman."

"How long will you be?"

"Two hours."

"Promise."

The sun was pouring into the apartment. The light on the river hurt your eyes to look at it. It glistened more like the Aegean beneath an early afternoon sun than the East River. I could close my eyes and imagine us back on the island of Paros. That was nice, that was lovely, that was free and easy: Paros, Greece, our hotel off by itself and seldom anybody else there but us. The town was like squares of lump sugar. The Greeks proud and unbending, not like the island's few trees, bent like suppliant hags along the shore by the relentless Meltemi wind.

"Truman, remember Paros? I was just thinking of it. Of course you remember it."

"Of course I remember it. That's where Bunky chased a donkey."

"Yes, and I chased the two of them, and fell and scraped my hands on the rocks. I still have the scar. But it's a happy scar now when I look at it, Truman."

There did not seem any connection for him between times past and now, but there was for me. He could only see me skiing in Switzerland when he thought of foreign places now, and he hated that, even though the mountains had been his idea in the first place, his desire to please and amuse me, since he knew I loved to ski, but it came from a need in himself as well, to get away from peacocks and work. His rucksack is always with me, wherever I go, yet it was Truman who used it first, climbing the mountain paths through the snow under loads of provisions he had bought for us down in the town of Verbier. Our view across the valley to Mont Blanc was uninterrupted. At night we closed the shutters and played Mahalia Jackson records. We ate supper in the kitchen. Truman had his room, I had mine. That was all there was to the apartment, really, except for the cabinet et douche. No bathtub.

I was doing my exercises the morning of the day I was to

leave for Switzerland. I had already told Truman, so I was surprised when he came into the living room from the bedroom and stood there in the hall doorway next to the japanned secretary that I was always afraid he would crash into and hurt himself. He watched me as if my exercises were all that concerned him. I'm very self-conscious about exercising, feel silly doing it, and so on, and I positively loathe being watched. Truman, who is sensitive to all my idiosyncracies, knows this and has forgotten about it, or else simply doesn't care. His expression is benign, sweet. He's wearing a pair of dirty shorts. He has forgotten I'm to leave for Switzerland, obviously. Now I'll have to break the news all over to him again. It was painful enough for the two of us the first time. Why am I going? After all, what's the difference whether I ski or not? It doesn't matter if the apartment in Verbier just stands empty. Or does it? I'm about to tell him I'm going again when he says, referring to my exercises:

"I wish I could do that."

Later on in the day, when I was actually leaving and he knew it, he faced me bravely enough. The tears appeared without any other indication of what he was feeling, they were more like glass globes than water, and there were just two of them.

My departures weren't always like this, oftentimes he would stay in bed, his writing pad propped on his knees, as I went out the door. Open hostility to my departures came as the rest of his life receded far to the background and I stood in the foreground, the only one he seemed to want to know anymore. He used to write me when I was away, but then that too, like all his letter writing, stopped, except for a valentine—the only saint's day that ever meant anything to Truman.

Precious Beloved Baby,

I'd just sat down to write you when the
mail
~~mail~~ came with your little note....about how bad the weather has
been, and that you are feeling bored and nervous; you always stick
to things too steadily, why don't you break it up, go to the
Ritz in Paris for a spell...it's stupid not take more advantage of
<u>having</u> an apartment in Europe and get around on little trips once
in a while. Even Diotima likes the Ritz! Anyway, I'm glad you
are feeling more deeply drawn into your book; as for your not
being sure now what it is about, does anyone <u>ever</u> know completely
what they are writing about?---if they are any good.

No, we're not going to have a Bull Dog
Farm. Maggie came through fine. She and Charlie really get along
famously. He loves to play with her, and now even instigates the
games once in a while.

My hemmorhoids are really bothering me
again; the only cure is an operation (painful, but not serious) and
I suppose I ought to face up to it, but ugh...what thinkest thou.

Gosh, I wish you would get a phone
installed there so we could talk.

I notice that some of these bills
(Animal Shelter, for instance) have been appearing month after
month. Haven't you paid them?

Hugs and a kiss and all the love in
the world...

T.

Chapter 11

"John, John, the person is not your concern, God forgive me. Your problem is more to be thought about than his. Just how friendly are you two, anyway?"

"Not enough."

"You don't mean that, John. Go to Paris. There's nothing like travel. One look at Notre Dame will give you back all you've lost."

"What have I lost, Father Colfaxen? As my confessor, you should know of course. But I don't remember telling you I lost anything."

"You don't have to. It sticks out all over you."

"What sticks out all over me? That I'm in love with a man?"

"Men have always been in love with men and always will be, John. No man was ever greater loved by other men than St. Thomas More. Even that selfish old bastard Erasmus loved him. His son-in-law, John Roper, loved him. The king loved him and felt betrayed in his love for him."

"He's very precious to me."

"If he is a way back to your faith he is precious indeed."

"How do you mean?"

"Why, John, that's your problem, not this or that person you helped home out of your kind concern for them. You have lost interest in being a priest, John. Am I right?"

"I don't know."

"John, let me tell you that when I first saw the great Catholic city of Paris…"

"Oh, Paris."

"It did wonders for me, John. If you think you're in trouble, you should have seen Stephan Colfaxen in *his* halcyon days. I wanted power, I wanted wealth, I wanted everything a poor, tough, not very bright boy from Hell's Kitchen would want and, not only that, believed heart and soul that he had a right to."

"Father Colfaxen, you never doubted your vocation."

"Never, John. But I thought it gave me that right I'm tell-ing you about to have more, much more, than I needed."

"Why, what did you want?"

"I wanted to be high with the high-ups. I scorned poor parish priests. I wanted power, John, power over souls. Not just power over Mrs. McThing and her servant girl, but power over untold millions of souls, John. I think I would have given my own soul, my own immortal soul, in return for that—that chimera!"

"Why, then, whatever happened to you?"

"Happened, John?"

"Yes, to make you the wonderful person you are."

"I was at the end of my first European tour, paid for by my old man, who used to show me the blisters on his hands he got from digging ditches all day long for the lot of us. I'm a great believer in peoples' hands, John. Yours are very fine and dodgy, but will turn steady enough when the day comes for you to show your true metal. My dad's hands were ready for any work, as you may well guess, but there was a shyness about them—he never threw them around, not even when he was drinking. Most of the time off the job he kept them stored in his pockets like they hurt him. But once at mass he put them together, palm to palm, and I never forgot the sight of them. I hit Paris, yearning for home and all the big things I meant to do when I got there. But it so happened that God had other plans for me. I found myself at evening mass in a little chapel behind the choir at Notre Dame de Paris, surrounded by tired people like myself, only most of them bent under the rod of a hard life. One old joker in particular caught my attention. He wore a pack on his back that he seemed afraid to take off for fear he'd lose it or it would be snapped up by somebody no better than himself. He'd been through the mill, John, but when he prayed, he became for me transfigured. His hands especially seemed to me to drop all foulness and to turn pure and unwanting. His head was bowed and he knelt all the time, but it was his hands, empty as a pair of poor old cracked cof-fee cups, that hoped and prayed and did their simple best for Our Lady, John. Notre Dame de Paris. She changed me. Give her a chance, John, and she'll change you."

Chapter 12

As Father Colfaxen's study door was always open and all his doings known and generally approved of, though not always, not at first, Father Scarpia told Father Devine and Father Schenck of what he had just overheard, and all three hurried to the pastor to stop him from sending Father Synge away for awhile from St. Roses, where the trio agreed that he was wanted more than he would ever be in Paris.

"He's already gone," Colfaxen told them, already saddled, in his turn, with Juan and Maria, back home from Mexico, jobless, penniless, but still pregnant.

"I count very much on the child. I'll do anything for it. I'll tell you what, I'll stand for it, I'll be godfather to it."

The two young people, tired and broke and close to falling out of love with each other, regarded the big, red-faced Irishman as their ancestors might have looked on their first white men—gravely, questioningly, and not scaredly as they are supposed to have looked on them at all.

All four whites were silent before the dark young handsome couple's adamancy. To argue with them would be like casting words at stone, old carved stone, sacrificial stone that knew blood, human as well as animal. Looking at them, Father Scarpia felt he was in a jungle and could not find his way out. Fathers Devine and Schenck remembered their trip to Cuernavaca and its heat. Father Colfaxen alone thought of what action to take with the Mexicans. Something violent. Yes, like rushing at them with two sticks tied together in the form of a cross. St. Thomas Aquinas had done as much when his family had urged a girl on him to try and keep him from the Dominicans, a bunch of beggars in their eyes, unworthy of a rich, aristocratic youngster like Thomas.

"Father Colfaxen, what are you thinking?" Maria asked, her lips scarcely moving. "That we are children, unused to the ways of the world, the wicked world?"

Father Colfaxen's frame doubled at the middle as if the little Mexican girl's words had struck him like iron. He re-

mained bent over himself as though he hurt all over, but
when his fellow priests moved to help him, something came
off the pastor that resembled no sound any of them had ever
heard from him before. It was a low, hurt, almost snarling
sound, of a cornered fighter, perhaps even bleeding inside,
but wary of help, of ties, betting on himself still—or something.

"Leave us alone," he said to the priests, and they did. They
went out, leaving the study door opened as a matter of
course. The little stone-like images before him—so young
and yet so old, children of infinite persecutions, of suffering, a boy, a girl, flying from country to country in their
search for food and jobs, a place to welcome their baby—
smiled. They were cold, even cruel smiles, and Father Colfaxen supposed they were meant to send a chill through
him. He straightened up, pulled the phone to him, called
Annie Bushnell, Sister Secret.

There is a monument somewhere in Mexico whose base
is a huge square, but the top of which, reached by hundreds
of stone steps, is a flat surface hardly bigger than your average kitchen table, on which the blood of countless victims had been purposelessly spilled. Father Colfaxen wanted
no more sacrifices, not in the whole wide world, if he could
help it.

"Sister," he said, over the telephone, settling his great
shoulders in a bellicose stance and biting his words before
they were half out of his mouth, his lips slits, fighting, fighting, since that was what it was all about, "Sister, say you
won't help me, and I'll come over there to Brooklyn and kill
you, I swear."

"I'll help you, Stephan. What is it you want now?"

"Jobs. Two jobs for two kids who have a baby coming
they don't want."

"Send them over, Stephan. Send all three of them."

Chapter 13

"It was better when the El went by," said Sister Secret to herself, glancing up and down the dumpy, winter-wounded street from the door of her Shelter of the Sacred Heart of Jesus. "Here they come now," she said when a taxi pulled up at the curb. "Just like them to take a cab when they haven't got a penny to their name. There is nothing equal to the pride of the poor." But the expected Mexicans did not appear. Instead a large woman arrayed entirely in grey emerged from the dirty yellow vehicle. "Annie," she called out familiarly to Sister Secret as she climbed the steps of the Shelter of the Sacred Heart of Jesus, "I can't tell you what it cost and how long it took to get here from Willow Street. I could have walked it, and did, many a time, when the Malloys lived here, and not you and your riffraff."

"Come in, Nora. I'm afraid I can't offer you peace and quiet."

"Don't tell me you ain't got a corner of the kitchen you can call your own where you can share a pot of tea with an old comrade, Annie?"

"I'm afraid not, Nora. I've given up everything I have to the poor."

The two former rivals for the hand of Matt Malloy lingered in the cold on the top steps of the ugly old brownstone where in times past they had danced together and never dreamed they would reach sixty. Somehow, out here in the grey morning cold of the city, they felt more at home with one another than they would ever feel again in the old immigrants' house where they had had so much fun when they were kids.

Nora never could get over it that it was Annie's house now, though not in the way Matt would have wanted, not the two of them married and living in it with their kids, but Annie's alone, since Matt had given it to her when she had "changed."

"There's no end of what you can get if you make it your

life's work to beg for others," Nora thought, following Sister
Secret into the house, which still smelled of beer and wine
and spirits to her, for then, the stuff had never stopped flow-
ing. What poor Mr. and Mrs. Malloy would think of the place
now there was no saying. A dozen beds in the parlor and
dining room. The walls were covered with signs saying not
to take drugs and not to drink and to love God and your
neighbor.

It was enough to make Nora Synge forget what she had
come for. To complain. But how could she when everybody
else was complaining, too? A little black boy, tugging at Annie's skirts, complained how he couldn't get into the toilet
on the second floor because some boys had locked themselves in there out of devilment.

"Did you try the toilet here on the first floor?" Annie asked
the kid, who said he hadn't, but would now, and away he
went, as carefree as if he was in a home of his own.

"They're mischievous, it takes patience handling them,
but they like being here, most of them, since it's a change
from home and all that entails."

"Like what in his case, Annie?"

"Well, they beat him for wetting the bed."

"Why, John used to wet the bed. I never beat him for it."

"Of course you didn't, Nora."

"His father wouldn't have stood for it. Harry was more
understanding and forgiving than I was or ever could be. I
miss him. I especially miss him now."

"How come, Nora? Sit here at one of the tables in the kitch-
en. I'm afraid I can't offer you anything. If I did, the children could clamor for something, and it's not their time."

"Annie, John's taken off for Paris."

"Oh, Paris! I'd give anything to see Paris again."

"Why, you could, Annie. All you've got to do is drop this,
ask Mattie for the fare, and you'd be there."

"Leave this, Nora? All I worked for? Surely you don't mean
that."

"No, I suppose I don't. That's no life. Living in hotels, eating meals other people prepare for you. Give me home any
day. My own home, on Willow Street, Brooklyn, where I was

born and raised and where I'll die—if you and your good works don't drive me out first, Annie."

"Why, how could I do that, Nora?"

"That Italian couple you sent me are about to drive me up the wall because they are living in such close proximity to the pair of blacks you also sent me. How long is it going to be, Annie?"

"But your house is so big, Nora. Three stories, as well as a livable basement, to say nothing of the attic, which, if it was straightened out..."

"How 'straightened,' Annie? Straightened for what? Are you about to take the house I was born and raised in away from me as you took the house Matt Malloy was born and raised in away from him for your good works? I like my house, and I like my life. Or did. Annie, you're a torturer. If heaven is filled with your kind, I'd be afraid to go there for fear I would never get a minute's peace. I can't run my house on Willow Street with those four people you gave me in it, Annie. I woke up last night thinking maybe the best thing I could do would be to go around the corner to the hotel and live there until you get rid of them for me. The idea wrecked me. To think of giving up my home, the home my parents worked their fingers to the bone for, to strangers."

The little boy came into the kitchen buttoning his fly ever so proudly; it took him a time, since they were his big brother's pants or somebody's, anyway not his, and he was not used to them or their size. Annie kissed him as if she meant it, and Nora Synge supposed she did.

"Annie," she said after the boy had been sent away smiling, "do you think John will be all right? I don't. He's all right with a book and a desk and a chalice, but most of life is a matter of handling weapons. You know that, Annie, but John doesn't, and never will. You see how he's got himself mixed up with this celebrity, don't you?"

"Whatever became of it?"

"Why, John's very involved, Annie, very involved indeed. The guy's become a cause with him. Now, Annie, you know yourself..."

"Maybe some good will come of it, Nora. You never can

tell. Hold on a minute, won't you? Unless you want to go. There's the doorbell."

Seeing her free, children rushed at Sister Secret from all over the big old brownstone that she had known in other times and in such different circumstances. Hardly ever a black, and then only to clean or serve at parties.

The beauties at the door did not surprise Sister. She had been to Cuernavaca to study in the university there and was acquainted with the sullen handsomeness, the diamond-black eyes, and the seemingly depthless spirituality of Mexican Catholics.

"Come in and be welcome," she told Juan and Maria, who had not come in a taxi, but by subway, and carrying a cardboard suitcase containing all they owned.

Annie's no different than she ever was, thought Nora Synge to herself, as Sister Secret ushered Juan and Maria into the kitchen as if they were island people of royal blood from some jeweled archipelago in the Pacific. Why, she used to walk dogs who had trailed her home from school as if they were prizewinners, and maybe they were, but I never knew any of them to win anything.

"Now, Nora, I don't want you to say no to what I'm going to say. I want you to think about it first."

"No," said Nora right away. "I'm up to your dodges, Annie Bushnell, and I'm in no mood to be taken in by another one of them. My house overrun by racists ready to kill one another as soon as my back is turned. Isn't it bad enough John has left the country? A boy whose whole life is a mystery to me, even though I am his mother. I feel I'll never know him now. Everything is unsettled. It's worse than when he went into the priesthood. Now I'm afraid he'll pull out of it. Picking up people on First Avenue. What next? You're not listening to me, Annie. Who are those people? Don't pretend to be praying."

"Actually, that's just what I am doing, Nora."

"Praying for what? Right in the middle of the day, too. You don't care how you behave and never did."

"That's true, Nora. I can't help it. When I get an idea, I must see it through. There's nothing to do then but pray that I don't make too much of a fool of myself. We've got to go now, Nora. I must settle these young people some place...if I can only find the room."

"Well, you won't. I can tell you that without even looking. The place is jumping. To think of how peaceful and quiet it was when Mr. and Mrs. Malloy were here by themselves. It was like a shrine then, after the kids had all left them and there were no more parties. Well, maybe it's better this way, every room crowded, every room a'jump."

"Not every room, Nora. I still have Mattie's old room, the smallest in the house, because he was the last to come along. He used to call it his hideout. It's my hideout now."

"Well, you deserve it, Annie, I'm sure. I'm glad you have it. I'm going now. Call me a taxi. Do what you can about the people you sent me."

Sister Secret put her arms around Juan and Maria, the veil of her hood hiding one from the other, for she kept to the old way of things in dress. "Run out, one of you, won't you, and hail a cab for Mrs. Synge. It's quicker than phoning." As the two young people broke away from her, Juan tripping over their poor suitcase, Sister told them that they did not both have to go.

"Yes," said Maria, "we'll both go. That way we will make sure that no taxi goes by without one of us seeing it."

"Why," Nora broke out after the Mexicans had left, "it's no wonder you get along as well as you do, Annie, considering you have nice kids like that around. Where are you going to put them up?"

"In Matt's old room, I guess. There's no other place."

"But I thought you just told me it's your hideout? Where will you go for peace and quiet if you give it up?"

"I'll find a place. I always have, Nora."

And here Sister Secret began to pray again, or seemed to.

"At least let me see that room again before they take over, Annie," Nora pleaded at the front door of the Shelter. "Let me see what you're giving up. Your whole life is a story of what you've given up. Sometimes, Annie, my heart aches for you, at all you've missed."

Sister turned and looked back on her friend as they

climbed the steps of the old house together. "Oh," she said, brightly enough, "I often think of things like that too, Nora. Yes, and who wouldn't? Why, I don't think I could ever love another man the way I loved Matt Malloy."

On the second floor they stopped at rooms familiar to them but changed and noisy now.

"Don't tell me these kids are with you night and day, Annie?"

"No, their mothers come and take most of them home after work in the evening. I don't have all I should. There's hundreds knocking on the Shelter door, Nora...like this one."

The little colored boy who wet the bed and got beaten for it appeared at the door of what used to be the master bedroom of the old Malloy house. Now it was a classroom of sorts. The kids were making clay things under the guidance of a bearded boy. "Don't worry, Sister Secret," the little colored boy said, "I know better than to touch you now." That he should talk so old, and be so wary of such a little thing as colored clay, bothered Mrs. Synge.

"Why, it would be no great thing if you were to get some color on us," she told the little boy, much to his surprise. "Come now," Nora coaxed, "I'll show you I'm not afraid of it. Give me your hand."

But he would not.

"No, no. I'm a mess."

On the third floor there was one door that was closed, the only one that was, and it was here, in Matt Malloy's old boyhood hideout, that Sister Secret hid out herself, but no longer, since she was about to give it up to Juan and Maria.

There were no rallying cries in prints and pictures on her walls. Here, it seemed no one saved you but yourself. It was a place of total self-reliance, a cell in a brownstone, containing a few books, a turquoise crucifix. A window framed the icy boughs of a naked tree of paradise outside.

"I hate to think of you giving it up, Annie."

"I'll get it back. Don't worry. You know young people, Nora."

The friends' voices were low and conspiratorial, as if they were plotting. Not so the voices outside in the hall. "Taxi is waiting, Sister Secret." "Taxi outside." The entire pottery class stood outside clamoring in the hall, their little stained hands waving in the air like autumn leaves.

"There's my taxi, Annie. What a clamor they raise over nothing! To think you have to put up with it day in day out, with no recess but this room, and now even this will be taken from you."

"Taxi! Taxi!"

"Well, let's go. Else they'll break in the door. Oh the peace. And to think you're giving it up. It's more than I'd do. Well, everything you do is more than I would do. For heaven's sake, keep those kids away from me or they'll have my grey squirrel a mess."

The bearded boy maneuvered the kids back into the classroom, and the two ladyfriends descended the stairs to the front door, where Juan and Maria waited, still with their suitcase, as if they did not know where they stood without it, which they didn't.

"So you found me a cab, did you?" Nora asked them, sternly. She could not forgive their taking Annie's room away from her, knowing what it meant to her, meant to both of them, really. Say what you would, it was a kind of shrine, that room was; why, it would break Mattie's heart if he knew Annie was giving it up, after he'd given her the house on the condition that she would always keep some part of it for herself, no matter how small, where she could go breathe freely for a spell, or even pray for that matter, but that she seemed to do everywhere and at any time. "Now, Annie, this is no time for that sort of thing, if that's what you're up to. Is it? Are you praying, Annie?"

"I was, actually, Nora."

"For what? That I should take these two with me?"

"It was something like that, Nora. They could live in the basement."

"Yes, and complain about it in a week."

Maria made a move, the first it seemed since she had gotten the taxi. "No, we wouldn't," she said, giving Juan a shushing look. "We'll be very good, not only for you but for your son, Father Synge."

"Ah, so you know my John, do you?"

"Yes, and we sympathize with him, having Father Colfaxen over him as he has, directing his every move. Father Colfaxen is very bossy. He sent Father Synge to Europe against his will."

"Of course he did. You're right about that Colfaxen. Why didn't he go himself? Why did he have to push my poor John?"

"He's saving him, Mrs. Synge."

"Saving him? Who does he think he is, God the Father?"

"Yes, that's what we say, don't we, Juan?"

Juan regarded Maria with a look of utmost inflexibility and said nothing. Nora rather liked him than not for it. For she addressed Juan when she next spoke and not Maria.

"Well, come on young man, if you're coming," she said. "You too, miss," she told Maria.

Now what, Sister Secret demanded of herself after they had all gone, made Nora assume they aren't married? She is the limit. She'll never get over not getting Matt Malloy, and that's the truth, and this house with him. Then Sister Secret looked up and down the street, praising God and waving to passersby at the same time.

Chapter 14

Considering today's ruthlessly supervised voyages, Father Synge's arrival in Paris was remarkably romantic. No room, no lodging of any sort, no luggage to speak of—in the rain and cold, hugging wet walls, yearning toward lighted windows, gawking after lovers glued together under an umbrella, or in the communism of one raincoat.

It was the last light of day glimmering through the colored glass windows of Notre Dame de Paris that emboldened Father Synge to reprimand a floozie flaunting a lighted cigarette and tell her to jink it. She did so, but not before another young priest, a Frenchman, emerging from the sacristy carrying a covered chalice, withered her with a hard, tough, intellectual look. Then he continued on his way, vestments flying, to the altar behind the choir, hidden and haunted and as if underground and militant, to say mass for the benefit of a few bizarre types, the night flowers of Paris. One twitched as if she would dance and probably had danced her head off, in her day. Grey, gnarled hands hung over the backs of pews like racked gloves in a thrift shop window. The priest himself hardly seemed part of the powerful wave of redemption coming from his parishioners and breaking against him, but played out the ritual like a doll, loquacious only when wound up. He was a boy of today, they were yesterday's children, believing in their sins' gaudiness if in nothing else, trying to unstick themselves from them for heaven, or merely to pass the time left them here below. All the same, one of them pinched Father Synge's bag.

He was lost. What should he do? Without a hotel room, too. How his mother would laugh at him. The first thing a traveler does arriving in a strange city is to register himself at a hotel. This Father Synge had failed to do; now, wet and without baggage of any kind, he was ashamed to try. He had his money and passport and was grateful for the warm overcoat and well-made shoes his mother had bought for him. His return ticket home added to the bulge in his pocket, but he had no intention of using it yet. Outside, he fancied himself a clochard, one of the bums of Paris, though unlike them he had money in his pockets. Assuming a camaraderie with his newly adopted brethren that did not exist except in his own head, Father Synge demanded in broken French of an ambulatory bundle of rags the way to the trains for Switzerland.

He was answered as if he had approached a windmill in a gale, by flailing arms, kicking legs, which told him better than words not to accost a touchy stranger in the wet and dark. I'll wait until morning, he thought, and he crossed the Pont du Carrousel and walked where kings had walked, though probably not unguarded. Father Synge felt prodded toward a renewal of his vocation, and the night and rain stimulated him rather than not. He felt dramatically close to finding himself in a way that mattered, not just superficially, and stood shivering with appreciation as well as from the weather in the Place des Pyramides in the shadow of the gold-painted equestrian statue of St. Joan of Arc, the girl who had put France back on her feet again.

The arched Rue de Rivoli, enclosed and dry, made him feel cloistered and safe. A policeman in a gleaming white slicker in the Place Vendôme put him in the hands of the doorman at the Ritz Hotel, who shirked him at first as if Father Synge was poison, but was soon put straight by the cop, who ordered the lackey to speak English, Father Synge not knowing much of any language but that and Latin.

"You want to eat, no? A place to sleep, yes? You English?"

"I'm an American on my way to Switzerland."

The doorman threw his back at Father Synge and faced the policeman with a grin on his face and a good one to tell him. "Figurez-vous que, Monsieur l'agent, un homme sans bagage qui voulait aller à la Suisse!"

"Ça, c'est bon," the cop said, also grinning. "Pas un sou, sans doute."

"Money? You got money? You? Money?"

"Yes, I have money."

"Moi, je me méfie des américains," the cop said.

"Moi aussi, Monsieur l'agent," the doorman agreed, keeping well out of the rain and seeing to it that Father Synge stayed in it. "Ils sont les blagueurs. La ville de New York est plein des blagueurs."

"Vous avez été à New York, vous?"

"Pas de tout, Monsieur l'agent. Ce pays là, il vient à nous par la TV. On n'a pas besoin d'y aller pour le voir."

This reply of the Ritz doorman, confessing he had never been to New York City after calling its citizens a bunch of jokers, displeased the cop, who took Father Synge gently by the arm and led him to the curb.

"Vous voulez un taxi, Monsieur, n'est pas?" he asked in a nice quiet voice, at the same time throwing dirty looks over the shoulder of his white slicker at the Ritz doorman. When a cab pulled up in front of the hotel, the nice cop said to

Father Synge, "Voilà, Monsieur l'américain, un taxi." He opened the door of the cab and Father Synge climbed in. "Gare de Lyon," the cop told the driver. "Au revoir, Monsieur l'américain," he said to Father Synge. It was not until early next morning that Father Synge actually boarded a train for Lausanne, Switzerland. He felt lightheaded from lack of sleep but happily free for the first time in his life. Everything seemed new to him, even the Hail Mary he said to Notre Dame de Paris.

Chapter 15

I had not been long in Switzerland when Father Synge showed up. Well, I thought to myself, if he thinks so much of Truman, why is he hounding me in the Alps? I said nothing of the kind, of course, but was all false breeziness with him, thus assuring myself that I was infinitely more socially adept than he was, which doesn't say much for either of us, since I've always told myself that I would give anything just to be able to come calmly into a room full of people, as any blackguard can do.

"Well, Father Synge, if it's Truman you're hunting, he isn't here. Verbier bores him stiff. He doesn't do anything when he does come here now but go to the clinique, which does him no good at all, except, of course, that it robs him."

"Oh! That reminds me. I lost my suitcase. Could you lend me a change of shorts and socks and a shirt?"

I gave him the stuff, wondering at his nerve, thinking he could handle himself alone abroad.

"Where are you staying?" I asked, not hearing where he said it was. Two o'clock was the time I was out to ski. Here he stood, blocking the door. It's amazing how dumb a change of scene can make some people.

"Come to supper, Father."

He looked poor but clean when he did, the way he wanted

to look, perhaps. He looked thinner, though I did not think he had ever been fat. Something had happened to him. He'd got religion again, I supposed, and I did not want to hear about it. Up until now I'd found him rather uppity with me. Now, because he was in a strange place amongst strangers, he tended to humble himself, without, of course, giving way an inch to me, really, as why should he?

We sat down to dinner in the kitchen with its stone floor and overhead light. Truman always saw to it that we dined by candle light in our little kitchen in Verbier in our hardy days.

In the days that followed I tried to get to like Father Synge, but I could not. I felt he wanted to take my place in Truman's life for his own good, not ours. I felt he believed that in saving Truman's soul, he was saving his own. But of course I was much too shy to say this. Not only was I ashamed to show my ignorance, but I felt saving souls was a priest's business. I knew nothing about it. I hoped he did.

Father Synge bloomed in a way I never expected him to in a shirt and sweater I gave him, the pants he had come in, and a borrowed pair of ski boots. Something in him snapped. He let go. He forgot about directing souls and saving his own. Learning to ski can wipe everything else out of your life but eating and sleeping. He was soaking wet by the end of the day, and his face had taken on some color. He looked better than I had ever seen him. He had fallen in love with skiing. He hardly seemed to know me when I came down from the mountain and found him in the act of love with his pair of rented skis. He had cast off my sweater. I was surprised to see hair, like fine copper shavings, in the opening of his shirt at the neck.

I can talk to anybody as long as we are out of doors. Houses kill me, and I'm not much better in restaurants. Bars I hate. In the Alps I talk to anybody who will talk to me, but nearly always out of doors, on trails, in lifts, at the turn of a forest road, or on the sidewalk outside the post office. What with the altitude gone to our heads and few restrictions but time, we tend to say more to one another than we would elsewhere. It's fun to figure one's way through the ubiquitous ski outfit to the man wearing it. And if you speak French, as I try to do, and the other does, much can still stay a mystery, even nationality and profession, as views are exchanged on Jean-Jacques Rousseau, Jean de La Fontaine, or Charles Baudelaire. That's the way Father Synge met me next day, as if we'd been talking instead of skiing, and close together instead of miles apart, me up on the mountain and Father Synge practicing on the kiddies' slope.

"That's the gist of the whole thing," he said right off the bat to me, soaking wet as he was from falling down into the snow nearly all day long, and cheerful for a change.

"What's the gist of what, Father? How's the skiing?"

"Damn my skiing. Are we our brother's keeper, or aren't we?"

"Yes, but suppose I'm not good for my brother?"

"Truman says you are. He swears by you on the radio, on TV, everywhere."

"I think I was once, but I don't know about now. I seemed to have abandoned him."

"Yes. Why? Does all this mean so much to you? More than his need for you?"

"He wouldn't want me anymore if I was the sort of person who sacrificed all this for him. I have to get outdoors some part of the day, a good part. I couldn't do anything if I didn't. Truman knows that. He wouldn't want me if I were somebody else."

"Yes, but he isn't what he was, and...you still are, aren't you?"

"No, I'm sadder. I'm my brother's keeper, but it's as if my brother isn't there for me, lots of times, even when he's in the next room."

"How's that?"

"Well, he just isn't, he wants to sleep so much. He's happiest when he's in bed and knows I'm beside him, not at the opera or ballet, not in the library writing, not swimming or walking, not sailing, not skiing—but beside him."

"The way it used to be."

"No, it was never that way, it has *fallen* into that way in his mind now. There was always a difference, a distance, between us, as there had to be. We aren't like other people. Constant proximity to each other would have killed us. It would have stopped whatever there was in us that God meant to come out. To have had one room, one bed, would have been like putting two racehorses in the same stall."

My proud talk hurt Father Synge. He had been taught the virtues of resignation. He looked across the valley at the sun sinking into the teeth of the Alps; down the valley, the way out to cities where men work and build things; out, way down the valley past Lausanne and Geneva. He picked up my sweater from alongside the piste where he had cast it earlier in the day before I had made him unhappy with my worldly talk of worldly, ambitious people. He turned his back on the sun and me, the sun sinking into the teeth of the Alps, and went back to his hotel carrying his rented skis. Those outlandish skis, when I thought of it, considering he really should have been at Chartres or Beauvais or even back at Notre Dame, pilgriming and at the same time checking on the possibility of retrieving his purloined suitcase.

I took off my skis and hurried after him, but I was too late. He'd gone back to his hotel, but he'd set me worrying about what I had done, what I was doing, and what I should do with my life with Truman, when it wasn't my nature to worry and fret. I stopped and watched the sun and the dark valley. I remembered when we came here for the first time. A November night in pouring rain, Truman driving. Verbier was all mud roads then. The car slipped and turned as if it had a will of its own, but we were not due to go over the side of the mountain. We had years ahead of us, happy, productive years. That was the only night we ate out here, the rainy night of our arrival. Nobody would have noticed our Peugeot, our dogs and cat. But we were making history.

VERBIER, 19 NOVEMBER, 1960

Snowing. All the tops of outdoor things are white. The air is the color of fat left to grow cold in the frying pan. The chalet next door, where Diotima hangs out (though today she is very much with us), looks sullen, stranded.

Weeds and things, however, wear their snow with an air;
the telegraph pole has a white guardsman's hat; the
branches of the pine trees look like stacked wings.

How deep is all this snow? It came to Truman's knees as
he left the chalet to shop. He's been gone an hour. There he
is now! Here he comes! I help him off with his backpack.
"Winter wonderland! Winter wonderland!" he shouts at the
door. "There's a letter for you," he tells me.

Chapter 16

I should never have shown Father Synge the telegram from
Truman. He had so little. His progress, even in skiing, was
lamentable. He was tied up in knots, if not actually self-
trapped in doubts and confusions, where almost anything
might appear to him as a bridge to light and peace and re-
pose.

"What does it say?"

As a priest he thought he had a right to ask. I handed him
the telegram submissively. In it Truman wanted to know if
I would meet him in Paris in February. It was now the middle of January. Father Synge's reaction to it was odd to say
the least.

"Oh, I couldn't stay here that long. I have to get home.
Besides, I haven't any clothes. I'm beginning to feel a mess.
I wouldn't dream of trailing around Paris in this state."

February was a long way away. I had my writing. I wasn't
sure I wanted to meet Truman, though I knew I would. Hosts
of people in our past would have been aghast at my hesitation as Father Synge would have been had I let on to him.
I was used to that. That lots of people could not see me without seeing Truman as well was their business, as it was Father Synge's now.

Sometimes, when people are weak, they can walk in on

your affairs with the greatest show of strength. This is because they are throwing themselves at you, really, begging you to pick them up, give them guidance, return them to something they feel they have lost and that you may help them find again. Self-reliance is in that case thrown out of the window. Their point is to make you feel their state is your fault.

"Besides," he said, "he wouldn't want to see me."

"No, he wouldn't," I said, sorry but saying it all the same. Then, to ease things, I added, "I'm not sure he wants to see anybody anymore much," which I felt was true.

My own feeling about his telegram and its urgent demand for a rendezvous in the dead of winter at Paris (Hotel Ritz) was that he had broken with some bum and was racing hell-bent-for-election back to me for clarity, ease, the way things used to be, protection, penance—I could go on, the list of things he came to me for being endless, though I would never say so to him. Nor he to me, for we liked to appear perfect in each other's esteem. This had its shortcomings like any other ideal. It made us lonely and cut us off even from one another. It was perfectly all right for ordinary people to use the same bathroom at the same time, but not us.

What I felt about Father Synge was that he wanted everything to come to a head with us so he could cut it out, like a surgeon. The worse he thought our situation was, the surer he seemed of himself. He gloried in the telegram, but it left him nowhere because he did not know what I was going to do about it. He could learn nothing of our life, its past or present, and so he wanted to get his feet in the door of our future with a vengeance.

Just to turn the tables on him a bit, I brought up the subject of his stolen suitcase. The weather was bad; it was rotten, in fact. Rain, something unbearable during winter in the Alps. It bends everybody over and gives us the appearance of beggars, which we are, having come up out of the gloom of the plains, the varying greys of Paris and London and Amsterdam, for sun and fun and not this: daisy-making rain. Father Synge caught on to that aspect of the ski station if to nothing else; he looked the most beggarly of all of us.

"I'd check with Notre Dame on my way home, if I were you, to see if they've got your bag or not."

He didn't like it, he wanted to be poor and saintly, with money in his pockets.

"What has Notre Dame got to do with my lost bag? It would be as if I was accusing them of having taken it if I were to ask for it now. They're not responsible for the belongings of people who go in there. Anybody could have taken it, even by mistake. A tourist wandering by as we others were up at the altar receiving communion."

"It must have been impressive."

"It was all right."

"It was all right, but you can't say impressive."

"I didn't say that."

"What snobs you priests are! But I forgot. You're not a priest anymore, are you?"

"I'm sorry I ever told you that. You've probably told Truman."

"No, I haven't. I've never mentioned you to him."

"Never mentioned me. Fine help you are. And him? Hasn't he ever mentioned me either?"

"Never."

"What a pair! The two of you are in cahoots against me."

"Truman probably doesn't remember you brought him home. In any case, he wouldn't say. He never talks about people who have played Good Samaritans to him. I don't think he likes them."

"That's why he likes you, because you don't play the Samaritan—do you?"

"Not so's you'd notice. I think it would be in the worst taste. You see, Truman is still Truman to me, and probably always will be. I have more than thirty years of us against these last years. Am I to forget them?"

"In a way, yes. What good are they if they don't help you to fight present evil?"

"Oh, it's not all evil, if indeed any of it is, Father Synge. Our strengths are still enough to overwhelm this little present. Truman is terribly admirable. If you watch him up closely, he bears up. So few of us do."

I could be seductive enough, and Father Synge seemed to think so. He threw up his hands and backed away from me as if he considered me foul. His sudden show of strength and determination was refreshing and made him look better, though not good. Saving souls can be a pretty athletic affair. He was putting as much into it as he did into trying to learn how to ski. I had to give him credit, though he gave me pig shit for my money, going way back to mass at Notre Dame, where he had lost his suitcase. When I'd asked him had he found the ceremony moving, he had replied in a stumbling, defensive, selfish fashion, hoarding his mystical experience for other ears more worthy than mine.

"No, I don't think you are worthy to share what I felt about mass at Notre Dame. I don't trust you. You're too many things to too many people. You could have done wonders for Truman, brought him into the church."

"I daresay."

"Things are different now. It doesn't matter if he likes you anymore."

"I'm only human, Father, and glad that he does."

"Surely you see he must have more than you."

"Oh God, yes! Much more. But what? None of us can go back. No matter what we do, we are always in the present. Truman lives for the future now and loves me for our past, but the present no longer exists for him in a constructive, enjoyable, creative way. He can't wait for the day to end so he can be in tomorrow, except that tomorrow is never tomorrow when he reaches it, but today, and today he refuses to accept."

"I don't know what you are talking about. Practically speaking, you are nearly always way off the beam."

"I know. I'm not a very practical person, though I am pragmatic, I guess. I guess that makes me atheistic, or agnostic, which is the same thing to you."

"I don't care what Truman is, I know I could get through to him, but as far as you're concerned, you're beyond me."

"I'm beyond redemption, you mean."

"From my point of view you are. You're a sentimental Christian, in it for all the kicks that you can get, your own private drug-kitty, which you refuse to share with anybody else, even the person closest to you. How do you expect me to take you seriously, tell you how I felt about mass at Notre Dame, when you don't think enough of being a Catholic to try and make your friend, your best friend, a Catholic too?"

"I think it would be wonderful."

"Then *do* something about it."

"It's not our way."

"What is your way?"

"To love one another and respect one another's differences."

"Well, I don't suppose I'll see you much, or even know if I'll want to," he said. "You take me too lightly, almost as if you considered me an intrusion in your lives, whereas I feel that your entrances in my life were as radical as could be. The night I picked him up I had decided to quit the priesthood, as you know."

"And now?"

"Now I don't know."

"So you are searching an answer for yourself as well as for us."

"Yes. Maybe. I don't know. I'm not sure. I hope so."

"Or are you searching the answer in him?"

"He can help me. He can help me much more than I can help him."

"Like everybody else," I said. "No wonder he's worn out."

"Is he?" he asked, eagerly. "Then I have something in common with him. I feel worn out too."

"'Something in common with him.' How often I have heard people say that. People who want to have something in common with him, because they have nothing. Father Synge, it's not in me to say to him, 'Here's this priest. Maybe he can help you.' Can't you do it yourself?"

"You see, you're not your brother's keeper, after all, are you?"

"I suppose not. The role doesn't rest easy on me."

"You'd rather see him perish."

"We all perish, Father. Anyway, I'll die before Truman. He is not about to perish yet, don't worry."

"He's suffering."

"Yes, that's true. But he's not alone. All's not over."

"You take it so lightly."

"I take it."

"Yes, it's probably more than I could do in your situation. Well, I'm going now. Thanks for the shirt and shorts and socks. You don't mind if I keep them, do you? As for your hospitality, I'll have to keep that. You've been very kind, even though you may not have meant to be. I can see a little more now what Truman sees in you. You're there, you see—there, the way no one else has ever been in his life. The only trouble is..."

"Is what? That I don't do more?"

"No, that you don't do anything, as far as I can see; just nothing at all."

"I never said I was best."

"Do you think he's religious at all?"

"Why, sure."

"You're the limit."

He went out. We both did, but in different directions. I flung open the doors to our balcony and watched him from above picking his way carefully down the white road. He was alone and so was I. It was a sunny morning, between ten and eleven o'clock, and everybody was up the mountain, even most of the kids. There weren't even any cars moving; all of them were parked and lumpy-looking under snow that had fallen during the night. The sky was blue, the earth white. Across the valley the mountain crags were crowned with sunlight. Fir trees, stopping at the tree line, looked like multiple pointed shawls, irregularly draped over the mountains' sloping shoulders. Nor was it all so grand as to be inhuman, since kids could be heard going up and down their slope nearby. Still, the peace was striking, and Father Synge seemed to be fleeing it, his head lowered and determined-looking and his arms close to his sides. He seemed to be saying to himself, I'm going where trouble is, where I'm needed most, let others enjoy this earthly paradise.... Suddenly he stopped walking, which is what I wanted him to do. Next he lunged at the new snow on his side of the road, scooped up a handful, made a snowball, and threw it at me, very wide of the mark but making me see him as a boy again. He stood there smiling, open, his arms swinging freely at his sides, his feet planted solidly in the snow of the road. For the first time I realized how much he had achieved so far in life. I felt what a sting it must have been to him to feel he had a vocation and to go ahead with it. I realized as much as I could, which would of course never approach the reality in endurance and pain, what a hell of suspense seminary life must be, doubts flying like bats in the night over every cot, the sweet fragility of boyhood friendships and the fears of eroticism. I wanted to run to him on my knees and did, actually, though not on my knees. But when I reached him, he was Father Synge again, and the boy from Willow Street was once more drained out of him.

I didn't care. I was still riding on what I had felt watching him from the balcony. Before I knew it I was down on my knees. I couldn't resist it, even though I was laughing uncontrollably at myself, I felt that ridiculous.

"What in the name of God's come over you?"

"I don't know, Father. I really don't know. I just felt like it, I guess. I even feel like asking you to give me your blessing, but I won't, of course. It would be too embarrassing for you, wouldn't it?"

"I should say it would. To say nothing of yourself. Get up off your knees, please. Remember you have to live here."

"That's all right, Father. I feel I can endure anything sometimes, and this is one of those times. Come on, nobody's looking. One, two, three, and it's done."

He raised his hand, then let it fall. He put out his hand and crossed the air where his hand had fallen, as if to erase all trace of it. His lips did not move. He was frozen stiff with shock and shame at what he must have considered my brazen clowning. Was it a blessing? It was too late to ask him. He was off and away with all the airs of a young man who knows where he is going. I hoped he did. To make matters worse, we had been watched. No sooner had Father Synge disappeared around the corner chalet than Madame Grimper appeared before me. She was all clutch and probably always had been so. She had married the pastor of her

parish when she was young, and had had three children by
him. Now her teeth were gone and so was the man she had
made an apostate of. She was bent and old, but like an old
short tree that would not fall, but continued to send forth
green shoots in spring, for her eyes seemed to me to be full
of desire, and her great hands seemed to feel me all over
when she helped me up.

"Ça va? Are you all right, Monsieur?"

"Mais oui, Madame. Just fine. Merci bien."

She turned and looked after Father Synge.

Perhaps, she seemed to be saying to herself, this is the
way some Americans say good-bye to one another, one
kneeling, the other standing. Tiens.

"Au revoir, Madame Grimper."

"Au revoir, Monsieur. Et bonne journée."

Chapter 17

In Paris we lunched every day at Maxim's and I forgot all
about Father Synge, never even mentioned him, in fact. Truman was troubled enough without me telling him some
vague tale of a soul-saver bent on redeeming him. I felt they
were both pretty troubled people and the last thing they
needed was one another. Our tables at Maxim's were never
the same and never good. They were in fact rotten. The head
waiter outdid himself in his efforts to hide us until the owners found out about Truman and we were this time invited
to lunch. I didn't go, but after that the dope outdid himself
trying to please us.

We had drinks at the Ritz bar, where they bowed and
scraped, and swells came in and were interesting to watch.
Truman seemed to have built a mental moat between himself and all that was happening to us, commenting very little on things, and looking most of the time as if he felt his
coming to Paris and having me meet him there was a total

flop, which I expect it was. He seemed very hurt, very broken up and put out about something, and obviously would have liked to tell me about it. It could only be the reason he came over.

He did not like Paris, and never had much, except for our first time there when we stayed up in rooms under the roof at the Pont Royal. It was summer then, bright and hot. Now it was winter. When I told him I was going home with him, I could see he had not expected me to, but to go back alone to Verbier. I think he was pleased, but he hid it. Or touched. He was very emotional but kept strict hold on himself. I talked a lot, but without interesting him much, I felt, since what he most wanted from me were questions asking why he had come to Paris, but I could not bring myself to ask him, fearing, perhaps, that his reply would hurt me.

One strange, slight thing happened to us at the Ritz. We were invited for drinks by Anna Wiman, whose father, Dwight Wiman, used to produce shows in New York. Anna was half dead and could hardly walk or talk, though she tried to talk, and in a tough way, unsuited to her. She died a short time after, but she was a ghost then anyway, so it was like meeting nobody. I drank nothing but Perrier, so I saw things clearer than ever.

It was rather as if you had been out sailing, and a fog came up and a sailboat went by, barely visible, though close enough for you to hear its stern breaking the surface of the water. A ghostly, sketchy thing. Seemingly no thicker than vapor. Fog on fog. Then nothing. Nothing because she literally drifted away. Got up with the aid of her companion and shuffled off in her loafers.

I'd known Anna when she was young, in her teens, and we danced in the Ford Show at the New York World's Fair. Tall, with great, pale, sunken eyes. It was rumored even then that she was ill, but few pitied her, since it was assumed she had everything that money could buy but her health. I did not see her again until the meeting at the Ritz. She was angry and with cause; fate had not been kind to Anna Wiman.

We were ghostly ourselves compared to the way we used

to be. We shared the same room, the same bed at the hotel. We ate breakfast, at least I did. I went for walks—had to, actually, since I had Maggie with me. Truman got up and dressed for lunch and dinner, but mostly we did not have dinner. We ate well enough at Maxim's to tide us over until the next time we went there, which was always for lunch the following day. This existence lasted just a week. Truman was sad, but would not say why, and I felt I would only burden us if I put questions to him, though I also felt that he wanted me to. I began to think of his coming over to Paris as an effort, a need to purge himself of his immediate past. Maybe he did, maybe he didn't. It was a good pitch, anyway, and we did a few things, or half did them, before we went home together on a terrible Greek airplane.

One time there in Paris, where it is almost black at nine in the morning in winter, Truman showed a bit of his old spark. This was when he took me to see a blind woman who had an apartment on the Isle St. Louis. The only reason I went was that she lived on the Isle St. Louis, even though she couldn't see it. That she could not struck me forcibly. The most beautiful place to live in Paris, and she couldn't see it even if she did live there. It made me angry with Truman, because he could see it, and had so much besides, and yet he was so sad, so morose, so secretly melancholy.

Then we went one night to a restaurant that was all the thing. Tom Curtiss was there with some people including Janet Flanner, it was Tom's treat, sans doute. None of it meant anything to Truman. Tom dropped his party for us and we went to some dreary gay bar, but none of it interested Truman. Though he didn't like Paris, not really, we had good times there, and had even done some work. Tom asked me what was wrong with him, as though he had the cure for everything or knew someone who did. Because I liked Tom, I arranged for us to have lunch together the next day. It was a disaster. Suddenly I was caring about social things, when I never had before. I wasn't really. I was doing it for Truman, to see if I couldn't bring him around, and of course I was doing everything wrong. I suppose we stayed in Paris as long as we did because of me, because Truman knew I liked it. I should have stuck to following the Seine for miles and haunting the marché in the Rue des Saints Pères. I knew more about the pictures at the Louvre than I did about arranging a luncheon with an old friend, not dreaming that the old friend would turn up with still an older friend, which Tom did. He brought along Jennie Bradley, who had been Truman's Paris agent until he ditched her for another. Truman met her without turning a hair, but it was a nuisance because Jennie raged through lunch in a low, rumbling, gastronomic sort of way, holding her big gases in readiness. She looked like a general in severe drag. Square-jawed and a marching air. There was no beholding anybody else when Jennie pointed out the window of Tom's apartment (Quai Tournelle) at the Seine and exclaimed without the shade of a smile, or the slightest shadow of a suggestion that she was perhaps claiming what few kings had dared, "My river!" Jennie was full of her generalship that day. Proust was hers, too, though not available for pointing out. When we went upstairs to lunch and I complimented her on her rings, Jennie tore them off and threw them across the tablecloth at me like a pair of hot dice.

Poor Truman. And they used to be such friends. But he had ditched her and she was a woman scorned. There was scarcely a trace of the handsome vieille dame with a rare sense of chic who had had us to lunch our first trip to Paris together. There was no Tom then with his mandarin manner of treating everybody exactly like everybody else, as if the world was a great green billiard table and all of us but Tom as alike one another as billiard balls. Then there were just us, Truman charming Jennie, Jennie charming Truman, and me charmed by both of them. I remember Mrs. Bradley saying she considered envy a virtue and how convincing she was. Today at the Tour d'Argent she looked as if her corsets would snap on her. They almost did, I think, when Truman, halfway through lunch, rose and departed, leaving Jennie sputtering into his wake of whispered excuses. He had not liked the way she had thrown her rings across the table at me, for one thing.

But next week, in New York, he told me he could not write

anymore without drinking. Whatever it had been he would have liked to confess to me in Paris was nothing compared to this. We were in a restaurant called La Seine, a big, ugly place with blood-red banquette seats, where people from the clothing industry wandered about with glasses in their hands as if they were home, while waiters stood about as well, more like spectators than men with jobs to do.

Long before his unhappiness was apparent to others Truman was aware of it. It must have been like a bombardment to him that he only heard away off in the distance now, but knew was coming his way day by day and there seemed to be nothing he could do to stop it.

He hated drunkenness like poison, too. Hated it because he had seen it in his family and friends. So had I, of course, but ever since I had known him, he had a special vehemence regarding inebriation. Perhaps he saw his mother at her worst in people who were drunk.

Two waiters looked our way as he cried; I saw them as two flinty-hearted devils motivated by scorn and envy, slaves who remained within the law out of fear of going to jail. Had they only known it, they were witnessing courageous behavior under fire.

"I can't write unless I drink."

These were his words, as honest as he had ever been in his life. His face was a mask of control. He was obviously sorry for me, probably sorrier for me than he was for himself, since that was his nature. As usual he was not generous with his tears. There seemed to be only two of them, two at a time, and they stayed on his cheeks as if they did not know what to do with the freedom Truman so begrudged them. Then, as always, he assured me that everything would be all right, and we went home.

VERBIER, 12 DECEMBER, 1960

Said to Truman that I thought the men here drank a lot, and he said people drink a lot everywhere. True. I suppose when I first met Margaret and Jerry French and Paul Cadmus in Provincetown, summer '48, they were gay drink-

ers; but now they've settled down; Margaret, in fact, tak-
ing little or nothing much to drink anymore. We too are
what some people would call strict in our drinking habits
now. Three a night. I remember Slim Hayward sounding
a bit miffed about this when we were all three arriving at
a restaurant in Spain. We'd already had two drinks at
home, and Truman made the mistake of saying we "could
have one more." It was then that Slim acted miffed. She
likes going out.

Chapter 18

Father Synge slipped into St. Roses first thing on his return
from abroad, not daring to appear at the rectory without his
suitcase. He sat down in a back pew and thought, I'm home.
There was a fog in the streets outside and it seemed to have
drifted into the old church, with its balcony three-quarters
the way around from a style of architecture long gone out
of fashion. St. Roses wasn't a very warm church anymore,
but it used to be. Before Father Synge's time it used to smell
of burning wax and dance with the light from hundreds of
candles. It was doomed to go now. It creaked and it was
cracked. It felt abandoned. Father Synge wondered what Father Colfaxen would do when they tore it down and put up
something new in its place. Black marble, probably. Then
what would happen to the painting of the Last Supper that
all those who did not know any better thought was so good,
and all those that knew...
    Father Synge guessed it would go too, but where? Who
would take it in? Who could? Few were able to afford the
space these days. Besides, it really wasn't very good, was it?
It amused him to think that they did not know he was here.
Not even Father Colfaxen, who knew everything. A shiver
of love went through Father Synge when he thought of his
pastor. That he would not be nearby some day, that he would
go with the building, saddened him.

He drew out a notebook he had taken with him abroad. As he did so, a flood of memories of his short trip came to his mind, but when he started to write, it was about the old church he sat in: "It's a little church, the family sort, a neighborhood church, full of statues and burning candles. Petitioners spend their time here—and their money. Over the altar is a painting of the Last Supper, when Christ broke bread and poured wine for His disciples, first telling that when they ate this bread and drank this wine, they would be eating His body and drinking His blood. The colored glass windows are pretty though undistinguished. Somehow, one's values fall away here at old St. Roses. One's thoughts of painting and sculpture no longer matter. All around are people scraping their pocketbooks for change to buy candles, as if it was a question of life or death to them, as it very often is. There are areas of peace whose matrix is some woman in black, her eyes resting on the depiction of the Last Supper suspended above the high altar. Her attention is so concentrated that it is as if she was saying to herself, 'That's the way it was, all of them gathered there, and Him breaking the bread and pouring out the wine. It's lovely enough to see; none, not even Himself, knew altogether what was in store for them. Just as well. Let them eat and drink in peace.' It's a neighborhood church, but the neighborhood has fled. It's not what it was. High-rise buildings have been built over the blasted ruins of tenements, where the poor of First Avenue lived, loved, and died. It's a neighborhood church without neighbors, you might say. Now office workers from Third Avenue flock in on holy days of obligation. They help keep the church up and ease the thorn of taxation. But the drift to the suburbs did not take all; left behind are some like the woman adoring the painting of the Last Supper, people who act as if the world outside hardly exists."

It did, though. Over his shoulder a voice demanded, "What are you doing, John? What are you doing home? We thought you were in Europe." He turned to look into Father Scarpia's round face, whose rounder eyes were trying to read what Father Synge had just written. "You haven't even come into the rectory yet, John. I don't blame you. They've made a monsignor of him. Did you have a premonition of it?"

"Father Colfaxen?"

"Yes, and he's ashamed of himself and won't look at us, but to the rest of the world he's all right. I don't know how he'll be with you, John. How was Paris? No, I mean, really. Did you get anything out of it?"

"Well, I lost my suitcase there."

"You should never have gone, John. Your mother's wild that you did. Have you called her? She's got a houseful of people Sister Secret dumped on her."

"I better call her."

"She asked *me* to pray for her. I didn't think she went in for that sort of thing. I always took her for an Outsider."

"Oh she is. Definitely."

The first thing Father Synge did when he met his pastor was to congratulate him.

"Congratulations."

Father Colfaxen, who was Monsignor Colfaxen now, gave him a look and parted from him as if he meant it to be forever. At dinner Colfaxen made an unanswerable speech.

"People come at me with words like 'Congratulations' now, instead of 'Hello Father,' and so on, as it should be and as it used to be. I want it stopped. That's all."

"Then stop getting yourself honors," said Father Devine, to which Father Schenck said, "Yes, everybody knows congratulations follow honors like…"

"How are you, John?" Colfaxen asked Father Synge, as if no one had talked but himself. "How was Paris? I want to see the notes you made of your trip. Not voluminous, perhaps. But enough to go into the parish bulletin. I'm sure your experience of Notre Dame was as memorable as mine, if not more so."

"He lost his bag," Father Scarpia butted in.

"Your suitcase, John? Why, where could that have happened?"

"Notre Dame."

"Notre Dame? How's that possible?"

"I never leave my things down for a minute in church.

Not today I don't," said Mrs. Wallop, as though she was sitting down with the rest of them. Actually, she leaned in the doorway waiting for the end of the meal so she could clean up and go home. "Why, what happened, Father Synge?"

"Just what you'd expect, Mrs. Wallop. When I went up to communion, somebody lifted my bag."

"There's the French for you," said Mrs. Wallop.

The monsignor stirred in an authoritative way.

"Mrs. Wallop, we'll take our coffee in the rectory parlor. We'll get it ourselves," Colfaxen told the cook.

"We'll get it," Father Devine and Father Schenck said, rising together.

"You won't. You'll only make a mess," Mrs. Wallop said, blocking their way into the kitchen.

"We don't make a mess when we get breakfast, and we get our own breakfast lots of times. We all do."

"If you don't need me here, then tell me. Don't kick me in the teeth," said Mrs. Wallop.

"Bring my coffee to my office. Come with me, John," said Colfaxen.

"This is new," said Mrs. Wallop after they'd gone. "Well, what do we expect? It won't be the last of the changes. The building's coming down. Yes, and we'll all be scattered to the four winds. It's time I retired anyway. Everything's for the best. Now I want the three of you to sit there tight and I'll bring you your coffee just as always, not all the way into the parlor and out again."

"I wonder what they're talking about. I wonder if it's about Paris. Or what?" Father Scarpia said. "Maybe Colfaxen will take John with him wherever he goes."

"Oh, they're thick as thieves again," said Father Devine. "No sooner back than they're off whispering together again."

Mrs. Wallop came in with coffee.

"Now shush and be still and drink your coffee like old times and manners was back again and no signs of lordiness yet to be displayed. Why go miles away to have your coffee when you can drink it here like you always have?"

"You better bring them theirs, Mrs. Wallop," Father Scarpia said.

"Oh, I'd better. You know I'd better if I don't want my head snapped off. It won't be for long. It's all coming down, and us with it. I don't know where I'll go if they tear down our building. Yet there's talk, and there's agents. And where there's talk and where there's agents, there's bound to be blasting and knocking down. It's not like it was, and can't be, I guess, because there is such a thing as progress. Am I right, Fathers?"

They were used to her talking to them, and Mrs. Wallop was used to their not answering. There were no hard feelings on either side.

She was as bad when she brought Monsignor Colfaxen and Father Synge their coffee. "I never expected to see you back," she said to Father Synge. "Is it as bad as they say? Sure it is, because you lost your bag there, didn't you? Now what'll your mother say? Well, I'll let the two of you alone now. You've got a lot to say to one another, and you don't want to hear me. It's nice to have you back, Father Synge."

"It's nice to be back, Mrs. Wallop. Thank you."

Mrs. Wallop went out.

"I've asked everywhere for her, John, but nobody'll have her after the way I complained about her for years."

"Is she really going to be without a job? Are all of us?"

"I'm afraid so, John. I'll miss the old place. You won't, because you haven't been here that long, and, well, you're young. This is my last parish, John. I'm going out in glory. They've made me a monsignor. What would my old man say? I love my religion, John. I hope you will some day. Look what it's done for me. I mean even in the worldly things. I wish my father were alive to see me. I really do. I'm proud, John. God forgive me, but I am."

"I hope that wherever you go, they'll find a way to send me with you, Father."

"That could never be, as things stand, John. They're very much against your behavior with the celebrity of yours. Oh, it's much more than helping somebody across the street, John. Much more. But we'll talk about that later. How was Paris? I feel the trip did something for you. Did it?"

"In an unexpected way it did, Father."

"That's always the best way. God's ways are devious ways. He's a hiding God, the Old Testament says. The whole point is we must lay ourselves open to him."

"Yes, that's what I felt I did when I went to Switzerland. The Catholic part. His friend's there. I...I think I made some headway between the two of them."

"To separate them?"

"I hadn't thought of that."

"John, drop it."

"I'll never do that...now."

The two men rose at the same time and faced one another over Monsignor Colfaxen's desk.

"As your immediate superior, I command you to drop that guy, John, his friend, too, and all interest in them."

"Never."

Father Synge let himself softly down in his chair. He felt he had just made the strongest statement of his life, and he meant to stick by it.

Monsignor Colfaxen came around to him from behind his desk and placed his hands on Father Synge's shoulders.

"It's power, John, both of us misusing our power over one another. I'll never get over my desire for it. I thought I had. I've read. I've prayed. But to no avail. I'm no better than I was when I was a boy and wanted above all to be a bishop. John, you have power over me. I think you have it in you to go far in the church. Let me help you. Let's help one another. A man feels the need of a son. You fill that need for me, John. They're giving me a nice parish out of the city. Come with me, John. I'll see that you do. But you must drop this other thing. After all, what is it compared to what we've done together, and will do, God granting? I love you, John. Don't misuse your power over me. How was Paris? Let's talk about Paris."

As Monsignor Colfaxen left Father Synge and went and stood behind his desk again, he saw fit to pick up his copy of Thomas à Kempis's *Imitation of Christ* and hold it in front of himself like a shield.

"Digame, Juanito."

Father Synge raised his eyes to Colfaxen. He looked his best, as we do, sometimes, when facing the one we feel cares more for us and our welfare than anyone else in the world. But what he had to say to his pastor was so strong and so unlike him, he felt, that he lowered his eyes again and looked away at the dark window, which seemed to reflect the world, but all the same it did not deflect him from his purpose. If the world is dark, I'll speak out in it. Anyway, it is not true that it is all dark, he thought. And he remembered Switzerland. What he remembered about it was how he felt when the friend had showed him a rucksack Truman used to carry on his back in their strong days there, their purposeful days, when they both were writing, and where Truman would come in from town, having walked a mile uphill through snow, sometimes heavy snow, falling snow. What he most remembered was the friend telling him, albeit reluctantly, because Father Synge knew he was not wanted there, nor liked, how Truman never complained of having to go to the store or to the post office. If he could have done all that, he was worth worlds, Father Synge thought, seeing at the same time his life with Colfaxen going up the flue.

"Father, we're fighting for a soul."

"That's right, John, your soul."

"No, Father, his soul."

"I'm afraid he is a lost soul, John. Him and his friend. They have the devil's pride, the two of them. You see how they inveigled you into going to Switzerland, don't you?"

"Oh that. That was the high point of my life. I even went skiing."

"Good boy, John. But next time in better company."

"I was alone all day, Father. He was up the mountain."

"Yes, with the rest of the ski bums."

"I confess I don't think much of him. I find his books unreadable."

"He writes too, does he? Oh, John, it's all a trap. You want to be a writer yourself. Maybe that's all it is. This interest in these two characters. You want to be with writers. Well, go take a writing course somewhere. I'll put in a good word for you. I've read your stuff. For all I know it's good, very good. Did you keep notes while you were away? I'd like to see them if you did."

Father Synge showed Monsignor Colfaxen the writing he

had done just now while sitting in the old church of St. Roses before he had dared show his face at the rectory door sans bagage. The pastor read it attentively, then returned it to Father Synge.

"No, give it here again, John. I'll have it printed in the parish bulletin." After Father Synge had done so and Colfaxen had pocketed the piece, his pastor's manner altered; it softened. "John, I see where your heart is after all. It's with us, not with the elite riffraff down in the high rise on First Avenue. Confine your caring for souls here, in our parish of St. Roses, John, and in our new parish—wherever that will be."

"I could never leave New York, Father Colfaxen."

"John, I don't know what's got into you. You've changed. I feel I've lost you."

"You almost did."

"Out with it, John. What happened to you in Paris?"

"Switzerland."

"Switzerland, then. You went skiing. Is that such a big deal?"

"I hope to learn to really ski someday. I'm not all that old."

"Old? You, John? Of course you're not. Of course you'll learn to ski. Look at me, a monsignor at my age, when I thought all was over. What happened in Switzerland?"

"It was a letter I came across, addressed to him, when the going was good. It wasn't that I was nosing around. I was looking through some translations of his books when the letter fell out from between the leaves of one of them. No one could have resisted looking at it. At least I couldn't, and didn't. It was the salutation that struck me. The rest of the letter, from a friend, obviously, was gossipy and innocuous enough, except that it began, 'Dear Genius.'"

"'Dear Genius,' huh? That's quite an order."

"Yes, and to think..."

"To think people like you have to guide him across streets now."

"Oh! I didn't do half for him what he did for me."

"For you, John? Got you into trouble as far as I can see."

"Well, yes. But it's trouble I'm willing to face, since, you see, I feel I owe it to him."

"For what, John? He's fallen way beyond your efforts to save him. Leave him to his ski bum friend."

"He's vain and bellicose and thinks of nothing but himself. How leave him to anybody like that? He admits himself that he's no good for him, that almost anybody else would be better."

"Like you, only you must ruin yourself to do it. John, you're pursuing a chimera. The man is no longer there. I saw him on TV lately. He was all right, but something was missing. He's not slipping. He has already slipped."

"He saved me. The least I can do is try to help him."

"Saved you, John? You mean he was helping you out of Rajah's Bar and not the other way around? Come, John, you don't expect me to believe that."

"It was worse than that. I felt I was giving up all this, that all was over for me. I'd lost my vocation—if I ever had one."

"Oh, John, that's a common experience, a coming and going thing in the life of a priest, especially a young man like yourself."

"Did it ever happen to you?"

"No, not that I know of, John. But you must remember where you and I come from. I felt I was raising myself to unbelievable heights in becoming a priest. A poor boy. A ditch digger's son. Not too bright, just ambitious. You weren't ambitious, John. You could have gone on to be anything. But Stephan Colfaxen was priest material to the manner born, as things went in those days. Quit? Of course you wanted to quit. But I noticed you never did."

"I didn't because of him. As long as he lives, I'll stay a priest. I'll never leave him."

"'Dear Genius,' huh? It means that much to you."

"More than you know, Father Colfaxen. More than I know."

"John, I still see him and his would-be writer friend as traps of the devil."

Monsignor Colfaxen went to the door, pretending more anger than he felt.

What he felt was hurt.

"As your pastor, I command you to drop them both, first of all, and especially 'Dear Genius.'"

Colfaxen left his study before John Synge could say "Never" again.

Outside in the hall, the big man put his hands to his red face and wept, feeling in all sincerity that the fight was not with the boy he loved, but with the forces of evil, over which he felt for the first time in his life that he had lost all control.

SAGAPONACK, 8 JUNE, 1981

Truman: "Somewhere there must be a place for me, a place that will take my problem away and leave me free to do as I please again—and as I deserve. After all, who have I hurt? Nobody. Not really. Or anyway, not much. I haven't exploited people like the Gimbels have. Why shouldn't I be able to drink as I used to and enjoy it?"

Chapter 19

I was restless and wanted to go out to Sagaponack, but Truman did not. I thought that if I asked him why he had come to Paris that it would break things for him, so I tried, but it wasn't easy. He was not used to my questioning him, he did not expect it of me, though it would have been better lots of times if I had, I guess.

We had always been so free, going our own ways but never too far from one another. In this respect I have met no one like us, nor do I think anyone else has.

I could always tell when he had fallen out with someone, a peacock he did not talk to anymore; things like that were often in the papers, but I skipped reading them. Truman talked and acted differently with me than he did with others. He was less worldly. He was simpler. Attentive lest his naiveté show in front of others, he could not have cared less about that charming and touching aspect of himself with me, since he did not think I would notice it, but I did, of course, and I appreciated it deeply, since it was the source of great beauties in his work.

There were new photographs of him taken with people I did not know; some of them had their arms around him and Truman looked as if he did not care where he was or what he was doing or who it was he was with. These snapshots were unlike any ever taken of him before that I was aware of, and ordinarily I would have said he would be ashamed of them. I wondered what I should do. Here Truman was changing for the worst before my eyes, and as far as I knew I was acting the same as I ever did. No wonder Father Synge said I was no good for him and should get out. I was too vain to speak of these changes I saw in Truman to his face or to anybody else, since I felt I would be attacking our way of life. It didn't seem smart, it didn't seem right, it didn't seem like me. Also, the dreadful thing of hurting him stopped me. It would be like calling him names. It would turn me into an enemy. It was a game of nerves we were playing with one another. I was afraid that someday I would blow up and take every ounce of his self-respect away. Only I could do that. And I felt that if I slipped in that respect and fell, he would fall too. When he looked at me, he must see all his aspirations reflecting from me. I couldn't ask him to cure himself when neither of us knew what ailed him.

He always said he would be all right, even when despair looked at me out of his eyes. I guess we were both naive. At such moments I longed for the courage to say: "Look, there's this priest, Truman." But I did not. I did not because I felt Father Synge would start analyzing him to his face, and Truman could never take that for long without seducing the analyst himself. The necessary distance between physician and patient never existed for long. I had the feeling that Truman crowded these birds into a fighter's corner where they could no longer operate. None of them ever bothered me. None questioned me. Maybe they should have, maybe they were right and shouldn't have. The only thing positive from these encounters that I was ever aware of was the bills.

Truman, who had advised others, was now seeking advice himself, and he couldn't take it. I hoped our silences regarding these psychological seances would act like rain to an eventual harvest, but though I kept mine, never saying a word, Truman would inevitably break his, in trickles first, then in storms of disillusion and disgust.

I felt it would have been very pushy of me indeed to have asked him to accompany me to mass. "How was mass?" he would say, the same way he inquired about my walks, the opera, or when I went swimming. "How was the water?" "How was the opera?" "How was your walk?" It was all one to him. He would question me as if he was making a study of my appreciation of these things. People he saw knew what I was up to because Truman kept them posted. We had not always been apart in our divertissements. On the Costa Brava we swam together. Our house was built above a cove, and through the pine trees growing in between the rocks on shore I could see him when I leaned out of my window in answer to his call, "Water babies! Water babies!" that being the signal for me to come for a swim before lunch. Sunday morning, coming from mass, I could spy him from a high hill cavorting in the inky blue water. And when he spotted me he would break out with "Water babies! Water babies!" That was at Finca Sania on the Costa Brava, the house itself sparkling in the piney coast like a sugar-coated almond. We had a fire every night in the long narrow living room with its white stucco walls and high-backed chairs and black refectory table. We were to wish on many a new moon, but not then; then the tides' runs were all in our favor.

"Truman, what was it you wanted to tell me in Paris?"

"Oh yes. Well, let's go to the Lafayette for dinner. I'll make the reservations. We can talk there. Would you like that?"

We went to the Lafayette, but somehow there was no story. Our exchanges were often like that, short stops and sudden starts. It isn't my nature to pursue questions and answers; I pride myself that I'll find out things anyway if I'm supposed to know about them.

We were still in New York when Sunday came around, and I attended mass at St. Roses, Father Synge officiating. Truman was still in bed when I got home. "I bought you the Sunday *Times,* Truman; it's in the kitchen."

"How was mass? Thank you. Or didn't you go?"

"To mass? Sure I did."

"Well, how was it?"

"All right. Father Synge officiated."

"Oh....What's he like?"

"Don't you know?"

"How would I know?"

"He brought you home one night from Rajah's Bar."

"He did? Good for him."

"He goes on about you, Truman."

"What on earth about?"

"Losing your way."

"I've never lost my way in my life."

"I know you haven't, but Father Synge thinks you have."

"Jesus. What next?"

"I know. I think we should move to Australia...or Japan."

"I hate Japan."

"Shall I bring you the *Times*?"

"No, I'll get it."

He got out of bed in his dirty shorts and stopped beside me on his way to the bathroom.

"Tell him I don't remember him. If I remembered all the people who come up and talk to me all over the world, I'd go mad."

I handed him a clean pair of shorts when he came out of the bathroom. "I just put those on," he protested, as usual, but he took them all the same and put them on. "What are we having for supper?"

I had no idea, but I made up some answer and he looked pleased.

"I've lied to you for thirty years," he suddenly told me, and off he went in his bare feet to the kitchen.

His feet were beautiful.

He passed me in the hall with the book section of the *Times* opened in front of him. "I never talked to no priest. What priest?" he asked, without looking at me. He never closed a door. Doors did not seem to exist for Truman any more than they did for Monsignor Colfaxen.

Chapter 20

*He has forgot everything, everything—everything he has
worked for and is supposed to be. It is as nothing to him. It
would not be so bad if I did not think that in some sort he is
right. But I think he is more wrong than right. He is misusing his sense of his own autonomy. We are so unalike. I should
not be over him, since there is something in me that envies
him at the same time that I am reprimanding him.*

At that moment the telephone bell rang in Monsignor Colfaxen's office. It was his bishop. "Stephan, you've heard
we've found just the thing for you. A little parish on the North
Shore of Long Island. Nothing to do with the Hamptons or
anything like that. You'll like it. It will like you."

"I don't think so, Bishop. I'm not the man I was."

"Honors tear a man down, Stephan. Come, you'll get used
to it. Before long you'll begin to feel you always were a monsignor."

"Bishop, what would I do in the country? I'd feel exiled."

"But Stephan, when I talked to you last, you liked the idea
of moving out of the city. What's changed you?"

"A good look into the mirror at myself, Bishop."

"You sure it's not something else, somebody else? Tell
me if it is, Stephan. At my age I've heard everything."

"It's...the boy I sent to Paris. We've talked about him. John
Synge?"

"...Yes?"

"He doesn't want to leave the city, and I don't feel I should
leave him. He feels he has a mission here in New York to
watch over somebody and to bring them around."

"A priest with a mission, huh? That's nothing new, though
it can prove dangerous. Send him to me, Stephan."

*If only "Dear Genius" would meet Father Colfaxen. They're
both so strong, so pigheaded. They would be good for one
another, but they would never admit it. As far as Father Col-*

faxen is concerned, he's damned. How awful. I could never feel that way about anybody. I think excommunication's a horror. None of us have the power to damn another. We ourselves damn ourselves, and that is what he has done, "Dear Genius." My newfound friend, who does not know I exist.

Father Synge looked around his little room at St. Roses. He loved it. It meant more to him than his room in the house on Willow Street or his house at Harvard or his corner at the seminary. This was home to him and Father Colfaxen was father, but a home and father he would give up now, though not gladly, for the new thing that had come into his life, "Dear Genius."

I could never quit New York. No, it would be to abandon him. This way, being a priest, I can always gain access to him, especially through prayer. Even if he doesn't realize I'm a priest. Or believe that I am, since he must come across an awful lot of phonies. It was a miracle that he called me Father when we first met. I had no collar, I don't think. Even if I had, I was buttoned up and covered. I wore my scarf. I don't look like a priest yet, do I?

Father Synge stared into his dim mirror but took in what of the room it reflected rather than himself. He had been proud to come to St. Roses. Everybody said how lucky he was to have Father Colfaxen for a pastor. Not that he had been ambitious. No, but his idealism was strong then, not tattered, not faded as it was today. Then, when he had first arrived at St. Roses, his pastor used to regard him ofttimes with an indulgent smile. Father Synge had felt coming from the older man a love he needed, something that would be enough. He knew now that a thing like that is seldom if ever enough, that love never stands still, but must either diminish, leaving one wanting, or increase, leaving one burdened. Father Colfaxen's love, though it did not exactly diminish, did spread so as to include others. Father Synge soon felt himself left out of the picture. Was this why, in the final analysis, he felt he must leave St. Roses? In any case it was not erotic. It was sentiment. Monsignor Colfaxen was for Father Synge a father, the father he had never had but continued to search for—a strong father, an almost God-like figure who would take him up when he was hurt and console him, who would straighten him out in his long, tiresome dispute with God.

But Colfaxen, now monsignor, with his great red-haired chest like a burnished shield, his prole background, his faith, his touching love and knowledge of great painters, wanted no son, not really, not even a spiritual son, as far as Father Synge could discern. It was as if the pastor did not trust any youth but his own, feeling, perhaps, that therein lay a trap for him. Physical contact between man and man did not shock Father Synge, anymore than did the freedom to abort a fetus, both being recognized as possibilities by the younger, less passionate priest, whereas to Colfaxen they would be unheard of, at least theoretically. What the boy from Hell's Kitchen would do in actuality was an open question. For you never knew what might spring from the man whose kindness and concern for others seemed infinite to all except himself.

I'm jealous.

He called Sister Secret and told her the whole story.

"I'm jealous. Of his youth, his attachments. Everything he does is a sin to me because I'm jealous. Jealous jealous jealous."

"Don't rant, Stephan. Of course you're jealous. But admitting you are doesn't mean you're going to give it up. Send him to me."

"You're going to steal him."

"I've never stolen a thing in my life, Stephan Colfaxen."

"No, you pray for them to come to you and it's just as bad."

"His mother's leaving her house to us."

"Thief! My God, you are a thief, Annie."

Bishop Fashoda was a mystery to most. Some people said his was a coal-mining background. Others swore he was the son of German immigrants. He was dark and Teutonic, but he could be soave as an Italian. Perhaps it was his sometimes laid-back American way that made people suspect he was not a native son, but a newcomer convinced that America was the best of all possible countries in the best of all possible worlds.

Some found him causey, others considered him a greasy dodger. One unchangeable and sure feature about the bishop was his smile. He smiled at everything, yet it wasn't a tic, a nervous quirk. It was real, too. It wasn't a painted smile. It liked you, but at the same time it seemed to tell you to beware. Another thing about this smile of the bishop's, it made no wrinkles, yet it did not come only from the eyes. The eyes seemed to be of a velvet texture, tranquillo as a pair of dark purple pansies.

He was the sort of man people come to, or are sent to, saving the bishop the trouble of summoning them. He was very churchish, yet his leanings could be towards the underground of things. He came out for amnesty to draft dodgers, for example. Fanatics thought his stand on abortion fishy; he was all right when he wrote letters about it, but one lost sight of the enemy when he talked about it. When the airplane people struck and were automatically released from their jobs for life, Bishop Fashoda appeared to take their side.

If people were lost down in mines, if houses caved in because they were not kept up by greedy landlords, if a bus rode over a cliff in Peru or insurgents were shot down by the military in Chile, the bishop claimed he could not sleep, and sent baskets begging amongst the pews.

To some he was like the Tree of Jesse, forever shooting green, but to most he was a wonder and a pain, a regular nuisance, who was all things to all men and whose fingernails, some said, were so highly polished that you could see yourself in them if you had a mind to. This was the man Colfaxen sent Father Synge to, the most beautiful man in the American church. Everything he wore looked as if it had come from Hermès, the old Hermès, before it spread out and opened stores all over the world, when Hermès meant the Faubourg St. Honoré, and not Main Street. He was a work of art with the sympathies of a libertarian.

"Long time no see," were his first inexplicable words to Father Synge, the words of a man who knows everybody and assumes that they all know him. "A cause! A cause! Something to wake us all up. I envy you, Father Synge."

This is combat, thought Father Synge, girding himself mentally for a fight.

"I hear you have a cause, Father?" the bishop next said. Then he broke off. "Aren't you going to sit down? Are you going to continue to stand and stand and make me feel older and older?"

"I'm sorry."

"You're not. You're superior. If I were the Pope, you would still act superior. Spurning all comfort, appearing before me in ragged but good clothes, though tasteless."

Father Synge sat down. The two men smiled at each other.

"They are my mother's taste, not mine."

"Oh, your mother. Now your mother. I'm glad you brought her up. She's leaving her property on Willow Street to the Shelter of the Sacred Heart of Jesus."

"She is?"

"You seem surprised. Why? Did you expect to get it? When I heard of it, I went over to Chinatown to a little church I like and said a prayer for her."

"For my mother?"

"Yes, for your mother. As for you, I think you should go over to Sister Secret. What do you say?"

"I...!"

"She's branching out. She has the house next door now to the one she began in. God knows how she does it. She says she prays. I want her down in South America, or Nicaragua. I don't see why I should let her play it safe up here. She's not being used to her capacity. Who is? Go on over to her, Father Synge. I'm no good to you."

"But Father Colfaxen..."

"Stephan?"

"Yes."

"What about him?"

"I mean, I'd break his heart."

"It was your mother's heart you broke when you became a priest. You're used to breaking hearts. You'll probably do it all your life. It's hard for some of us not to. Come, I'll walk you over to New York."

He left the room to change from his soutane into something he considered suitable for the streets and came back wearing a trench coat which gave him the appearance of having dropped years in the interval.

Father Synge did not feel comfortable with him. The bishop made him feel he was in the company of a dandy. He was used to educated Americans who played themselves down, who acted tall even if they weren't, and who tended to be stoop-shouldered and dopey-faced. Bishop Fashoda left no doubt that he felt himself to be the center of things.

He stopped in the middle of Brooklyn Bridge and surveyed the scene as if he had made it himself. Indeed the traces left by men were everywhere evident, from the crowd of river traffic to the construction of the bridge itself ("The best thing Americans ever built," he said) to the crumbling pilings off South Street.

New riverfront dwellings vied with one another for a place in the sky. Old South Street brick buildings, with all their gold lettering, were gone, or going. Instead of all that was once loud and striving, riotous nights and slumbrous days, sailing ships and scows, sailorish jamborees, bouncing bars, and all sorts of languages spoken and songs sung—there had now been built in place of that mishmash of salty things, of wandering, pale-eyed men and sun-dyed boys, museums of these beings, their things, and what they'd done. Adventure and adventurous men would be enclosed behind glass, as it were, like exotic, captured fish in aquariums, doomed, both fish and men and all their wild ways, to be looked at or read about now for what they had been, not for what they were or would be. South Street, where bowlegged sailors once predominated and grinned to hear their parrots swear and their little monkeys chitter.

"I used to come at night on the bridge when I was a boy," the bishop was saying. "I used to swear that God would not get me, but that I would be a wanderer to the end. I cried after ships and for times past. I even got a job in a fish market down below. Well, you know yourself youth is a time of love. I was in love with all that used to be here. The mackerel, the cod, the whiting, the beautiful Norwegian salmon were like brothers to me, brothers who had left home and whom I envied; for though they were only fish, and dead besides, they still glistened as if with life. And such life! After all, they had come from farther than I had ever been....But come, I want to show you my church. It's on Mott Street. You probably know it."

The heat of hundreds of burning candles met them as they opened the old church door. "It used to be all Irish down here on Mott Street, but as you see, it's Chinese now. Don't you feel how Oriental it is? The Orientals must have light, and tinsel, and pink paper. But especially light. Especially candles."

Suddenly Bishop Fashoda grew silent. He roved up the nave of the old Irish immigrant church smiling at everything. Smiling when he looked back at Father Synge to make sure he was following him. Smiling when he encountered figures, smooth of visage as he was himself, praying with the palms of their hands together, which one rarely sees done in "white" churches.

"Here's where I wrestled with Our Lord for my immortal soul and Our Lord won, Father Synge." He smiled and shot to his knees, indicating with a pat at the air with the palm of his right hand for Father Synge to follow suit. "You might ask if I feel a prisoner of God now, when I think of ships I might have taken, Father Synge. The answer is no. The other day, for example, when I heard of your mother leaving her house to the Shelter of the Sacred Heart of Jesus, I felt I had been let in on the end of an adventure, a struggle, a struggle where Our Lord was the winner."

The bishop stopped at the door of the old Irish church on their way out and put money in the poor box, first coins, then bills. Then he turned to Father Synge: "Give me your money. All of it." Father Synge did. The bishop stuffed all of it in the box. "Now walk home," he said.

Father Synge didn't, though. He had saved a token for himself to take him back to Brooklyn to the Shelter of the Sacred Heart of Jesus, which now consisted of two houses, not counting Mrs. Synge's house in Willow Street, but was still crowded as ever if not more so. Father Synge was let into the Shelter by an overworked-looking young woman who told him that Sister Secret was not available at the moment but that she would be with him as soon as she had finished her business. Father Synge smiled. The free-swinging atmosphere of the Shelter made him feel liberated after the restricting visit he had just paid to Bishop Fashoda.

"What business is it this time?" he asked the overworked-looking young woman, who appeared willing enough to talk, as indeed everybody did at the Shelter. Voices voices voices. At the bishop's there was only the bishop's voice, but here one felt suddenly plunged into the heart of a great multitudinously inhabited tree—the tree of life, of now, not of sailing ships of long ago nor of great motherly old cathedrals like Notre Dame de Paris, but of today and today's children. Suddenly he knew that Truman's story was a child's story, after all, and he felt that in helping these kids here, he might be helping him, he might even be able to get at him. But how get in? Sister Secret would never take me. And how leave Father Colfaxen? Then he thought of Truman again, and how his story was a child's story after all, and he felt he had hit on something, and he smiled and even laughed.

"My God! I don't see where there's anything to laugh at. If you only knew," said the overworked-looking young woman.

"Knew what?"

"Why, what they're trying to do to this cheeild."

"What 'cheeild'?"

"This cheeild. Lord, Father, where are your eyes? Don't tell us you left them in Paris, tired and no good to you, blinded with looking at the sights?"

"Oh, you mean him, this 'cheeild.'"

Father Synge squatted down so as to be on a level with the little colored boy who emerged from behind the overworked-looking girl.

"What's your name? My name's John Synge. What's yours?"

"Robert."

"Now it's more than Robert, Robert, and you know it is. Robert what?"

"I don't know."

"That's his mother you hear," the young woman told Father Synge. "She's moaning and hollering how she won't let us have him anymore. She wants to go to school somewhere in the South and take Robert with her."

"I want to go, too," the boy suddenly burst out, throwing his arms around Father Synge and becoming ever so talkative, as if he would never stop, his slightly upturned, wide-apart eyes looking over Father Synge's shoulder as if he saw visions of things wished for and dreaded. "I want to go, but I'm afraid she'll leave me nights. So I think I'll stay at the Shelter."

"Listen to her, just listen to her, though. She's a minx and always was. Of course he wants to stay, but what can we do against the law? The law's on her side."

"You bet it is," said a great-sized woman, coming out into the hall followed patiently by Sister Secret. "The law is on mah side and Ah'm aimin' t'keep it theah. All this talk 'bout me beatin' thad chile. I nevah beat thad chile. Robert, you answer yoh mothah now, did Ah evah beat yawl foh bed wettin', Robert Devereaux?"

Robert turned to answer his mother, but before he did so, he winked at Father Synge.

"No, Mama, you never whipped me, except..."

"'cept whut?"

"Just except."

"Chile's grow'd uppity since he came to the Sheltah. Ah don' want no uppity chile."

"I don't blame you," said Sister Secret, speaking for the first time.

"Now, Sistah, no wheedlin' Robert outa me. Jus' foh tonight, maybe, 'cause Ah got me a mess o' things t'do."

The thought of having a mess of things to do rattled the big woman from head to foot, and she took no more notice of the boy, but flounced out of the Shelter as if she suddenly felt the place was a danger to her. Sister Secret waved her off as though she was her best friend.

"Someday she'll go away and never come back. Not because I wish it, but because it's her nature."

"Then what will happen to Robert?"

"Why, Robert will be all right, Catherine. Don't look so startled, John. I've learned a lot about mothers since I opened the Shelter. Sometimes I feel most children are better away from home, though I don't say it. Catherine, take Robert and teach him manners."

"Manners! Manners!" cried Robert, jumping up and down. He stopped suddenly and held himself in the crotch.

"Come, Robert," said Catherine, "you don't have to do it that way. You can just excuse yourself and go to the bathroom."

"That's right," said Robert. "Excuse me everybody. Good-bye, John."

"Father Synge, Robert."

"Good-bye, Father Sing. Sing a song of sixpence, a pocket full of rye. Four and twenty blackbirds baked in a pie," sang Robert, going off with Catherine and forgetting all about holding himself.

There were lots of children running up and down the stairs between their little classes. You could see that they had been dressed carefully by their hard-working mothers, most of them, clean white stockings and plaid skirts and polished Mary Janes. Many sang a song of sixpence after Robert Devereaux, but few got it so exactly and passionately as he did.

When all was quiet—comparatively—and doors had been closed, Sister Secret said to Father Synge, "I wish I had real teachers, John, learned boys like you. I could make wonders of my children. Robert, now. Robert Devereaux can read and write like lightning, but he needs a catalyst in his life, someone more than me to teach English, say. Well, there's no sense dreaming. I can't afford the company I dream about, John."

"I don't see why not," Father Synge heard himself saying, and he knew he was lost, that she had him hooked.

He felt his knees were shaky, but he wasn't sure. His mouth felt dry, too. He suddenly felt that he was taking the most terrific exam, though he had given no thought to it before. He felt he was being tested. He felt he must prove himself. He felt that it was a matter of now or never.

Sister Secret appeared to have forgotten him, which was

just as well, since he could have sworn he looked very foolish indeed.

He went into some ridiculous sort of trance where Truman and Robert Devereaux got mixed up in his mind, and where he was convinced that by helping the one to begin, he was helping the other to continue.

"Hope, Sister, is an awful burden to put on others," he managed.

"Yes, John, if only I could let people alone."

"Me too."

"I mean, John, that humanity's none of our business, is it?"

"I know. Sometimes I feel like nothing but a buttinsky."

"Me too. I'm glad you tell me this, John. Till now I've always felt I'm alone in feeling that I ought to mind my own business. After all, who am I to tell others what to do? Have I done such wonders with my own life? But, you, John, are a different matter. An educated man, a learned man. You wouldn't be telling people what to do, you would only be handing on knowledge come down to you from the ages, the magnificent ages of man, John. Then think, John, there's always one who catches on, one of them who is the reason why."

"The reason why I'm doing it, that I'm there at all: yes."

"When do we begin, John?"

The woman who only a little while ago stood in the lower hall of her Shelter of the Sacred Heart of Jesus complaining of how she could not afford the company she dreamt about appeared to be rich enough to outbid the highest bidder.

Chapter 21

"Oh, she's tricky, very tricky. Too tricky. Not to my taste at all," was Nora Synge's comment to Father Synge when he told her of his latest commitment.

"Teaching English to babies. Don't tell me you had to go all the way up to Harvard to learn to do that, John! Well, maybe you did. Will you still be a priest? Or what? I don't understand things like that, having little or no interest in them except what is forced on me. Why, it's never occurred to me how I'm to be buried. Now how do you like that? How do you feel about it, John? Don't you care? Or are you like your father?"

"Oh, I don't care."

"Yes, you're more me. Though it wouldn't be like me to lose a suitcase in Paris. I heard you went chasing all over the place looking for the guy you were photographed with on First Avenue. And all the time he was here, ruining himself. John, you can't do anything about a man like that, so forget him. Colfaxen's right. Colfaxen feels you've forgotten everything you ever learned because of him. Not that I trust Colfaxen. Father Colfaxen, Monsignor Colfaxen now, mind you, gets carried away. You're no good to him, John. You confuse him. He's a simple man who liked to think he'd made something of himself before he met you. Now he doesn't know what to think. He says that you told him the only reason you're still a priest is because of this Truman. Is that true? That you were ready to shoot the works before you met in Rajah's Bar and got to talking. It's a wonder you didn't fall down yourself when the two of you hit the air, John."

"Nobody fell down."

"Is it true you were about to quit before you went out with him?"

"Yes, it's true."

"Just tell me why, John. In a word or two."

"Because he called me Father."

"Why, that'd been done before, John. What was different about him calling you Father and hundreds of others calling you the same thing? You've been called Father for five years, John. Surely you should be used to it now. If I'm used to you being called Father, I don't see why you aren't. I'll admit it was a shock to me at first. I felt outraged, though I never let on. I never thought much of priests and I still don't. Priests and sisters. Why, they come a dime a dozen. I thought you were different. I counted on you. I'll tell you when I was proud of you, John. I was proud of you the day you graduated from Harvard. Up there under all those trees. Say what you will about New England, there's heritage there. There I was, Nora Synge, and you, my son, John. I cried."

"He called me Father as if out of a great need for somebody, anybody at all, who would try to help him and not screw him, exploit him. He called me Father without knowing I was a priest, at the very moment I was on the point of giving it all up."

There was a stir in the hall outside the parlor door, startling both mother and son, who were so intent on their conversation with one another that one might have been forgiven the assumption they were conspiring, which was not the case, of course.

"Sometimes," said Nora Synge, composing herself, "I quite forget I have someone living with me. Come in, Maria."

Maria did so, but not quietly, as was her nature ordinarily; instead she threw herself on Father Synge, laughing and crying all at once.

"I have been listening to what you said, Father Synge, and I am so happy. If anyone was meant to be a priest, it is you."

"Well, Maria," Nora replied to that with a light laugh. "I'm glad you think so. You're the only one of the three of us who seems to."

"But that's not true, Mrs. Synge. Didn't your son just tell you he had decided to remain a priest because he had experienced a miracle?"

They all laughed at this, and the subject was let pass without further talk about it. Maria seemed more intent on her own physical being than on anything else, pushing her belly out so that no one could miss the fact that she was enceinte, and furthermore proud of it.

"She was ashamed of it when she first came here," said Nora after Maria had left them to prepare tea. "She didn't want the child at all. Nor did Juan. Who can blame them? They had no job, no home. There was no room in the inn."

"How do you like their being here with you on Willow Street?"

"I think they have made me older with pampering, John. Especially Juan, even though he is out of the house most of the day. It turned out he knew a little about carpentry and has found a job. Of course Sister Secret takes all the credit."

"She doesn't. She's not like that, and you know it."

"Annie Bushnell can wind a man around her little finger and always could."

The telephone rang out in the dark old-fashioned hall where it was kept under the stairs, as people used to do, as if it was something shameful, talking into a metallic instrument and being talked back to, and so it was considered best by all to do it in the dark.

"I wonder who it could have been?" Nora Synge asked, since Maria failed to appear. "She's talking Spanish, so it must be Juan. I hope nothing terrible has happened. You don't think she could have had a miscarriage in the little time she left us to go make tea, do you, John?"

Maria came into the parlor at last, looking pale as she could, which wasn't very, and without the tea.

"It was Father Colfaxen. I mean Monsignor Colfaxen. He's all upset and didn't want to talk to anybody, but was relieved all the same when I told him you were here, Father Synge."

"Why, where did he think I'd gone? I'm not about to run away, Maria."

"Sometimes it seems you are, Father Synge. That's only my impression, of course."

"What has upset Father Colfaxen, Maria?" Nora impatiently demanded.

"Oh yes. They had started work on the church, St. Roses, and Father Colfaxen is worried about the painting."

"What work, Maria? There's never going to be any work on St. Roses."

"Yes, of course."

"I know the painting," said Nora. "I can't take it in, though. There's no room in the inn, John."

"I know, Mother."

"I sit here trying to figure out would it go there, could it go here? The only place I can think of is the cellar."

"Shall I call Father Colfaxen and tell him, Mrs. Synge?"

"No, Maria. I didn't mean I would put it down the cellar."

"Father Colfaxen wouldn't care. Just so long as it has a place. It would be like Juan and me when we came here, Father Synge, and your mother took us in. It's only a painting, but it means so much to Father Colfaxen. That's how he is. You know. Driven. Candlesticks you can hide. The painting is big. It is ungainly. It should have been moved before, of course, but it wasn't. Now it is almost too late. That's all poor Father Colfaxen seems to care about. It's not true, of course. It is just the fact that the painting is his focus now in his hour of need."

"You better get over to him, John. And John, get the painting over here. Maria's right. We'll find room."

Nora's eyes targeted in on Maria's growing belly, and she thought of the kid the enterprising little Mexican was about to spring, wondering could she stand the noise and worry, the excitement of a brand new life in her quiet house on Willow Street. Suppose it was a boy, a little brown firebrand with characteristics of a Zapata, a little revolutionist revolted by the quiet gringos of Brooklyn Heights? It was all so foreign.

"Get me a cold beer from the icebox, Maria. You can call Colfaxen about the painting later on. No, you better do it now. If worse comes to worse, we can always take the canvas out of the frame and roll it up for storage."

"That would be sad, Mrs. Synge. Besides, Sister Secret wouldn't hear of the picture being rolled up and stood in a dark closet and forgotten."

"What's Sister Secret got to do with it?"

"Well, you know how she is."

"Get me a beer, Maria. Have one with me, John. Father Synge. Imagine me being able to call you that."

"Yes, I never thought you would," was Father Synge's reply after Maria had left them.

"I never thought I could, John. Who knows? I may even go hear you say mass someday. Me, brought up the good Lutheran that I was. Good German stock, all of us, up and down Willow Street. You had your fun with them, you and your father. Will they still let you say mass—if you go over to Annie Bushnell, that is?"

"Oh yes. Everybody's with me."

"John, everybody always has been with you. You're a very lucky young man, if you only knew it, but you don't know it, do you, John? Now what are you up to? You were always doodling with a pencil and paper when you were a boy. What is it you're writing about, John?"

"If I'm to teach those kids, I should have a plan. If only one knew where to begin."

"Begin with love, John. Your own love of reading and writing. They'll soon catch on. I don't know what's happened to Maria and our beers. Go see what she's up to. It's not the baby so soon, I don't think, but it will come along any minute now, and I'm all on pins and needles about it. If it's a girl, I refuse to have them in the house a minute longer."

"Why, Mother!"

"I want a boy, John. Yes, I want a beautiful bronze little Mexican running through the house, flashing and passionate, as if the sun itself had come to see me off. I've had a good life. Harvard was a bonus. Then there's mass left me, if I should choose. You're worth a mass, John."

Maria put down the telephone in the dark hall and caught hold of Father Synge as he was about to pass by her into the kitchen for a can of beer for his mother.

"Maria! The light is so bad here under the stairs that I didn't see you. What are you up to? It's not the baby, is it?"

"It was Sister Secret, Father Synge. There is no need to roll up the painting. Sister has a place for it at the Shelter."

VERBIER, MAUNDY THURSDAY, 1981

If Truman were here, we would have left long ago for the Costa Brava. We would not be here smelling dust. We would have been on the road, or already in Perpignan, where the people are dark and handsome. We would be winding down the coast to Spain and water!

PARIS, 22 APRIL, 1981

There is an Englishman's red Jaguar parked outside on the Quai Voltaire in front of the hotel with a sticker on the back window: RESTORE NATIONAL PRIDE, RUN A JAPANESE CAR OFF THE ROAD TODAY.

NEW YORK, 30 APRIL, 1981

Truman bad when I got to the apartment. He did not seem to realize that I had just come home from Switzerland. "Do you know me, Truman?" I said to him just now. He looked at me for a long time. "Of course I do. You're Jack," he said then. He appeared here in the library trying to button on a shirt. He said Cocteau had done the pillow on the sofa. I told him that it was the embroidery work of George Platt Lyons. I think he'd picked up a biography of Cocteau in the other room. He cried softly as if over the past, past glory, telling me how he admired me and always had. He was thinking of photographs of himself. Everything he saw made him sad. When I went into the bedroom, I saw he had wet the bed. It may be that's what made him cry. He knows he's mad. He knows I know it. "Something one's thought and thought about," he said. Then he looked at me, rolling his eyes, holding back tears. "You know what I mean?" he asked. I said that I did, my heart breaking. The both of us cried, but as I did not want him to see me doing it I left him and went into the library where he followed me.

"You weren't here last night."

"Yes I was, Truman."

NEW YORK, 6 MAY, 1981

"Come out, come out..." was the war-cry through the streets of Catholic Belfast yesterday when Bobby Sands, the

hunger-striker, died in Maze Prison after sixty-six days without food. I saw a great crowd, 10,000 the papers say this morning, though it didn't look anywhere like that much to me, march by the British Embassy on Third Avenue. They were a wild looking lot, many with relatives over there, I guess.

Truman was better yesterday, much better, thinking and speaking clearly, but he had to ruin it all by drinking more than a pint of vodka after he went to bed. He was, as usual, all right at first, talking about Oona and Gloria and Carol just as he used to do. Then, suddenly, he asked me did I know Gerald Clarke. Well, of course I know Gary. This morning he read the papers for the first time since I got back from Switzerland.

A mass was said for Bobby Sands across the street in front of the U.N. under the budding trees as night fell at the end of a clear day. Seven priests officiated. The crowd of five hundred or so was subdued. There was music of course. A boy played a silver flute for a great length of time. It was funny how long the music went on. It was typical. As if none of us had anything else in the world to do but stand there on the sidewalk and listen to it! How Irish!

During mass the beatitudes were read as if their meaning was secret to all but clergymen. By then, Maggie, bored with standing so long, threw herself down on the cobblestones and rested her chin on the curb, her eyes closing and opening by turns on the ceremonious gathering of mourning priests on the improvised platform across the street.

Chapter 22

The old doomed church of St. Roses on First Avenue did not mean much to me until I saw it being torn down. Like others I wondered what would happen to the painting of the Last Supper that had hung over the high altar and had acted as an obvious consolant to many that I myself had seen studying it. It was more of an historical work than religious, putting me in mind rather of the big things Baron Gros did of Napoleon, or even the great propaganda paintings of Jacques-Louis David. I did not think much of it, oddly enough, unless I was looking at it directly. Then it used to hold me, rather. I did not think it was very good. Perhaps no one else thought so either. But it represented St. Roses in essence to me, as it obviously did to others. For all around me through the din of the roar of tractors and the thump of the demolishing iron ball, I heard, or felt I heard, since the noise at times was deafening, little people trying to console themselves in little ways for the passing of time, in which they knew they had no say.

It was a remorseless scene. I suppose that amongst us there were those who had seen their own places go, where they had lived, just as St. Roses was going. They had never said it belonged to them, but now they seemed to be saying just that.

"It's the way of the world," said a lady to me, but seeing that I was about to answer, she fled.

It so happened that she bumped straight into Father Synge, who stared at me as if he felt it was all my fault. Everything. The demolishment of his church. The noise. That the woman had inadvertently bumped into him. Everything. Even the grey day.

Newsmen with their cameras were around, but they soon went away, and their stories never appeared.

I had come by at about four o'clock in the afternoon, out for a walk through Central Park, when the sounds of the wreckers drew me back from Second Avenue to watch with others, though the dust and malodorous fumes rising from the site were choking the lot of us, even with sprinklers going to keep down the dust and lessen the possibility of little stones flying in our faces and those of the people passing by on the run.

"I wonder what happened to the painting?" asked an old thing of the dusty air, looking at no one but meaning to be heard and even answered. She had a dog on the leash and another dog in her arms, she had a shopping bag too, and she was wearing bedroom slippers, not shoes. And she had left her teeth at home, if she had any, and was enjoying herself in that brown, bitter way of New Yorkers, catastrophe-hungry and taking no pains to hide it. She talked through the last bombardment of old St. Roses for the day, so all her words were lost to me except the final one, delivered in the sudden quiet of quitting time:

"...Vatican."

Working men passed us on their way home without looking back at the havoc they had wrought.

"Sure it's in the Vatican."

She pulled her dog on the leash away from Father Synge as if he was enemy and cuddled the one in her arms away from me.

"Everything of any value they can get their hands on over there is stored in the Vatican. We've seen the last of it."

Here she gave the leash a yank, causing the spidery creature on the end of it to twirl in a forced pirouette, after which he swayed, wobbling in his little way from side to side on his hind legs, until he was pulled forward to his mistress so very energetically that his collar slipped over his skeletal neck, leaving him free for the first time in his short life. Now it's an accepted fact that given freedom, few creatures know what to do with it. Such was not the small dog's case. He tore into what was left of the old church of St. Roses between the legs of the last of the departing wreckers. By this time Father Synge had been joined by his fellow priests, and the lot of us trooped into the remainder of the church after the old woman, whose interest in the recovery of her pet was superseded by the discovery that the cherished old painting of the Last Supper, so long connected with the neighborhood parish of St. Roses, no longer hung in its place over the high altar, though both altar and roof above it were still intact.

"There now, didn't I tell you it was gone?" the old woman cried, collaring her dog. "Didn't I say they had it in Rome? Ah, leave it to them to take what we prized. 'Tis no use crying over spilled milk, though. Let's remember past times with pleasure. It'll come back to us, Fathers."

She peered through the unsettled dust of demolishment at the five priests, huddled together with the exception of Father Synge who stood apart with a half-smile on his face, sad, accepting, and grudgingly mature. He looked a bit more like a man now who had been abroad in the world and could take in the old woman and her dogs, her prophetizing out of a broken heart. As for the other priests, blasted out of their sense of security, it seemed to me that if wishes were bricks, there would have risen between them and the old woman and her dogs as undemocratic a wall as any tyrant could have wished for.

"We who have nothing are used to living in the reflection of holy things. To call them our own would be unheard of. In the long run, Fathers, what does it matter where it is, so long as we can see it plain as if it was before us still, still lit by the burning candles of old St. Roses?"

The tallest priest took a decisive step forward as if he owned the place. "I'm going to say mass, Mrs. McLavery," he called out to the old lady across the dusty pews. "Stay, if you like, but it will be at your own risk. Benito, run across the street and get the necessaries."

"Is that you, Father Colfaxen?" the old woman calmly replied. "It's as smoky as a gambling casino in here. Sure, say mass. You're still pastor. St. Roses deserves a mass."

During mass plaster fell from the walls and ceiling in a tired sort of way every once in awhile throughout the church, reminding me of the war, of Rouen, where the wind and rain ran through the cathedral like the unvanquished spirits of former choir boys. The single candle Benito had brought from the rectory across the street sufficed. Monsignor Colfaxen passed pieces of bread amongst us, but otherwise it was a dry run.

Chapter 23

Father Synge caught up with me outside Rajah's Bar on my way home. I had not talked with him since his visit to Switzerland, where I suppose I had been pretty rough on him, and was as a consequence shy with him now. Father Synge's manner, on the other hand, was combative. I had felt something different about him at mass just now at St. Roses, but I was unprepared for what I considered a sharp change in him.

"How is he?" he demanded straight off. He even glanced into Rajah's in a blaming-me sort of way, as if he saw Truman sitting up at the bar in there.

"Oh, all right, Father. Actually, he's been very good."

"Really. I'm glad to hear that."

He didn't sound glad. He sounded disappointed. He might have been a surgeon who was ready to cut but was put off by a turn for the better in his patient.

"Whatever happened to the painting at St. Roses, Father?"

"I know perfectly well what happened to it. It's over at the Shelter of the Sacred Heart of Jesus in Brooklyn. He's all right, huh? Any chance of putting him away for a cure?"

"I don't know. I'll have to ask him. Did you ever get the bag back you lost in Paris?"

"No, but I don't care about that. Everything's changed for me."

"It has? And...how do you feel about the changes?"

"You ask as if you didn't believe in them, as if you felt you need a sign of their veracity, that there really have been changes. You're right. They should show on me. I should appear more sure."

"You seem to me to want to appear more sure."

"Yes, I...want to learn to accept things, as you seem to be able to do."

"Me, Father? I'm at odds with everything. And always have been."

"No, you're not, you only seem to be. Left to yourself you have a kind of peace. It is only under questioning that you are restif. Questions make you unhappy."

"Only because I don't know how to answer them."

"Weren't you afraid of the ceiling falling in on us just now at St. Roses? I was."

"No, I was thinking of the war, of fallen plaster. That's what makes the mess. Fallen plaster mostly."

"And nothing else? My God. Nothing else?"

"I remember the plaster mostly. The smell of it. I think it was a sour smell, but I'm not sure."

"And not bodies? Did you see bodies? Dead boys' bodies?"

"Yes."

"I don't see how you can be a writer. You're so inarticulate. Unless—does it come out in your writing?"

I said nothing. I thought he was a snobbish sonofabitch and would never read me.

"What are you thinking?"

Of what a lot of shit all the people were who were trying to help Truman. No wonder at night, when I took his hand, he seemed to me sometimes to heave a sigh of relief that we were away from everybody, at least until morning came.

"I'm going to start teaching over at the Shelter of the Sacred Heart. I want you to come see us over there. If I believe in anything it's that. I won't be doing anything worse than St. Francis Xavier did when he walked through the streets in India and rang his bell to call the little children to him to teach them to pray. You probably don't see it as anything, but I assure you the sight of those kids does something to you. Aren't you going to ask me anything about it? Oh, I forgot, you don't like questions."

"It all sounds wonderful, Father. I hope you'll be happy over in Brooklyn."

"I wish I could take Truman with me. He must experience conversion again as, for example, when he first decided he had a vocation to write."

"Yes."

"You see, he must aspire again."

"Yes, I know. He does, too."

"Aspires?"

"Yes, it's a sort of yearning back towards what he feels is

right—to a way things were before he published *In Cold
Blood* and sold the movie rights and we did not live in the
palace across the street."

"What does he do when he aspires?"

"He gets washed and dressed and presents himself to me
for approval."

"That's very touching."

"Yes, and he says he's going out for some pencils and paper, that he'll be back in a few minutes."

"And does he come back?"

"Always."

"And has he bought pencils and papers?"

"Yes, and magazines, sometimes as many as six magazines."

"To read after he writes."

"I suppose, except that he reads them first, for hours."

"Until it's too late to write."

"Well, I take a walk, and by the time I get back, he's usually asleep. I sit down to work in the library and he comes
in calling me to come to bed, even though it may only be
eight o'clock in the evening."

"And do you?"

"No, it's too early."

"Here I am asking all these questions. Do other people?"

"Not anymore. They assume they already know the answers. Sometimes they do. I must go now, Father. I'm glad
about the painting. But what about the lady with the dogs?"

"What about her?"

"I wish she knew of its whereabouts, since she seemed to
care more about it than any of us did."

"I wish I'd said that," Father Synge said, coming close to
me, a troubled frown on his young, unmarked face. "Why
didn't I say it? Why can't I say things like that?"

"Why should you, Father Synge? You must say your own
things. If you're not satisfied with things you say, you must
try to make them better."

He fell back from me as if I'd hurt him. You could see he
wasn't afraid of how he acted in the streets. Nothing much
had happened to him on them, obviously.

"It's very undermining of you to give me advice, you know. I'm supposed to be the one handing out advice, not you."

"Yes, to think you're a priest again, and all because of Truman. That should see the three of us into heaven."

"You don't believe in that sort of thing, do you?"

"In miracles? Sure."

"You say such things, yet you're not cynical. It seems to me you don't care what you say."

"That's true. At least it's true a lot of the time. Talking's a game I don't play to win. I like doing it, that's all."

"Am I your conscience, you think? The thing that tells you you're your brother's keeper?"

"I don't need you to tell me that, Father. I know that now."

"I know you do. You know it better than I do. Well, good night. Don't forget Brooklyn. I want you to see Willow Street, too, my mother's house as well as the Shelter."

"Willow Street I know, Father. We lived on Willow Street, in Brooklyn Heights, in Oliver Smith's house, for seven years."

"Seven years! Seven years and I never saw either of you."

"That's Willow Street for you, Father. Each house is a fortress."

"Yes, it's depressing. But it's true. Well, good night. I feel closer to you, now you told me the two of you once lived on Willow Street."

"Good night, Father."

When I got upstairs, I looked out the library window before settling down to work. The river was dark, but Brooklyn lay stretched out flat as a rug all the way to the horizon lit by little, unpretentious lights, and with no glory whatsoever like Manhattan, but all the same we had been happy there. I saw Truman in the bathtub there, lying on his back in a tub full of warm water, shaving himself. He was going out for the evening. I was probably having somebody in to dinner, but maybe not. The apartment was lovely, with no view at all, since it was on the ground floor. We did not need a view, we had a world view. We were taking off next a.m. for Europe and were all packed and ready. Bunky, Kelly, and Diotima knew something was up, though not exactly what.

They followed us everywhere. And when I took Bunky and Kelly out for a walk, Diotima was waiting anxiously for us at the front door when we came back home.

"I'll be home early," Truman said.

He always said that.

Chapter 24

On Willow Street, if anything was lost, it was found again. Permanent leavetakings were unthought of. Diotima was lost, but I found her again, because that's the way things were then; everything came back; nobody went away for good. When Truman called me on the telephone from Russia, I felt he was close by. Then a Christmas card from Leningrad.

I wasn't so sure of Diotima. Besides, it was summer when she got lost, the time for wandering. She had a way of staying put (perhaps out of fear) and waiting for me to come rescue her. She had done that in the Alps. I found her in the dark atop a mound of snow where I had left her earlier in the day during a walk assuming she would follow me home, but she had not. It could have been she was lost or that she was afraid to venture home at night without me. Not that it was easy finding a white cat in the snow, but I did.

Where was she in Brooklyn Heights? Summer, too, when she could wander clear out of my life and not miss me until it was too late, and the way back to Willow Street would be a blank to her.

The backyards on the Promenade appealed to me. I called into each of them in the dark. I went up and down Pineapple Street calling her. I called on Montague Street where I knew she would not have dared to venture. I gave up and went back to Willow Street to face life without Diotima, but she haunted me so that I knew she must be alive somewhere waiting for me, as she had sat trustfully on my hand

Air mail

Miss Joan Dunphy
300½ East 65 St.
New York, N.Y.
Komy U.S.A.

Leningrad, Dec 27
Dearest— Such a pity
the Hermitage is being
wasted on me (how you
would adore it) though I do
love to go and stare at the
jewels. Did I write that
I'd bought you an
Astrakhan Cap? Tell Joan
there is no such thing as a
"white peasant" coat. Love

as a kitten when I rescued her out of the Aegean where she had been tossed early one morning by children acting under orders of grown-ups. Brooklyn Heights being what it is, I went to bed without telling anybody. She was only a cat.

But in the middle of the night, the second night of her disappearance, I rose and slipped into clothes the nearest to me, sandals, shorts, and ran out into Willow Street, cheerless and ungiving as ever, with its ugly brownstones glued together in animosity and suspicion. Tight-fisted, middle-class Willow Street, with its rows of families all rigidly sleeping the sleep of the just.

What in the name of goodness would a half-naked man be doing out in the middle of Willow Street calling a cat in the dead of night except to be trying to have himself arrested, deported, decapitated, denaturalized? One thing, the street was blessedly quiet. I began to feel supernatural, as if I was walking on air. If anything, Pineapple Street was quieter than Willow Street. Quiet but not peaceful. It was the quiet of a miser counting his money on a velvet cloth. It was a troubled silence. Or was it me? Sad as I was with the sense of loss, I was by this time calculating how I could surmount it as fast as possible and get on with things.

Still, something kept me outdoors, something kept me walking, even though I wanted to forget her now that she was gone. Animals teach you like something terrible. Love has to be learned like everything else. I don't know why I didn't go home, but I didn't. I didn't know why I stayed on Pineapple Street, either, or why I even had a cat, for that matter; why in the world I had dragged her all the way home from Paros, Greece, when, if I was really so mad for a cat, I could go to Bide-a-Wee, where they have cats by the hundreds and tens of hundreds to give away free for nothing to nuts who go in for that sort of thing.

I don't know where Truman was. Manhasset, maybe. Or New Hampshire. Or maybe he was on a yacht with the Italians. Good thing, too. He would have been in knots had he been here. Everybody would have known about it, which is not the way to go about getting something back you've lost.

The way to do that is to go out and stand half naked in a

dark quiet street and pray without letting on you are that a creature you adore will somehow come back to you, or else that she will stay where she is until something guides you to her.

That Diotima, with all her willfullness, might be taken up by someone who did not know her ways crushed me. I stood without hope, yet I waited. I yearned for bed and sleep, yet I could not move towards home. It was as though I had suddenly become hooked to the sky. I could not free myself. I was all hers, Diotima's.

It was a hot night, but I felt chilled. My hands were wet. I hated people for the possibility that they might appear and see me, and told myself a thousand times that I was dramatizing myself. The only thing that held me together was when I thought of what a good story it would all make to tell Truman. Except, if Diotima was lost, really lost, and never to return, where would be the story, and how could I tell it without hurting him, since we took things seriously that the world did not?

Something told me to turn left. When I did, I faced an alley that I had not to my knowledge seen before. All the same, there it was, an alley running surreptitiously behind the fat, brown houses across the street from us on Willow Street. I walked into the alley.

"Diotima…"

"Squeak."

"Diotima, is that you?"

"Squeak," again.

Then, as God is my witness, there stood a ladder rising out of that dark alley I had never seen before that I knew of, and that ladder was leaning against a fence. I climbed it, slipping out of my sandals first so as not to make any startling noises.

There she was. She was sitting in the middle of a yard waiting for me. When she saw me, she thawed all over as if she had been icebound.

Chapter 25

Father Synge entered the rectory of St. Roses to the sound of laughter. It gave him the chills. There was a moon outside and the old church never looked better to him, corroded and jagged as it was, with disturbed tenement life clipping in and out of the light and the shadows, people letting their dogs loose amongst the debris, where they sniffed and ran like wild or stood still and shivered, all at a loss what to do with their sudden freedom.

It was a ghostly sight, and now the sound of laughter from his confrères struck Father Synge as ghostly as well. He dreaded going into them, but Mrs. Wallop took care of that.

"Here he is! We thought you'd left us for the Shelter without saying good-bye. Talk about leaving a sinking ship. I never thought of you as ambitious, Father Synge."

"You didn't, Mrs. Wallop?"

She had done her worst.

Nobody was eating.

"Mrs. Wallop, bring us in a bottle of wine," Monsignor Colfaxen ordered the cook in a tone of utter desperation.

"I won't," said Mrs. Wallop, leaning in the doorway like a cowboy. "Wine'll only make you sad," she explained.

"Or merry," whispered Father Schenck.

"Well," said Mrs. Wallop, "that's just as bad. I don't know that I approve of merry priests. Look what happened in England when Henry the Eighth kicked them out and stole their goods, because he thought they might have been having a better time than he was!"

"Mrs. Wallop, we'll miss you," Benito told her.

"Now don't. Or you'll have me crying."

When Father Synge bypassed Mrs. Wallop and got the wine himself she said he had changed.

"I haven't. What makes you say a thing like that, Mrs. Wallop?"

"Well, I've been thinking," said Mrs. Wallop, propping herself more firmly against the doorjamb. "And what I've thought is..."

"John," said Monsignor Colfaxen, "see if there's some cheese and crackers. Go on, Mrs. Wallop. You were thinking. You were thinking what?"

"That's so, Father Colfaxen. And what I came up with is that he didn't lose that suitcase in Notre Dame, he *gave* it away."

"Not bad," said Benito, and the two old priests shook their white heads yes. "Yes," Mrs. Wallop continued. "He's given up all to go teach foundlings."

"They're not foundlings, Mrs. Wallop," said Father Synge, putting the cheese and crackers before his pastor, whom he loved, he recalled, feeling, at the same time, an echoing flush of physical love throughout his body. "They have mothers, Mrs. Wallop. And some even have fathers."

"We haven't any glasses," Monsignor Colfaxen dryly remarked.

"I'll get them," said Benito, and he jumped to his feet, then stopped and looked around at everybody in his pop-eyed way. "I'll miss this," he said.

"There now, even the thought of wine has made him sad," Mrs. Wallop remarked as Benito rushed past her out to the kitchen. "He'll be in no state to find glasses. I'll go get them myself."

She came back in a minute with some glasses, none too clean.

After Monsignor Colfaxen had poured the wine, Benito came in from the kitchen. Instead of taking his place at table, he walked around, touching his confrères on their shoulders, first the pastor, then Father Schenck, then Father Devine, and lastly Father Synge.

"I don't want any wine, Father," he told Monsignor Colfaxen. "But thank you anyway."

They heard him moving around upstairs, then all was quiet except for Mrs. Wallop singing in the kitchen. First Avenue traffic had long died down. Mrs. Wallop ran out of tunes. They heard Father Scarpia moving around again.

"He's restless," said Father Devine. "He doesn't know what's coming his way. It's only natural in a young man to want to know where he's going."

"He'll miss us, it's like he just said," murmured Father Schenck.

"He won't at all," said Monsignor Colfaxen. "He's young, and only thinks he will. He'll forget us before the dust settles on old St. Roses."

"I don't know how you can say that, Stephan," said Father Schenck. "I remember how I felt about lots of things when I was young, and those feelings were valid."

"Yes, Ben's at a loss. Not like John here, who knows where he's going," said Father Devine.

"Maybe I should go up to talk to him," said Father Synge. He was quiet after that, but then he could not help blurting out, "I would go up, too, except that I'd feel so inadequate. He doesn't want the likes of me talking to him tonight, and we all know it."

"Aye," said Father Devine, sneaking a look at his superior. "He feels he has nobody. I felt that way once, though I told nobody. I wish now that I had. There's always somebody, isn't there? To talk to, I mean, Stephan, don't you think?"

"Of course there is," Monsignor Colfaxen agreed, at his gruffest.

He looked down the table at Father Synge and thought of him as his son, a prodigal son, going away and leaving him with a son he did not care for half as much as he did him.

"Have some wine, John," he cried, as if it were the world he was offering to someone who did not care for him anymore. "How's your charge, anyway, John?" he lightly asked. "Has he stopped drinking? Is he writing? Of course he hasn't, and isn't."

"Remember when men used to take the pledge?" Father Schenck asked. "I remember that as if it were only yesterday. And you know something? It never worked."

"Father Colfaxen," Father Synge broke out, "I wish you'd go up to Benito."

"I will, John. Sure I will. If you think I should I will. I hope I don't wake him. It'll be on your head, John, if I do. Remember that."

The pastor left the table and went upstairs and knocked on Father Scarpia's door.

"My God, now what?" Father Scarpia cried, leaping out of his bed and flinging open his bedroom door. "What's the matter, Father? What's up?"

"Nothing's the matter, Benito. I want to talk to you, that's all. May I come in?"

"Sure, come in, but why?"

"Everything's going to be all right, Benito," Monsignor Colfaxen heard himself say. He stepped into the room and closed the door behind him and leaned his back against it, then the back of his head. Obedience, poverty, chastity, he thought, and the greatest of these is poverty, a vow I took when I was a thoughtless boy, full of feeling and prone to dreams of ambitions.

Make me poorer still, Lord. Let me be empty and unwanting. Let me give, instead, and help, and lift up. But leave me my heart, Lord. Leave me my memories. Let me remember hoping, though I do not hope anymore. Look, help me cut my cloak and give half of it to this poor boy here, whom I do not especially like and could easily do without ever seeing again.

"Father Colfaxen, what was it you wanted? If it's anything I've done wrong, tell me. Is it bad news? If it is, tell me. I can take it. I must take it, Father. What is it you came upstairs to tell me? Is it my family? Tell me. My mother, my father, my brothers, my sisters, my nieces, my nephews? I'm listening, Father Colfaxen. Or haven't you come to say anything but good night?"

Monsignor Colfaxen heaved a great sigh of relief. "That's it, Benito, you've guessed it. I came to say good night. I don't see why I've made such a big thing out of it. It must be the wine. Mrs. Wallop was right."

"Mrs. Wallop is always right. You know that, Father Colfaxen. Good night now."

The old priests had gone to bed when Monsignor Colfaxen came downstairs, and the table was cleared. Mrs. Wallop called out good night. Monsignor went into his office, where he found Father Synge standing over his desk turning the pages of Thomas à Kempis.

"Is he all right?" Father Synge idly asked, his mind elsewhere obviously.

"Yes. All he needed was someone to say good night to. He's young. He'll sleep."

Father Synge closed the book and raised his eyes to his pastor in a challenging way.

"And you, will you sleep, Father?"

"Me, John? Why, I should think so. What makes you think I won't?"

"Nothing. I was only wondering."

"Wondering about what?"

"Wondering why you don't ask Benito to go out with you to the parish on Long Island, Monsignor Colfaxen."

"Well, John, your trip has changed you, hasn't it?"

"It has? How come?"

"You're ever so spunky, John, since you came back."

"That may be."

"Oh, it's true, John, it's true. I'm...proud of you."

"Thank you, Father. Well, good night."

Monsignor Colfaxen listened to the younger priest's footsteps on the floor above as he prepared for bed, but at the same time, in his fancy, he talked Father Synge into accepting the assignment in the same parish that he himself was bound for on Long Island's North Shore. He forgot his prayer for poverty he had only just made while up in Benito's room, and was instead filled with a sense of gratification on having gotten his way, even if it was only in his imagination.

On his way to bed Monsignor Colfaxen fell against Benito's door and damned himself for a fool. Benito, out of bed in a flash, his door wide open, his feet touching in their nakedness, stared at him with such expectancy, such that only the power of youth can bring itself to express, that Monsignor Colfaxen heard himself inviting the unhappy boy out with him to the parish on Long Island. Benito, perhaps for the first time in his life, was speechless. All he did was shake his head yes, but the tears streaming down over his great round brown cheeks were witness to Monsignor Colfaxen that his prayer had been answered after all. And in spite of himself.

Monsignor Colfaxen went to bed himself feeling that there is nothing quite so wearing as witnessing other people's high emotional states, especially if they were young people, like Benito Scarpia and John Synge. How dreadful he had con-

signed himself to a life with Benito. Poor Benito. It wasn't
his fault that he was not John Synge. That he would have to
face him every day, every day be forced to listen to inter-
minable stories about his vast family. The only glimmer of
light Monsignor Colfaxen felt he could offer himself was to
get Bishop Fashoda to override him. Surely more education
should appeal to a boy like Benito. He hadn't the slightest
feeling for religion. It's dishonest of Benito to be a priest,
and it's dishonest of me to have him around when I feel he
should be doing something else, as far from me as possible.
I'd be a liar if I didn't tell him so. So I'll tell him, Monsignor
Colfaxen sleepily told himself. I'll put it to him as gently as
possible that he's mistaken in his vocation. Cruel? What's
cruel about it? No, it'll do him the world of good...

Monsignor Colfaxen was almost asleep when Benito
walked into his room without knocking. "Father Colfaxen,
you must excuse me, but this is a matter of the utmost importance. Did you mean what you just said? Sometimes, Father, you get carried away, you know. It's probably Thomas
à Kempis. There's only so much of that stuff a body can take.
Unless you're a mystic. It wasn't anything John Synge said,
was it, Father?"

"John? What would John say?"

"Oh, well, you know John. John can say the strangest
things. I'm sure you've heard him yourself. I don't believe
a word of that theft in Notre Dame, either. Another thing.
He says he's learning to ski. What's the place like out in
Long Island, Father? I mean if you really mean what you
said about seeing that I get out there with you. It wasn't the
wine, was it? Or mass tonight? We were lucky the roof didn't
fall in on us."

"Go to bed, Benito."

"I can't. I'm too excited."

Monsignor Colfaxen stared at the ceiling. He felt empty.
"All right, my lad," he said, "then don't go to bed."

Father Scarpia broke out laughing, as if he was tickled by
something, which of course he was, like a child. There was
a rustle alongside Monsignor Colfaxen's bed and he felt Benito's breath on his cheek.

"You've made me so happy. I know you'd rather have John with you than me, but I'll try to make up for his absence. I can't tell you what a sense of loss I was experiencing. I didn't believe in anything, Father. Nothing. I lost everything. Now it's all come back because of you. We have to have something to look up to, at least I do. I'm not really religious at all, you know. I wasn't meant to be a priest, but it made my mother and father, my whole family, happy, so here I am. But I'm worldly. I have to have somebody before me that I can hear and see, and even obey. Someone I can honestly look up to, like I do you. I'll confess this wasn't always the case, but tonight has made all the difference. I think you're extraordinary, Father. I really do. To ask me to come out there with you, when all the time it's John you want, is simply remarkable. You're a very religious man. You have a vocation, and you've never doubted it. Not like me. I doubt it every day. Matter of fact, I don't have a vocation, but still and all, I don't think I'd ever leave. I guess I like being a priest. A joker like me. I don't have the imagination to even think of leaving."

A growl escaped from the bed the former pastor of old St. Roses was lying in. No, it was a snore, but it sounded to Benito like a growl at first and it startled him, but then he smiled. "He's asleep," he said to himself, and suddenly all his good intentions were swallowed up in a bitter joke, though he himself didn't feel the least bit bitter, only... funny, and like abandoned. "That's the trouble with the world," Benito whispered, closing the monsignor's door behind him, "God's a grown-up too."

Chapter 26

Soon after his initial enthusiasm Father Synge began to suspect he had only traveled from one parent figure to another in going from Monsignor Colfaxen to Sister Secret. When he entered the Shelter now, he was remembering his own first school days so vividly that it was as if he was doing it all over again. So intense was his agitation that he was sure it showed in his gestures as well as on his face, since Sister began scrutinizing him even more sharply than was her custom, as if she was wondering whether in having him with her she hadn't bought a pig in a poke.

But the children swarmed around him and made him feel like the centerpiece of a newly gushing fountain in their lives. In some ways going back to the ABCs inspired him. Life was simplified as it is in a Matisse painting. Children of three learned to read under his tutelage and caused Father Synge to be accused of witchcraft. Mothers banded together and petitioned Sister Secret to let their children go back to messing in clay. Meeting their children in the evening after their day's work when they were tired, they did not want to compete with babies, their heads full of new words, reading every single sign they saw on their way home at the top of their voices. Robert Devereaux's mother was most critical of the higher learning at the Shelter:

"Mah chile is beginnin' to sound lak a preacher, swear me if he don'."

"Now what difference does it make to you whether Robert can read or not?" Sister Secret wanted to know of the big, sweaty woman with the big feet and little shoes. "You should be pleased."

"Well, Ah ain'. The boy's grown long and narrow. He's not mah chile, he is the offspring of books now an' stuck up like he don' know his mama no moh."

"That's the pride of new knowledge, Mrs. Devereaux. You must be patient."

"Ah'm run clear outa that commodity, Sister Secret. The

boy's tried me beyond patience's call. Here he comes now. Note how he don' know his mama? Oh, he's cold. He is cold. Hello, Robert."

"Hello, Mama."

"There! You heah how he said that, didn't you? How'd you say it, Robert? How come you talk so icy now to yoh mama?"

"I do?"

"Sho' nuf. You strut, too."

"I do?"

"Sho' nuf. Strut foh me, boy."

"I can't."

"Stubborn, too, like his father."

"How is his father? Do you see him? You seem to. If you do, you must see to it that he sends you something for Robert's support. We are hard-pressed here, not as you seem to think. There are others to feed here as well as Robert, Mrs. Devereaux."

"He don't look lak he eats much, 'less it's words. Is that whut they feed yawl at the Sheltah, boy? Words."

"No, Mama."

"'No, Mama.' Hear him? Oh, he is ice. I got me a mind to go home to Durham. *He* won' mind."

She had made him mind, even if he didn't really. Tears appeared in his eyes, and he did his best to suppress a sob. After which, seeing with satisfaction what she had wrought, the big woman rose and plunged out of the Shelter into Flatbush Avenue. But as she left, Father Synge entered, and Robert brushed back his tears as if they meant nothing to him in comparison to the arrival of his instructor and the things he had to tell him.

But there were so many others that he had to wait his turn, and when it came, Robert found his enthusiasm had left him.

"Well, Robert, haven't you anything to say to me today?"

The forlorn child replied with a shake of his head no.

"I haven't anything to say to you, either."

Sister Secret did not know what to make of either of them, but it was to Father Synge that she addressed her concern.

"Why, what's wrong with you today, John? You act as if you've seen a ghost."

"I've made a mistake in coming here," Father Synge told her. "I feel I ought to be back on First Avenue."

Why yes, Sister thought he should too, if he felt like that. Besides, there was his charge, he would be near him. "The celebrity," she specified.

"Oh him!" Father Synge gushed. "He's not there. At least I don't think so. They're out on Long Island."

"Long Island? Why, Long Island's where Stephan Colfaxen is being sent."

"I know."

"So I suppose you feel you should be with him."

"Oh it's too late now, Sister. They've already dispersed, or will be soon, the old priests into retirement, and Father Scarpia with Monsignor Colfaxen. There's no place for me out there. At least not with Father Colfaxen."

"Then...?"

"Then why did I say I should be back at St. Roses? When it's empty, when the church is razed? I don't know. It slipped out. Maybe it was Robert telling me he had nothing to say to me. He can get on your nerves."

"He can. He's high-strung. He's like a wayward little colt whose mother won't have him anymore."

"I'm not," said Robert, his good humor and self-confidence restored because he was being talked about and felt himself to be the center of attention, which is what he liked most. "I'm a horse, a fiery stallion, who doesn't need anybody anymore."

"Well, Robert," said Sister Secret, "that's a brave speech."

It was, and furthermore Robert seemed to be capable of backing it up. He was a well-made little fellow, and when he raised himself up on the balls of his feet, he appeared to have attained heights undreamed of by his two grown-up watchers, who, nonetheless, gave the boy what they could in the way of admiration. Not so monitress Catherine, who descended on the trio, demanding why Robert was not in his class. Robert went off with Catherine docilely enough, but not before Sister Secret informed the monitress that she supposed she would have to take over Father Synge's little English class for him, since the priest had urgent business across the river. "But before you go, John," she added when they were alone, "I want to show you something."

Father Synge, suspecting a ruse on the part of the seemingly imperturbable nun, smiled broadly, which gave him another look entirely—youthful, carefree, wayward. Though not for long: he soon looked tired and tried again, but better than he had when he came in.

In the meantime his hand had been taken and he had been led through a newly cut doorway out of the Shelter and into the house next door, where he encountered the back of a tall, trim, masculine figure posed thoughtfully before the painting of the Last Supper from the old church of St. Roses. Father Synge had not seen it up close till now. The day outside was bright, and the sunlight came aslanting into the parlor of the old brownstone, empty now except for the painting, whose personages appeared to be on the point of making themselves heard, even to rise from the table and mingle with the three who stood before it.

It was the sort of painting that could be best judged on its humanity, since it was not fine enough to be seriously considered a work of art. It was too sweet, and in places inept, but it told a story in a thoroughly acceptable way, not exactly a lie but nowhere near the truth. It was consoling rather than convincing. It made the unthinking think and the thinking feel, as was the case now, where judgment was set aside for wonder at the event that had engendered the thing in the first place.

"Well, Annie, you've done it again," said the tall, trim man, turning and facing them finally, with an air rather of having stepped out of the picture he had been in the process of regarding so privately and scrupulously.

"Done what, Mattie? You talk as if I was in constant competition with the outside world."

"That's it. That's exactly it, Annie. You've hit the nail on the head. That's just what you are: in constant competition with the world outside."

"For what, Matt? Constant competition for what? Now

you're talking as if I was a captain of industry. I want nothing for myself."

"I'm aware of that, Annie."

He spoke softly now, and in a somewhat surprised tone of voice, as if echoing old feelings, which he was.

Father Synge was pleased but saddened to find himself in the presence of lovers, old lovers but no less in love. He felt sad because they gave him a sense of loss of something he was never to have, and never had had. He watched them so intently that he quite failed to see that they were watching him, studying him, at least the man was, ever so intently, and wonderingly also, his wide, thin-lipped mouth hanging open, as if he was about to speak but could not because of a certain puzzlement of feelings natural enough in a man who has come home to the house he was born in, inherited, then gave away, along with the house next door, which he himself had purchased expressly for that reason, as if he had no more care for either of them than if they had been two sticks and a handful of stones.

"He don't look like a priest, Annie," he finally said. "He looks more like his father, who didn't look like anything much, did he, Annie? He looks like Nora too, though. Maybe that's the side of him that goes bar-hopping with celebrities. You've quit for sure, haven't you? It's written all over you that you've had enough of restrictions and restraints and have returned full-fledged to your mother, who went all over the place saying how she didn't want you to be a priest. Not that I blame her. She saw you weren't made for it. You're too good-looking, for one thing. Now, tell me, have you got what you wanted? That's what it is all about. Have you got what you wanted! That's the first thing on my mind when I meet a man, any man, high or low, rich or poor. I ask myself, has he got what he wanted? I haven't. Have you?"

"No, I haven't," Father Synge replied, which took Malloy aback. It was after all not a priestly answer Father Synge returned him. He was used to priests' acting more or less in stereotyped ways.

"Well, Mattie," Sister Secret told him with a laugh, "you've got your come-uppance at last. A priest who answers, whose predicament is as yours. Why, Matt, come now, we're all human here."

"I don't believe he is a priest," Malloy grumped, and he turned as if to go into the picture of the Last Supper out of disgust with the real world. "No, I don't believe he's a priest at all. Nora has led me to believe as much. She's as much as told me she doesn't believe it herself. She says he's come over here to teach these Indians their ABCs."

"Oh that!" Sister Secret laughed again. "That's all in the past."

"You mean to say it's not true?"

"Oh yes, but he's given us the gate. Haven't you, John?"

"I'm not sure. I can't say. No, I haven't. Not really. I guess."

"There's a priest for you. I thought priests were supposed to be sure?"

"No, Mattie. They are no more sure than the rest of us."

"Then it was all pretense—the way priests used to act when we were kids. So sure, so firm, so bossy. Pretending, were they?"

"For the most part, yes."

"Well, Annie, I don't care about all that, you know. I don't and never did. If priests have changed it's about time, I guess, but I still don't understand it when I know I myself haven't changed about them. No, nor about you."

"You've been wonderful to the Shelter, Matt."

"Oh, the Shelter. Yes, I suppose you'll give me a plaque after I'm gone."

"There's no telling about that. God knows you deserve one."

"I've been faithful," Malloy whispered, to which the nun, ever ready with words, had nothing to say for a change. From other rooms you could hear the sound of children singing now.

"I'll stay," Father Synge heard himself say.

"Of course you will, John," Sister Secret robustly replied. "But remember, you're always free to come and go. There are no ties at the Shelter."

A roar of voices and the tramp of a hundred pairs of little feet resounded throughout the Shelter as classes broke for lunch. Up out of the basement kitchen rose the perfumes of simple cooking, onions and turnips and steamed rice. Children streamed downstairs, some for the first time, wide-eyed with surprise that such things as order and cleanliness exist at all. Long benches, tables, scrubbed floors. Glistening heads bent over smoking bowls. After lunch Robert Devereaux came up to Father Synge.

"Hello, stallion," Father Synge greeted the beautiful little black boy, still holding himself despite his present bliss at being spoken to like this, with such obvious approval, holding himself because the memory of hard times, when they beat him for wetting the bed, would not let him go, especially when he felt he had to make water, and dread would rise in him of screamed recriminations and beatings. No matter what, he would be left alone nights behind locked doors, his window too high above the pavement to make a jump for it. Sometimes his mother would come home with a stranger and they would take up the whole bed. Then the little boy who now referred to himself as the fiery stallion would have to make out as best as he could on the floor.

"Fiery stallion!" Robert Devereaux cried, dispersing that other boy, and his brown hands dropped as if by magic from clutching his crotch and he raised them over his head as high as he could, aspiring.

Chapter 27

Truman began telling me about his purloined manuscript in an almost casual way, as if this was the way things were going now, and if I was unaware of the fact, it was about time I brought myself up to date.

I tried, but it was hard. Though shocked, I let on I wasn't. Half the time I did not know what it was Truman was talking about, and I don't think he did either.

This attempt at revelation and confession, for it was both,

had begun back in Paris, where it had come to nothing. He had retreated from this the purpose of his trip practically on his arrival in that city. Perhaps my appearance after having skied for two months in the mountains had put him off. Too, we were not as accustomed to one another as formerly. We were at times quite formal with each other, and had never been more so than in Paris the last time. And it was the last time.

Now, when I go there, I am all right so long as I keep moving, and it is Paris alone that concerns me, but the minute I start thinking of leaving, Truman pops up, calling me to wait for him, not to go without him; telephoning me from the Méditerranée on the Place de l'Odéon that he has a table for us in the bar in front of the little open fireplace; he's down in Les Halles at the restaurant Escargot in the Rue Montorgueil; or, I hear "Jack!" and he's out on the balcony of his room next to mine under the roof at the Hotel Pont Royal where we stopped our first time to the city.

Anyhow he told me nothing then of what was on his mind, why he might have flown to Paris at all and had me meet him there. He spared me as he always did until he could no longer bear it alone.

It was a mixed-up story at best, and he dropped it as suddenly as he had brought it up and was never to mention it to me again. Someone had taken the manuscript, he said, without naming the person. That he could not go directly to the police and get the thing back, but must hire detectives to try and do this for him, always had me questioning his story if not doubting it entirely, which I sometimes did but not for long.

He often said he could catch himself in time, that sooner or later he spied out a bad character. I never thought enough of his friends to be disagreeable to them; there were none I would not call if I feared Truman might be lying helpless with them. The idea that he had inadvertently glued himself to one of them stimulated me to many a one-man searching party.

It was as it was with Diotima, and no lie, that I rose out of bed one night and dressed and crossed First Avenue to some ridiculous saloon where I had no idea he would be in the first place, just a hunch, to discover him seated at the bar surrounded by grifters and drifters. He looked at me calmly, as if he saw *home* in me, and climbed down from the bar stool without a word and came to me. Outside he asked me how I knew where he was, as he was not in the habit of frequenting the dump, this being the only time he had gone there. "How did you know where I was?" We laughed as we crossed First Avenue without a car in sight. I was always glad to get him back, and so was he that I had. People he cared about well enough knew things about Truman that I did not, though sooner or later he would fly at *me* as if from out of the top of a high building, and I was supposed to be there to catch him.

Whatever the truth of the matter of the stolen manuscript, it tortured him. He suffered in the loss of a thing dear to him as no one I had seen suffer before. Yet all his measures struck me as half-measures. His interest in it came and went as well. I suspected that his sense of loss stayed with him. I know it did with me. It was a terrible thing to hear from a careful writer like Truman, such a clean writer, that his life outside, his public life, as it were, had found a way into his creative life and robbed him of what he had formerly treasured beyond anything, and still did, or tried to. I stood numb, as if beside a grave, for it was as inexplicable as death. And, as with death, that final thing, there was nothing to say, really.

Chapter 28

"Annie," Matt Malloy said to Sister Secret after Father Synge had left them to teach his classes after all, "how do you ever find these kids, these troubled kids? I was a poor boy, so I know how we used to hide the fact that we had less than others, since we blamed ourselves for our poverty, not fate or whatever, certainly never the government."

"The statistics of poverty are secret, Matt. Most poor conceal their woe, especially children."

"Good God, Annie, what have you become?"

"One of them, Matt."

"Well, yes. In any case you were never one of us, were you? You fooled us."

"I fooled myself."

"Sometimes I doubt you can add and subtract, Annie."

"I can, though, but I can't multiply. The poor, God help them, do that for me."

"Have you chosen them, or did they choose you? Without them you would have nothing to do. You would make a hell of an ordinary nun. You were, though, weren't you? Again you posed. You're not very honest."

"I could never afford it, Matt. No one with a mission can afford honesty. Honesty in a person implies the assumption of honesty in others. I don't hold that belief, Matt. I have no faith in it. Fighting poverty stripped me of any ideals I might have had. Sometimes I feel I'm fighting wickedness with wickedness. There's none so black who come to my door that I don't feel I could match them deed for black deed. It's as if I don't believe in the existence of goodness anymore, Matt. I know I can't afford to. Even the children I watch as though I were a jailer. They come to me already made, for the most part. Little rapists. Little liars. Little thieves."

"But surely not all are bad. It's this place that makes you despair. You're a happy, sanguinary person really, Annie. You no more belong here than I do. All this misery, day in, day out. Of course you're black. Who wouldn't be?"

Suddenly the cries of the children broke out in the comparative quiet of the Shelter, "Sister Secret! Sister Secret!" Catherine Lepore appeared in the doorway to the house next door. "Come down to the kitchen, Sister," Catherine commanded. "Have you forgotten why?"

"Forgotten what, Catherine? Am I expected to remember everything? Of course I've forgotten, if I ever knew. Well, lead the way. Come, Matt, you might as well join us too, as long as you're here."

"Why, what is it, Annie? No wonder you're so tired. Don't they ever let you alone?"

"Never. No more than you do, Matt."

As the three descended the stairs into the Shelter's kitchen they were met by the rising fumes of burning candles.

"Who's trying to set the place on fire, anyway?" Malloy grumbled.

He had no sooner uttered his last word than a chorus broke forth from the assembled children that fairly rocked the Shelter from top to bottom:

"Happy birthday to you,
  Happy birthday to you,
  Happy birthday, dear Sister Secret,
  Happy birthday to you."

"My God! I'd plumb forgotten," Malloy cried, reaching desperately into his pockets and coming up with a small velvet-covered box which he thrust on Sister Secret, who took it from him shaking her head no! no! as she was led away by ten, twenty, fifty little hands toward a pink cake crowned with a single burning pink candle. They've taken my girl away, taken her away again, Malloy said to himself.

There she stood next to her cake, surrounded by little rapists, little thieves, liars, their faces raised to her, as though she was some sort of light to them, though she saw that they were scrubbed till they were sore sometimes. She returned their holiday expressions with an examining eye, nothing escaped her.

When she opened the little velvet box Malloy had almost forgotten to give her and drew forth a small Swiss watch on a fine gold chain, she held it up over the heads of the enraptured children.

"Don't reach! Don't reach! It's not yours!" Catherine Lepore ordered them, to which her boss cried, "Yes, reach, of course, reach. Reaching is what it's all about!" "Reach!" the kids yelled, stretching their little arms, their hands, their fingers. "Reaching is what it is all about!"

The two old lovers stepped as a matter of course towards Sister's hideout at the top of the house; that the room had been Malloy's boyhood room seemed to encourage their intimacy. They were not the sort who must eat and drink when they met: their interest in each other absorbed them completely. It was easy to see how they could have dated others, gone on parties, danced, flirted with others, since that was the name of the game then as now, while knowing at the same time that they belonged to one another. There are such marriages, unconsummated in the worldly, biological sense, whose sole aim is friendship, whether the concerned parties are aware of it or not, a friendship way and above anything they had when young, and Matt and Annie had such a marriage.

Malloy had never forgiven her for having jilted him without actually wounding him, a rare feat. She had never dropped him. Her concern for him had grown with the years. Now Malloy felt he loved her precisely because she had not given into him. How tell a young man let us be friends without making him angry, breaking his heart, making him feel his very manhood has been lassoed away from him? But that is just what happened. In a way, one might say Matt had never developed as far as Annie Bushnell was concerned. He was still a boy. He still wanted her, or told himself he did. He burned for her, or convinced himself that he did. Though a grandfather now, there was seldom a rare thing he saw—a falcon over his place on Long Island, the windows of Chartres, a Sunday night in Mayfair when shop windows gleamed for him and him alone—that Matt Malloy did not think of Annie Bushnell. It was not so much a matter of giving as of sharing things with her, things that money cannot buy, like the falcon and how he felt like a boy again watching it, and thinking of the bird's fabulous history, and, inevitably, telling Annie. He had had his dark years concerning her, of course, when the thought of her turned him black and mean and competitive. They were his years of success, of begetting children and building houses, stacking mountains of material things between himself and Annie Bushnell. And while he built houses and robbed people of their homes, putting the old into the streets as they do as a matter of course today, Annie gave herself to a religious order in which she found no peace. The whole thing was driving her crazy until Malloy offered her his house on Flatbush Avenue, Brooklyn, and Annie obtained leave from her order as if to go on a trip, except that the trip was to last a lifetime.

She was young then, and when she met Catherine Lepore she had no idea she was ever to be known as Sister Secret someday, or that the empty old house Matt put at her disposal would ring with the cries of children from top to bottom, that babes would be left on its doorstep, and that its doorbell would ring day and night as if echoing not only the misery of the city but its hopes as well. She was known as Sister Secret because people always said of her that they did not know how she did what she did.

Catherine, who knew a thing or two, from street-walking to alcoholism to drugs to abortions, was the first to find refuge in the Shelter, though she had sought nothing so much as oblivion at the time. It was Catherine who brought out the steel in Annie Bushnell's character, Catherine who discovered the positive nun behind the blurred creature in veils bored to death by ritual and things generally that did not catch her up, but put most of her vibrant self to sleep, "which is the way the bishops like us, Catherine," Annie confessed while emerging from the cocoon she had inadvertently spun herself into.

The two women clung to one another, Catherine raising herself up, Annie lowering her sights to take in a world she'd heard of but which she had not actually seen. They dressed as men. In their search for subjects it was Catherine who turned away from the sight of little Robert Devereaux when they first came upon him sitting up in a wet, cold bed in an otherwise empty room, staring at them as if he had been clubbed.

It was days before they got the little boy to speak to them and weeks before his mother showed up to claim him. But by that time Robert had begun to shoot buds indicative of the possibilities of such treasures as he might never have exhibited had he not been found. Still, it was Catherine who knew her way through the labyrinths of poverty, who knew how best to talk to rough men and sly, lying women.

The greater the cruelty suspected, the harder it was to

wrench the child away from it. Often children would be brought by strangers to the Shelter's door, no names would be given, and a child would have to be baptized all over again, if it had ever known baptism in the first place.

Sometimes children would present themselves, only to be snatched back and thrust down again into the pits of misery where the laws of the city decreed they must remain until they had reached an age where no improvement could reach them, when they would be lost forever to order and cleanliness; when they would look back on the day they had made a dash for it, but had been driven back to crumble and decay, to harshness and no sign of grace, there to marry their likes and beget still more impoverished beings, grinning at opportunity, education, and the rest of it as though they were huge jokes they knew better than to fall for.

Chapter 29

Of course Truman never knew poverty of that kind; there was always food and heat enough. His people cooked country even in the city. But in the country, the real country on Mary Ida's farm, breakfasts were vast, from fried squirrel to pork chops, grits, hot buns, even pies. That his young life did not include his mother and father bothered him and made him feel abandoned. Montgomery, Alabama, the nearest big city, was to him what Oxford's lights were to Jude Fawley. Promises made and broken by his parents were to be remembered by Truman for the rest of his life. His one recompense was his friendship with his great-aunt Sook Falk. Sook was the first of the many addicts he was to know so well and even emulate. He used to run for her morphine to the corner drugstore and back in Monroeville, Alabama, where his mother had left him, breaking their promises to return and get him time and time again. When she did, finally, he had been marked with the sting of broken promises which he was always to feel. Years later he would talk to her in his sleep, demanding why she had not taken him with her, why she had left him behind to haunt the post office for news of her to enliven his life in the small town of Monroeville. He was always to hate the homespun baloney of small townspeople, and rusticity in all its forms.

When she did appear to take him away with her, it was the commencement of her life-long determination to dominate a spirit she no more understood than she did the turnings of the moon. At the same time she was to persist in leaving him alone but this time in hotel rooms at night without the solace of familiar surroundings no matter how hateful. She was to be forever trying to make him over, make a man of him. That she did not really want him, and never had, was only to surface with her later on, when drink bared her secretmost soul, not only to herself but to Truman as well. By then she had remarried, this time to a Cuban whose last name Truman was to take as his own, and later on was to be known by it wherever in the world books were read.

He was twenty-three when I met him, and I was thirty-three. I met his mother at a party Truman gave in the Park Avenue apartment he shared with her and Joe Capote, the man she had married, who more or less idolized her. She was a rather handsome little woman with short, stumpy legs, overexpressive eyes, bleached blond hair, and tawny skin. I disliked her intensely after I saw her kick her bedroom door closed on Joe Capote on his return from work one hot summer evening. After that, I took everything Truman said about her lightly. Seeing he could no longer pull the wool over my eyes about her, he confessed how he had almost pushed her out the window of the Park Avenue apartment once when she was drunk. He never said he hated her, but he did all the same. He despised and feared her somewhat as well. She had a crush on a doctor and used to be sick as much as she could to have him visit her.

Truman had a way of telling half-truths and whole lies, so I had developed a wait-and-watch attitude toward his stories of people. Gradually they would emerge as they really were, and not as Truman would have me believe they were. He did the same about me to others.

I would not write about Nina Capote except for the fact of her heavy influence on him. She would have liked to sit on him and smother him, roll over on him and subdue him utterly, as some animals, motivated by jealousy and competitiveness, do their young. Truman was an exotic, and she had no connection with him, really, except in the mere biological sense.

She was a great bore and talked of nothing so much as her aches and pains. She struggled to get to Park Avenue but had nothing to do when she got there, since she knew no one. This she tried to remedy by cooking. She cooked well in a country-big sort of way, but she ruined that as well, since she talked about it, and that was boring too.

He did not love her, but he wanted her to love him. I don't think Nina Capote was ever in love in her life. She struck me as being all for herself, whereas Truman possessed the gift of selflessness. Seated up in bed, fully dressed, supporting his back against some pillows, a writing pad on his knee, pencil in hand, he was an instrument. It was not easy for him to write, but all the same he was at peace when he did, the peace that comes from a sense of achievement, the only peace that counts.

When dreary people have a phoenix in their lives, their objective is to try to tear it down to their own dreary level. Nina and Joe Capote in Sicily were a sight. Joe was all right. He didn't try to stand out. He did not push himself. But Nina was obdurate about fitting in. She just would not. To hear her, it was all Truman's fault that she had come to Taormina, which of course they would never have done had we not been living there. Sometimes I used to feel that Nina felt they had come to take us home. Truman used to look at her as if he was no longer sure who she was. She wore high heels everywhere and constantly, even to bed, I suspected, so as to give herself height and make her ankles look less sturdy. There was too much oil in the food for her, too much caffeine in the coffee, the sun was terrible, the dust suffocating. Where was the rain?

Truman had given her his bed and had come in to me. Joe slept downstairs in the dining room on a sofa. Poor guy, he looked haunted to me, and as it turned out he was. I used to come on him seated at the kitchen table reading the *Herald Tribune* in his B.V.D.s, a cigarette between his rather sensual lips, smoke pouring from his hairy nostrils. He gave me the impression that there was something on his mind. There was. He was trying to make time with our cook, Graziella, who was seventeen or eighteen at the time. Graziella had always sung at her work. Now she was silent. So was Joe. I don't think he could get near Nina. She was too much occupied in trying to convince the Sicilians of her sensitivity, and that she was tout à fait like Truman. The doctor was forgotten, but Joe could hardly dismiss the horses, the numbers, and whatever else he had gambled on, because his debts, like blood vendettas, pursued him everywhere, and were to land the poor man in jail, finally.

How often I used to look at Joe and wonder at him for having left his native Cuba. He never mentioned his country or his people, nor did he talk of anything else, really. This trip abroad was his last fling. Afterwards, everything would be down hill for Joe Capote. His arrest for embezzlement. The works. But first there was Venice to visit.

Chapter 30

All watery places should be seen through fog. They are best then, they are most themselves. This is especially true of Venice. Then all seems water, and what is stone appears as shadows cast down to us from a long time ago. On a wet day in Venice you don't walk, you swim.

It is only when you get inside somewhere that you look around you like someone who has been kidnapped and wonder were you blindfolded or not through streets that were not really streets, and over bridges unlike any bridges you ever crossed before.

In San Marco priests, like rusty dolls, say mass at several altars. No other men are present. The cats, the pigeons, the occasional rat wait outside by sculptures so worn by time and water they could pass for figures on an undulating tapestry. Undulating is the word. Venice is like a great grey undulating wet flag, and its legends are its bâtiments. On sunny days it is still all Carpaccio, it is not so mysterious then, it is gala and historical, but no longer its true self.

For in truth, Venice is a mirage, an idea now, based on all we know of her, her grandeur, her glory, her greed; otherwise she is baseless. She rots and rocks as we watch. She is forever sinking, forever out of our reach. That is why we love her so much.

Nina and Joe got lost in Venice, they blurred out completely. I forgot about them before they even left. She never spoke to me if she could help it, and Joe said yeh to everything, his mind occupied with money matters that would eventually land him for a year's séjour in Ossining.

The next I heard of this rapidly disintegrating couple was that Mrs. Capote was drinking again. It was the following winter, and we were living in Paris at the Hotel Choiseul on the Rue St. Honoré. Truman only mentioned these parents very reluctantly, but they were like a slowly sinking vessel, and they made him feel guilty that he did not want to go to their rescue every time they signaled in distress.

One got the feeling then that at last this mother wanted her son—at last, after abandoning him as a baby, then taking him up again only to leave him alone night after night, so that he never forgot those lonely rooms, and their locked doors, or the window way above the dark pavements.

Realizing that the one way to get him back to her was to make him worry, she took to telephoning across the Atlantic, a fairly unusual expenditure to make in those days, or in any day, actually, since Joe Capote did not make (or steal) that kind of money. Maybe she knew by then that he was dipping into his company's till in order to pay his gambling debts. At any rate, she had Truman back. We were far apart from one another even though we slept in the same room at the hotel. I got up early and went to the dentist on the Boulevard Haussman. It was dark going through the streets even at nine o'clock in the morning. They were cleaning up

Paris at the time, and the grimy buildings gleamed, if not altogether, then in part. I had to pass the Madeleine and the flower market. They did not sell false flowers there then, but real ones, so that it was nice, something to look forward to each morning, like an open fire in the damp and fog.

I came back to the hotel from the dentist one day to find Truman putting down the phone in the bedroom. Nina was dead. I felt she killed herself but refrained from saying so. Truman was not sad, only stunned. He flew home alone. She had him, even if she did not know it. She had got him home, brought him down! She fixed it so he would have to sit by her coffin shaking hands and getting his full of banalities for hours, as she, let it be remembered, had never sat by him, not when he was little, not when he was growing up, never.

He would do it for her, he would do it for other grown-ups who thought he should. He would do it because he felt it was expected of him. He did it despite the price he had to pay, as he did everything that he should not have done, because the price he paid was too great. He was not like other sons. He was better. He was this instrument, this finely tuned thing made of nerves that helped him catch the nuances of things and record them. His sitting there beside Nina was a waste. He could never talk about it. It was too black a farce he played, the homecoming son who sat remembering how he came near to pushing this dead mother he was now dutifully burying out the window of their ill-furnished, nearly empty Park Avenue apartment. Dying she pulled him back to her, dragged the phoenix down to her level, but of course he would rise again. That was the beauty of it. I came home. Joe went to Ossining, where Truman visited him, but it was the end. When he came out, he married a mad woman, then died, swearing eternal love to Nina. The phoenix soared free, his wounds invisible to all but me.

SAGAPONACK, 15 MAY, 1981

Truman went to a hospital yesterday. He called me and said it was in upstate New York, someplace where the Hud-

*son turns and narrows. As always he wants out, sounds
withdrawn, says scarcely a word. I read where Rossini was
afflicted with something doctors diagnosed as cyclothymia,
highs and lows, euphoria followed by terrific depression,
thoughts of death, etc. They might have said the same about
Truman. Rossini was finally "cured." He no longer wrote
opera, only light piano pieces.*

SAGAPONACK, 4 JUNE, 1981

*I give him A for effort. No matter what, he still does try.
Talk about pride. Truman is so proud when he isn't drinking. He means never to touch it again, too, I'm sure. Someday Truman will turn around, I'm sure; I may not be here
to see it, more's the pity, for I'd dearly like to. I've watched
out for him, he's watched out for me; if I buy a shirt for
myself, I'm just as likely to buy one for Truman.*

SAGAPONACK, 15 JUNE, 1981

*Truman lost his leather envelope again. "Well," he said,
"if it's lost, and the two thousand dollars in it, I'll just have
to pull myself together and write a story and sell it for four
thousand dollars."*

SAGAPONACK, 16 SEPTEMBER, 1981

*Maggie rolled down the stairs this a.m., but I caught her
at the halfway mark, and she was none the worse off.*

> *"Fortune knows we scorn her most,
> When most she offers blows."*

SAGAPONACK, 29 SEPTEMBER, 1981

*Truman too sick to move this morning. Called me over to
his house. I fed him, then said I could not sit with him, that
he was a bore and had brought it all on himself by cadg-
ing drinks around the neighborhood.*

Later, in the afternoon, I saw the garage door open on my return from the beach. The Mustang was still there, however, since I had taken the keys—but had not hidden them; they were in the drawer of the hutch in my house where I always keep them. Certain that Truman was too hung over to figure that out, I supposed he had gone back to his house after opening the garage door. He was not in my place.

I decided to shop for food. It was near six p.m. I took the Mustang. Up on Daniels Lane near the Toppings' horse farm I made out a figure in red. It was Truman in his night-gown, shoes, dungarees. Tear lines streaked his face. He told me he was off to find a telephone and to get a car to take him to New York because I had left him, or had left him alone—I could not make out which.

I took him shopping with me. "Is there anything you want?" I asked him before I went into the store (taking the car keys with me). "Yes," he said, "arsenic."

Afterwards I drove us home by way of Bridgehampton and stopped at Emil Pape's store for a newspaper, but it was after six and the store was closed. I'd left Truman in the parked Mustang outside the liquor store across from Pape's. "Go get me a pint," he begged me, when I got into the Mustang. "Why," I said, "I thought you didn't drink. You tell me you don't drink. Never touch a drop." Anyway, I did not get him the stuff, but took him home and fed him. He signed some checks and left them with me to mail.

I walked him home and put him to bed. I can't forget him out there against the autumnal sky in his nightgown, two tears streaking his poor, dear, determined face. I suppose it is sometimes true as Heidegger says that

"Where danger is, there also grows the saving power."

SAGAPONACK, 25 OCTOBER, 1981

I pray for counsel as to what to do about Maggie. Truman tells me I must not think of her as being lovely now. How can I do that? It is not my nature to dwell on the weakest, sickest part of my beloveds, but the best, the strongest part.

SAGAPONACK, 26 OCTOBER, 1981
Adios Maggie.

Chapter 31

Old St. Roses was a wasteland like any other vacant lot in Manhattan. The rectory across the street was empty, its dining room silent, its parlor windows blinded by sheets of metal. Churches used to stand until they fell or caved in or went up in flame, but now they were swept away in the middle of a prayer. Mrs. Wallop thought so. So what? It was old. The thought consoled. There was talk of something else going up in its place. Good. Anything rather than this mess. She was without the wherewithal of the fathers, else she would have fled as they had done. Not all, not Father Synge. Brooklyn was only across the river. She knew he had it in him to be something someday.

The other night now she'd felt she ought to call him but she had not, taken up as she guessed he was by his new work. For all the joking that had gone on at the dining room table at St. Roses about the celebrated charge of Father Synge's, there had been something serious in it as well. To be cut adrift from friend and foe as Truman Capote seemed to be, wandering First Avenue as if he was nobody at all, gave a party something to think about. Especially if you feel you've been left behind, too, abandoned, as you might say. It was just that in seeing Truman this steaming July night, Mrs. Wallop felt they were aligned.

Now here was she that nobody knew, and here was he, a world-renowned figure, him rich, me poor, and yet we have this thing in common: nobody seems to want us anymore.

The long and short of it was that Mrs. Wallop helped Truman home. He was grateful enough. He talked, too, and that's what did it. That's what made Mrs. Wallop feel they had something in common, though he talked of things way out of her ken. He told her he was a wonderful writer, but in such a way as if he wasn't giving himself credit for it. It was as if he felt he had stood out in the rain and this gift had rained on him and into him, so that he was a little apologetic about having it. Otherwise, he seemed to say that he was nobody.

"You must be very careful of crossing streets," he had told her, when kings knew who he was, Mrs. Wallop had thought, and it was like being in church to her. Yet all this time this feeling that they had something in common together grew in her till she began to feel she was almost as tall as where he lived.

Father Synge did not recognize her voice over the telephone right away. It was only the thought of her displacement that, nicking him just as he was about to hang up on her, brought her back to him, not as she was now, quiescent and appreciative but garrulous and deprecatory, as she used to be when she cooked for them at St. Roses. Now she sounded little and old, not long and lanky anymore as if she could stand in for a cowboy, but boxed up in a simple, single longing for times past.

She wanted a job. That's why she was calling him. No, it was just to talk. She had no social life. Her social life had been the rectory at St. Roses. Now her social life was her Social Security check.

"It's good to hear your voice, Father."

"Yes," Father Synge told her, "it's good to hear your voice too, Mrs. Wallop."

She wanted to see him. My God! For what? He felt her advancing on him like a wave from his past.

"I must go now, Mrs. Wallop. You've no idea how noisy and crowded it is here. I can hardly hear you. Stay where you are if you know what's good for you."

But where was she? She had been displaced. Nobody would have her, of course. How old was she anyway? She said she had something to talk to him about and hung up. She did not say she was coming over, but that is just what she did. She arrived breathless, as though she had run across Brooklyn Bridge, and watched Father Synge teaching a class through a crack in the schoolroom door until Catherine Lepore discovered her and told her to go in and sit with the kids.

"You might have to sit on the floor," Catherine told her. "Are they all sitting on the floor in there?"

"Nearly all but not all," Mrs. Wallop replied, her eye to the crack in the door.

"Someone you know in there?" Catherine casually inquired.

"Just Father."

"Father Synge?"

"Yes, I cooked for him when he was over at St. Roses. I think it's wonderful what he's come to."

"We do too. Not that the parents like it."

"Too bad about them. They're lucky to have their kids learn anything the way things go t'day."

"Why don't you go in?"

"I'd be embarrassed."

"Well, it's over now. Some other time. Watch they don't mow you down."

A thousand legger with a hundred heads emerged from the classroom as another thousand legger with not quite as many heads took its place. During this change of classes Father Synge remained at his desk. Mrs. Wallop forgot what she had come to tell him about, then she remembered, then she forgot again. Well, it was all different from when she went to school. She looked around for Catherine, but Catherine had gone, leaving Mrs. Wallop feeling alone and left out of things. It was not Mrs. Wallop's way to hesitate, to hold back, or to put off till tomorrow what she felt was meant to be done today.

"Why, Mrs. Wallop!"

"Now, Father Synge, I know I'm taking up your time."

"You're not. Sit down."

"Sit down? Where?"

"Here, in my seat."

To her own surprise Mrs. Wallop found herself sitting before a roomful of expectant faces.

"Say something to the class, Mrs. Wallop," Father Synge
told her in his nice way.

Shyness not being one of her faults, Mrs. Wallop began to
talk right away, but she was not at all prepared for what she
heard herself say. But, having said it, she let it go in the
hopes it would be forgotten or dismissed or misinterpreted
for something else. Still and all, it was as if someone other
than herself had spoken up for her. The children, being the
kind of kids they were, accepted her plight, being as familiar with her present situation as she was herself. Their bright
eyes were killing, though, the way they had taken in what
she had said, even though she'd had no intention of saying
it. She had intended to say something about the painting of
the Last Supper, how she had come over to Brooklyn to see
that, and not to inquire about a job, for God's sake! It had
slipped out. Not that she needed the money. She collected
Social Security. It was really all a matter of belonging again.
She was sure they understood. As she talked, the nicest thing
happened. Father Synge put his hand on her shoulder without making her feel the weight of it at all. It was remarkable how light it was. It could have been a bird, a sparrow,
except at the same time Mrs. Wallop felt that he had given
her his heart, not so much the thing itself, naturally, but all
his heart felt for her at the moment.

Lunch was a big thing, and no wonder, considering the
homes that some of these kids came from. Mrs. Wallop
hardly touched anything. It was all too advanced, to her way
of thinking. No salt, of course. She could tell that just by
looking at it. Well, the poor little things, a lot they cared.
They ate like wolves. There were signs all over. It was
enough to make your head spin. Mrs. Wallop did not know
what had gotten into her to want a job in the Shelter. She
could never work under anybody. She could not believe it
when she saw that Sister Secret. Why, now, no captain on
a ship was ever more stern. Oh no, a body would do almost
anything than work under the likes of Sister Secret. You

could see at a glance there was no piety to her. Nor modesty either. Why, the way Colfaxen used to confide in her over the phone you'd have thought she was another St. Teresa of Ávila come to life as an administrator and advisor, a solace to those in need and a boost to those down in the dumps. No, Mrs. Wallop wouldn't work under her if her life depended on it. Besides, she had a marching way about her, more suited to a WAC or a WAVE than a bride of Christ.

"Why, there you are, Mrs. Wallop, I've heard so much of you from the fathers that I feel I know you," said Sister Secret, in a loud enough voice to be heard outside the Shelter, Mrs. Wallop thought, feeling strangely subdued by the power of the long-draped figure moving towards her as if she meant to take her up in her arms, though she was not all that big, she only seemed so. She seemed, thought Mrs. Wallop, melting, to have come miles to see me, just me, Edna Wallop, who nobody cares a hoop about anymore, whether she cooks for them or not, and never did, really, if the truth be known.

Mrs. Wallop felt her own eyes fill with tears, sobs rose in her, sob after sob, she cried and cried, and felt that's what she had wanted to do walking up and down First Avenue night after night, cry and cry, and not only for herself either, but for everybody.

Never, not since she was a little child, had she leaned against anybody and felt as safe and as wanted there as she did against the broad front of Sister Secret.

As for the children, Mrs. Wallop did not mind them. They understood. They had seen worse. Eyes grew still at the sight of trouble here too, trouble at the Shelter, where all trouble was supposed to stop outside on the front doorstep. Eyes shifted between Mrs. Wallop and Sister Secret. Unarticulated questions grew like sunflowers in August from the shiny heads. How had Mrs. Wallop been allowed into the Shelter to air her griefs, to cry, to carry on, to beg for a job? Their own mothers would not have dared as much. At the Shelter Father Synge played *Peter and the Wolf* on the record player, but everybody knew the wolf was not a real wolf, but a play-wolf, a toy. It was a clean world, where you sang and grew, and learned and grew, and ate and grew. Of course nearly everybody went home again at night. Then the Shelter did not seem to exist at all. It was a wonder to many of the children that it was still standing when their mothers brought them the next morning before going off to their jobs.

"Give her a job," Robert Devereaux pleaded. "Give her a job, Sister Secret."

"Yes, give her a job," the understanding voices of his comrades echoed Robert.

Mrs. Wallop felt she had only herself to blame. It hurt her that they knew so much so soon. Yet they were only saying what she herself had told them when Father Synge asked her to speak to the class. Now why had he done such a thing in the first place? Well, for one thing he would never have dreamed she would have said what she had. She surprised herself. Oh, the humiliation! Mrs. Wallop thought, looking to Sister Secret to carry her off, as if she could, as if she was as big a lummox as herself, when in truth she was a leafy little thing, really, with the bosom of a big woman, rising, falling, rising, falling, falling. Mrs. Wallop sighed, closed her eyes. Sister Secret motioned Catherine Lepore to direct the children to their tasks of growing, reaching, aspiring. When they wanted to know was Mrs. Wallop going to be given a job at the Shelter or not Catherine told them to shush and mind their own business.

Chapter 32

The summer I wrote *First Wine* I hardly saw Truman. I swam and walked a lot. I sailed on Mecox Bay. I liked the rock pools in the jetties down at East Hampton and the herons and egrets and flamingoes on the south shore of Georgica Pond. Truman called sometimes. It was especially important to him to know where I was. *First Wine* was full of the adventure of falling in love for the first time—not only with boys of my own age, but with older people, grown-ups, both men and women.

I did not see anybody much. I worked around the place, cutting back bushes. People were at me then as now to clear our driveway. I weeded around Truman's house, missing him. There were clumps of margaritas that would have to come up someday, but I did not have the time for that now. Vines cluttered his doorway. It was a wild, romantic-looking dwelling, nearly always empty, even when Truman was home, for he fled it like something he dreaded, though I never heard him confess to an honest dislike of his place.

Evenings on the beach I would feel I had nothing. The lights in houses would strike me as gala. If I closed my eyes, all I saw in the double dark were couples. The lights of fishing boats alone brought me solace. I would swim out towards them, but when I got out of the water I would have to walk at a clip, since I never encumber myself with a towel.

My way home is through high marsh grass, my path made by my own bare feet. I am warm again and looking forward to supper and a fire. Now the way is along the edge of the potato field adjoining our place. A sharp left turn through the briar bushes brings me out on the grass before Truman's house. His lights are on. He's come! A sense of elation sweeps through me. His house, so cold and neglected-looking when I weed around it, is warm to me now, the way it used to be when we first came here to live in Sagaponack. Memories rush me as I approach the front door in my bare feet. One happening stands out before all the rest. It is the day of the publication of *In Cold Blood.* I have printed a sign and colored it with pastels and tacked it on the screen door for Truman to see first thing when he arrives here from New York. It celebrates the day we've looked forward to for five years when the book he has worked on during that time will appear, that is, today, this beautiful day:

LE BEAU JOUR

"Truman..." He didn't seem to be home after all. "Truman?" If he wasn't inside the house, then who was? I was up the single stone step when a tall, red-faced man appeared at the screen door. His manner was large and leisurely. He acted as if he had been wanted everywhere he went so far in his life. The whole of him was in shadow, but when he opened the screen for me and I stepped into Truman's kitchen, I realized I was passing a priest!

The revelation stopped me dead. I faced him shivering, looking up into his crimson face, for he was at least a head taller than me and I am five foot eight. Whether it was his intention to scare me or not I do not know, but he did. He was another face of the establishment that encloses one in times of disaster, whether they be the police, doctors, lawyers, or, as in his case, a priest. I assumed from the beginning that he was the real thing and not a masquerade come to rob me, though he had done that without half trying. Whatever tranquillity I had achieved swimming in the sea just now was gone. All I could think of was that Truman had run into deep trouble and this ungainly man before me with the rough red hands was cranking himself up to come at me with it. Why a priest, a great maladroit bird of doom, someone I felt I could take better care of than he could of me?

In any case this was not the house in which to hear revealed disaster. Besides I was cold again, and shivering noticeably. All I had on was a pair of torn shorts, cut down from red summer pants Truman brought home from Capri.

"Come to my house, Father," I said, opening the screen door again.

He took my hand as he went out before me.

"I'm Stephan Colfaxen. John Synge has probably told you about me."

Truman's telephone rang and I ran to answer it.

"Jack? Jack, I've been calling and calling you. I almost got the police. Where have you been? Well, no matter. How are you? Are you all right?"

"Sure, I'm all right, Truman. I've been here all the time, except when I go to the beach."

"How is the weather? It's terrible here. Is the swimming good? Have you gone sailing?"

"Yes, sure. Where are you?"

"California. I thought I told you...?"

Cold as I was I did not bother to change into warm clothing back in my own house, but lit a fire that I had laid that morning and took warmth from that instead. As was invariably the case with me, I found myself striving to impress Father Colfaxen with evidence of order and continuity and symmetry in our lives. This desire did not go so far that I felt I had to change my dress for him. Not at all. I remained in my shorts, knowingly underscoring our differences.

"Father, you were pastor of St. Roses on First Avenue, weren't you?"

He had seated himself without ceremony in Truman's chair between the window and the fireplace. "Yes," he replied to my question, "and I wish I was back there still. But of course it's gone, as you know." Though he made no mention of Maggie or Diotima, and scarcely appeared to be noticing me, his manners were unceremoniously good. There was consideration of everything about him, really, though he did not trouble either himself or me to point this up. The way he looked off into corners of the small room told me he wanted nothing to hinder his thoughts or interrupt him in the pursuit of them. I did not think he had been sent by Father Synge to talk to me about Truman after all, though at first I did. He seemed lonely and out of sorts. He did not impress me as a man used to talking about himself, but one who had spent his life listening to others.

I was far from ready for him to tell me of his love for another man, but that is just what he did. The daylight, slow in going, hung like lanterns in my trees. I let do with that and the firelight, and refrained from making more light.

"I thought John Synge would be here. I was called to some business in Southampton. I stopped by on my way home in the hopes I would see him."

"I think he's in Brooklyn, Father."

"Yes, can you imagine? In all this heat. And he could have been with me on the North Shore. Well, he's not, and that's that."

"You're on the Sound?"

"Yes, it's not the sea. I hear the sea here. Not that I know about things like that. I don't. I've missed a lot, but never minded till now. Matter of fact, until now, I never felt I was missing anything. This move was bad for me. It would have been different if John Synge had come with me, which he had every intention of doing before he met your friend. He's not here, is he?"

"Truman? No. That was Truman on the phone just now. He's in California."

"I came here for nothing," he said, without a hint of malice towards me.

I put more wood on the fire and turned on a lamp. Father Colfaxen did not budge under extra scrutiny, but took mine as a matter of course. He gave me the impression that he was as sure of his destiny as any man could be, but he was unhappy now and not ashamed to show it.

"I have never seen anyone interrupt the course of a man's life as your friend did Father Synge's!" he exclaimed, rising furiously to his full height, within inches of my poor parlor ceiling, low in my eyes for the first time. Did he know no one else with whom he could speak to in this way? Enraged and frustrated by Father Synge's decision to go work in Brooklyn, he came to us, to Truman and me, to unload himself in a way he would not have dreamed of doing with anyone else, probably.

"Father Synge told me himself that he wouldn't be a priest today if it hadn't been for Truman, Father Colfaxen."

"Baloney! I never heard such balderdash. Who told you a thing like that?"

"Why, Father Synge told me so himself, and more than once."

"Yes, he's been bewitched. You saw them together in the paper, didn't you? You realize that John must have been weak and drunk to allow himself to be photographed like that. Why, it's a wonder to me the authorities didn't come down on him with all the power they have after such an exhibition as that. I never understood it. I never shall. If you had known John when he first came to me, the zeal, the purity of him. From the first I warned him to steer clear of this business. Now look where he's wound up! Teaching babies their ABCs. Babysitting is what it amounts to."

"It's better than if he had quit altogether, don't you think?"

"No! It breaks my heart to see him sunk in bohemian Christianity, when I think how far he might have gone. And still will go, if I have any say about it. I'll have him ordered out to me, commanded. Why not? It's for his own good. A Harvard education, and teaching babies! Why, anybody can do that, couldn't you?"

I put more wood on the fire and told him to sit down and I'd find something for us to eat. I fed Maggie and Diotima first and let them out in the dark under the stars. There were fireflies too. The ocean beat the beach, washing in and out; it sounded hoarse but comforting, like old women in Spain singing as they did their laundry. I wondered at peoples' fury against Truman, particularly those who were unacquainted with him, such as Father Colfaxen, a good man otherwise, and fairly without prejudices.

I gave him an onion, a tomato, and half a can of sardines. We drank tea. I let Maggie and Diotima in, and they went upstairs without me to bed. Having paid no particular attention to Father Colfaxen's car when we had crossed the driveway where it was parked, which is between Truman's house and mine, I now wondered what make it was and how Father Colfaxen felt about driving at night.

He ate neatly, using a paper napkin to wipe his mouth with remarkable frequency. "Well, it was a wild goose chase," he said, cheerfully enough. He stood up, it was then he said something about himself, about the two of them, the man he had come searching for, John Synge, and himself. Stepping out onto the brick terrace at the back of my house, he peered up into the black of the crowded, unpruned grapevine, the scraping sound of whose leaves seemed to strike him as discordant, as if it recalled to him the rub in his own life that made him miss John Synge the most. He might have pulled some leaves down on his head had he tried. But he was unused to country life, to an open fireplace and the dry rustle of vine leaves. His forming years had been spent on asphalt, and he was ashamed of his ignorance and his lack of appreciation of all this, he suddenly told me, though not in those words.

"With John, things would have been easier out here," he

said, more to the dark than to me, I felt. His tone was apologetic without being humble. He was not about to fall to pieces over John Synge's not being with him, but he perhaps leaned more towards his comfort than ever before, and Father Synge would have been more comfortable to be with than any other.

"I used to fear for John if I left him to fend for himself. His was not a rough upbringing, whereas mine was. I'll never forget the way he walked into my life at St. Roses. It was as if he had never seen the likes of me before. It was hard to tell at first just what were his feelings about me. Then an expression came into his face that I'll not forget. He appeared to me to have climbed a mountainside and was at last near his destination. His face had been tired, cloudy, angst-ridden, and full of doubt. Then, after looking at me for awhile, taking me in, as the saying goes, his face cleared and he smiled. He made me feel I was somebody, and nothing that has ever happened to me has either lessened the feeling John gave me then or equaled it. Is it any wonder that I've gone out of my way to find him again?" He saw well in the dark and drove off with scarcely another word, leaving me far from feeling I had made a friend, but rather that I had met and fed the enemy.

Chapter 33

Father Benito Scarpia did not like the country either. He sat waiting up for Monsignor Colfaxen to come home. He thought that if only Monsignor Colfaxen still had a mother, he would call her. Maybe I'll call Bishop Fashoda. They were friends, or used to be. He has no friends now. I don't count. What am I saying? Of course I count. He hates me. Without me I think he'd go swimming in the Sound and never come back. I fill a need. I remind him of how he would rather have John Synge with him instead of me. I'm not myself.

Not even in the mirror anymore. I can't go home. I won't go home. My mother would have a heart attack if I quit and went home. I'm lonely. I have nobody, not even God, or especially. I'm afraid to open a book for fear he'll hear me turning the pages. I'm afraid of making any sound whatsoever in front of him. I'm afraid to chew at table. I swallow everything whole. The other night I ate a pork chop without chewing it. I'm afraid to go to the bathroom and only do when I can't help it, when I'm bursting. God I have dismissed. We don't know one another anymore. I believe in the devil. He guides me, leads me. Who else?

When the telephone bell rang and Father Scarpia made a leap from it and fell, the noises he made echoed throughout the little white rectory so despised by himself and his pastor. He was a nimble, round, little fellow, though somewhat overweight, so he got up easily enough and approached the instrument with a smile on his face, both hoping and knowing it would be his mother, since he prayed daily to the Blessed Mother that she would keep in touch with him.

"Mama, I told you not to worry about me. Now get off the line. I'm waiting for a call from Father Colfaxen. I don't know what he's doing out. Is it late? All right, it's late and he's out. Running around, I guess. He's not so old. Well, things are different now from when you were a girl, Mama. What makes you think that? Of course I'm happy. People invite me out to dinner every night, only I don't go. I know their food is lousy, that's why I don't go. Now get off the line, Mama."

After talking on the telephone with his mother Father Scarpia went to the front door of the rectory and opened it and crossed the porch which, had it creaked, might have consoled him, as a bit of dust might have done, or dirt, or even a sign of human misery other than his own. It was all so white, so neat, the lawns so manicured, the windows so shiny, the Sunday take so lush. It was paradise gained, but who wanted it?

The small town of Restwell seemed to Father Scarpia to be out of touch with reality. "Lord," he prayed, forgetting he no longer believed, for it was a particularly endearing trait of Benito's that he could not believe that he believed, "Lord, get us out of this bliss. It's too perfect for mugs like us. Not that I believe in you. I don't. Slums!" he shouted into the telephone. "Give us slums. We miss them."

"Benito! What's the matter with you?" Father Synge asked over the phone. "Where's Father Colfaxen? How is he?"

"Terrible, John. Out looking for you, if you must know. John, it's love. He can't get over you. I thought maybe if I gave him Freud, he'd see the light."

"Benito, you sound wonderful. You must like it out there. Tell Father I called."

"I won't. Anyway, here he is now. Hold on."

Benito handed the receiver of the telephone to his pastor, who stood over him, he thought, like Frankenstein, and ran outside and through the town to the beach where he sat in the cold sand wishing with all his heart that he had grown up.

"John," Monsignor Colfaxen said into the telephone, "I've seen him. No, the other one. The friend. I made some excuse that I thought I'd find you there. He wasn't wearing hardly anything when I first saw him, and he didn't see fit to put on anything else by the time I left. I'll say this for him, he fed me. Not that I needed anything in that line. I don't see why he thought I did. I ate to please him. He looked to me as if he could have done with a bit of company. Well, you know the country. The country has a tendency to be gloomy as darkness sets in. And he had been on the beach. On the beach in the dark, John! Can you beat it? It wouldn't surprise me if he hasn't done time. What makes me think he's done time? Well, he strikes me like a guy who's sat alone thinking his own thoughts. Of course you don't know everything about him, John. Did I say you did? All I ever said apropos of those two birds was lay off them, John. They're bad news. You sure he isn't a lag? John! John! A lag is a jailbird. Where have you been? What are you doing in all that Brooklyn heat when you could be out here? It didn't do you any good to stay in New York if it was because of the other one. He's nowhere around the place out there. If I were you, I'd stay away from Sagaponack. There's an air of violence about it. Anything might happen to a man out there, John, and only the sea would know. The sea and the potato fields. There's these two houses, one of them unlived in, you might say, for all the other one's ever there."

Monsignor Colfaxen spoke over the phone in a breathless way, as though he was on the verge of a nervous breakdown, or as though he was strong and well enough but young beyond his years—too young and unsettled for a man who had once not so long ago seemed set in his ways, an example to all, thought Father Scarpia, back from the beach listening to his pastor from the front porch of the rectory. Benito felt that he himself had just been through an emotional crisis, and he did not want to undergo the experience of listening to another going through the same thing, more or less.

Suddenly the idea of going and spending the night on his knees in the little church next to the rectory appealed to Benito, and he smiled. Let him look for me, if he wants me, not that he'll ever think to look for me in a church. He stopped on his way across the lawn and removed his shoes and socks, both black, and left them behind him. Nobody in Restwell believed Monsignor Colfaxen meant it when he told his first mass there that the doors of St. Jude would always remain open as long as he was pastor: "We should not have anything of such value that we are afraid to lose it but our faith."

It wasn't so bad in the dark. It was less antiseptic. It wasn't so cleared and cleaned out. There at least were the shadows, and they seemed to Father Scarpia all that was left of the debris of other times, when no parish would have been caught dead without its St. Anthony and his pool of burning candles. The people in Restwell did not go in much for lighting candles, or for light of any sort: the blink of the TV was what you saw from the street, after the kitchen light had been hurriedly extinguished as if it was shameful to be found doing anything so common anymore as eating a meal together.

"Benito! What are you doing here?"

"I...lost something. A pen an aunt gave me for gradua-
tion. Here it is. What about that for luck, Father Colfaxen?"

"Yes, yes. Well, go along to bed now. I'll follow by and
by."

He listened to him leave St. Jude. They had been Benito's
shoes he had come on in the dark. What a playboy! God the
Father help me that I may not abuse him any more than I
can help it, if at all. It's not my fault that a boy without a
vocation has been hung on me like a resounding tin can
when I could have had a patient little scholar for compan-
ionship had he not been charmed away from me....I can't
get over his reaction to my calling the other one a lag! Why,
he told me that the old lag had been a dancer, and that was
as cloistered a life as you could find outside a prison or a
monastery—the world enclosing the people of the ballet theater. We had a good laugh over it. It was good to hear John
laugh again. I saw him as he was the day we sat on the steps
of the Met together and talked over the sounds of the fallen
leaves....

The vigil light suspended over St. Jude's white altar spread
in Monsignor Colfaxen's view way beyond the confines of
its small red glass cup and there was light everywhere, nothing but light, as he always expected it would be.

Chapter 34

They buried him from St. Jude. He had no family left. The
father who had pushed him, and whose memory he revered,
lay crumbled underground in a cemetery somewhere outside New York City in the most expensive piece of furniture
that had ever held him. Fashoda was heartbroken. The
bishop had loved Monsignor Colfaxen; despite their different temperaments they had been close. St. Jude had meant
nothing to Monsignor Colfaxen but exile, but the people of
Restwell did not know this. They looked on him as a man

come to them to reap the rewards of a good life. Where else on earth would have served him better in this purpose? That he had died in church put him high in some eyes and questionably low in others. At night too. St. Jude took on an extra glow, threatening to some, consoling to others. There occurred the tiniest hint of a religious revival, but most felt better when the monsignor was out of the way.

The town had never seen such a display of feeling, not that it was loud, it was too low and intense for that, and there were hardly any flowers. Strangers seemed to have come from everywhere, the poor as well as the well-off, lay people as well as religious. They made a knot, impenetrable in its pride, and though many did not speak to one another, they had this in common: they had made a pilgrimage together and were gathered in a ceremony, the richest known.

Sister Secret and Catherine Lepore came by train. Matt Malloy drove from his place on the South Shore with two of his sons, who stared at their mother's rival with eyes they could not have made friendly had they tried. Bishop Fashoda arrived looking old and frail, and as if he did not care what he wore, though he was impeccably turned out all the same. Nora Synge made an obviously reluctant appearance dressed in grey as usual. She came in a hired car and left in it. She looked glum and said she did not feel well.

"Mother," Father Synge told her, "I don't see why you came at all."

"Curiosity. Curiosity killed the cat, satisfaction brought him back. I feel no satisfaction. There's Annie Bushnell, there's Matt Malloy, lovers still, though your average congregationalist doesn't know it. There's Catherine Lepore, a former prostitute. Poor Colfaxen!"

"Why 'poor Colfaxen,' Mother?"

"Stephan Colfaxen was an ordinary average man. They make the best priests. If he had his doubts, he didn't say anything about them."

"That's true."

"The baloney suited him, but it'll break you, because you can't take it in."

"I try, Mother."

"Go back to the Shelter. This is deadly. Go back to your Sister Secret. She won't let you rot."

"I'm not rotting."

"To go into mourning for a man who died two thousand years ago. That's the whole point of being a priest, and it's a ridiculous point, proving nothing. I'm going, John."

She did soon enough, having spoken to no one but Father Synge, and passing Juan and Maria with their baby as if she did not know them, even though they lived with her in the same house on Willow Street in Brooklyn Heights.

"It's the funeral," Maria confided in Father Synge. "She has been fighting herself ever since she heard and felt she had to come. She will be all right when she gets home and misses Esperanzo." Maria held the baby boy close to Father Synge. "He's beautiful, Maria. Aren't you glad, after all?"

"For Esperanzo? Of course we are, Father Synge."

Mrs. Wallop came by bus. She was impressed with Restwell, as its residents would have expected her to be. It was only at the end of things, when "the last rose was thrown," as she said to herself, that Mrs. Wallop confessed what she had felt all along: that the place smelled of exile. He should never have died here in this cold, quiet place, far from the noise and dirt of the city he loved and knew so well. She took Benito by the arm, and made Father Synge come with them under a tree behind St. Jude, where they were joined by Father Devine and Father Schenck, and Mrs. Wallop did most of the talking as of old.

"He should have died at the Met," she said.

"Mrs. Wallop, it's good to hear you again," Father Schenck told her.

"He should have died at the Met," Mrs. Wallop repeated.

"Why, now, Mrs. Wallop, why should he have died anywhere?" Father Devine asked. "Why not us? Why not Father Schenck and myself? Why, we're no good to anybody, not even ourselves."

Father Synge threw himself down on the grass and looked up at the rest of them with a smile, thus rousing their curiosity and chagrin, though they said nothing. He was the object of all eyes, and he seemed to know it and even like it.

"Well," Father Devine told him, "you've lost a pal."

"There's no gainsaying that," said Father Schenck. "He cared for John like a son."

"And so they were, father and son in all but name, until Father Synge went to Paris and came back changed," opinionated Mrs. Wallop.

"That's true, John. There's no gainsaying that. What changed you?" Father Schenck asked, to which Father Synge laughed and rolled about on the grass, causing Benito to stir loudly in his chair.

"I wish I were John," he complained. "John knows where he's going. I don't. I don't know what's going to happen to me now without Father Colfaxen. I don't. I really don't. I feel it's all my fault, in a way, and that he'd be here today if only I'd stayed with him in church. Instead, I left him to die!"

"But you've said yourself he told you to leave him alone and he'd come into the rectory by and by, Benito," said Father Devine.

"Father Scarpia, don't blame a thing like that on yourself; it'll only give you dreams," warned Mrs. Wallop. "People," she sagely added, "die when they want to."

"Oh! That's not true," Father Synge cried. "That's not true at all, Mrs. Wallop. Nobody wanted to live more than Father Colfaxen did. Why, we laughed so when I last spoke to him! We had such a good time. He was so happy."

"Why," said Mrs. Wallop, her eyes wide with surprise, "that doesn't say because he was happy he didn't want to die. What do you say to him dying because he was happy?"

Father Synge knelt up on his knees in the grass and directed all his attention to their former cook. "I never thought of that, Mrs. Wallop," he said.

"And now? Now what do you think now?"

"I don't know. I don't know what to think. For some reason the thought that he was happy to die makes me unbearably sad. I know that it shouldn't. I'm sure you're right, Mrs. Wallop."

"Ah," Mrs. Wallop replied to all that with a slow smile. "I'm not all that sure I'm right," she said. "It was only something to say, you might say. I'm not so sure as I used to be when we were altogether at St. Roses. I say things now, but I'm not sure anymore. Besides, who listens to you on First Avenue? They're building, you know."

"Building?" asked the old fathers, alerted out of their dreams. "Building what, Mrs. Wallop?"

"Why, a church," responded Mrs. Wallop. "What else do you expect they'd build? A church over where St. Roses used to be. Our old St. Roses. It's fitting enough, when you come to think of it."

"Yes, it's fitting enough, as you say, Mrs. Wallop," said Father Schenck.

"It's as it should be," Father Devine agreed. "The old gives way to the new."

"I don't see the logic in that at all!" cried Father Synge, rising excitedly to his feet. "All this passivity in the face of so-called progress. Why not say change is inevitable and profitable and let it go at that? Churches in America are not beautiful, but custom cannot be denied. Look at St. Roses. What can ever take its place?"

"A better building, for one thing, John," Father Scarpia told him. "For another, a different way of looking at the people who come to us."

"What's wrong with the way we look at them, Benito?"

"We might give them more to do than light candles, John."

"Well, John, none of us are saying anything about progress. None of us here believe in progress. I hope not anyway," said Father Devine.

"Don't let Restwell hear you say that or you'll be tarred and feathered and run out of town," was Benito's laughing response to that.

"Well, now, weigh your words. Here comes the boss," said Mrs. Wallop, indicating the approach of Sister Secret.

"A nice place to die," said Sister Secret, causing the group under the maple tree to stiffen somewhat, but only Mrs. Wallop saw fit to take her up on it. "It's not," she said. "It's not at all. Not for Father Colfaxen it wasn't, anyway. Why, the silence alone is enough to deafen you. Hell's Kitchen would have suited him better, what's left of it. He ought never to have been yanked out of St. Roses as he was. Let's see what they put up in its place. Let's see if it'll be worth casting a man as good as Father Colfaxen was to the four winds. He didn't want trees, but stone, and to be left alone with his pictures at the Met. He should have died at the Met."

"He was alone all right," Benito said. "I didn't count. He wanted John."

"Oh John!" said Sister Secret. "Everybody wants John, Benito. John's the most wanted man in the church."

"He's no more in the church than Father Colfaxen is... now," Father Schenck opined. "I don't see how you can say he's in the church when he's not. As far as I can see, he's not. It all began with Paris, of course. And that was Stephan's fault. John would never have gone to Paris if it had not been for Stephan Colfaxen urging him to."

"He wanted to get him away from the other thing," said Father Devine. "How is the other thing, John? Is it true Stephan went over to see them the night he died?"

"That's right. John called and caught him just as he got in. I should have known there was something wrong with him the way he was that night."

"There's a pity, Father Scarpia. You might have saved him."

"He died in church, Mrs. Wallop. What more do you want?"

"It was no place for him to be at that hour. It was outlandish. All sorts of things probably came to him. And nobody by to tell him to get a grip on himself and go home and go to bed. An empty church is enough to give anybody the pip. What made him go in anyway?"

"He came looking for me, if you really want to know."

Consternation seized the group at Benito's words. Everybody but Sister Secret and Father Synge spoke up at once. Finally, in the comparative quiet, Father Devine repeated what had already been said: "To you, Benito? In church? Why? What were you doing there at that hour?"

"I...lost something. A fountain pen. Anyway, I found it and

left. Father gave me to understand that he wanted to be alone."

"And you left him?" Father Schenck asked.

"Why not? He was in church, wasn't he?"

"Well, for goodness sake, Benito!" Father Devine exclaimed. "Surely you would have said something if you thought he was going to die."

"Sure I would. He looked to me like he was sleeping when I saw him next morning. He looked as if he was dreaming. When I touched him I felt he'd wake up with a smile on his face. After all, what's wrong with falling asleep in church? I do it all the time."

Groups of people were breaking up. The parishioners of St. Jude, Restwell people most of them, had all gone. It was as though the New Yorkers hadn't the heart to leave him, go home without him, pretty though the graveyard by the church was, for they lingered in silence, with nothing more to say to one another.

Gradually a certain restlessness took over and people said they ought to be getting back, but no one did so more forthrightly than Matt Malloy, who came striding towards the gathering under the maple tree followed reluctantly by his two sons.

"Annie! Don't think you're going back to Brooklyn by that god-awful Long Island Rail Road, because you're not. We're driving you, and it will be late enough at that when we get there."

"Why, Matt, I thought you left long ago, you and the boys. Catherine already has our tickets, Mattie, but we thank you all the same."

"Here, you give me those tickets. I'll show you what I think of them."

"Control your ill temper, Matt. Besides, I haven't got the tickets. Catherine has them. Don't, whatever you do, give them up to him, Catherine. He'll only destroy them."

"I don't mean to give them up, Sister. We can get good money for these tickets."

"Not if we use them, Catherine."

"N-no. That's true."

"Get the car, boys. Drive it right up here on the lawn. It's good for the grass, so I'm told."

"Oh it is!" exclaimed Catherine. "It's good for the grass. Everybody knows that. Of course not always, not every day."

No one but Sister had ever seen Catherine so excited before, but then few, if any, had ever seen her on holiday, free of the Shelter, before. You could see she had been pretty. She was well made, too. There were all sorts of stories about Catherine Lepore, none more believable today, from the looks of her, than the one that had her rumored amongst the fastest set in Manhattan at one time. Not that she ever moved an inch away from Sister. She didn't. It was just that she had a certain way today that suggested another Catherine, one whose hair was brighter, longer, whose eyes held hope and delight equally in both of them, a Catherine who weaved in and out of plush rooms pursued, pursuing.

She was still enough now. No one there, not even Sister, who'd known Catherine longest and had taken her into the Shelter even before it was the Shelter, had ever seen Catherine look at anything the way she did the car driven by the Malloy boy. It was as if she saw her whole past in that galaxy of metal and glass, of glittering spoked wheels, heard things that no one else there did in the running sound of its powerful motor, soft as a lion whelp's purr.

Sister was watching Catherine along with everybody else, the boy at the wheel especially, since it was as if Catherine was beseeching him to run over her.

"What's the matter with her anyway?" Matt gruffed.

"Oh!" said Sister Secret, "she wants to drive, that's all, Matt. Surely you can understand a passion."

Malloy looked at Sister Secret as much as to say, "Are you kidding me, Annie? Me with my devotion to you, and you asking me can I understand a passion?" He thought of his sons; one was beside him, the other was at the wheel of the motor car. He did not think it was fair to them for him to be acting like a young man, a very young man, so he said nothing in answer to Annie's taunt. Besides, she had helping people on her mind as usual—this girl, for example, who was standing before his car as if it was her own.

Malloy motioned to the son at the wheel to get out of the car. When the boy had done so, to his own obvious bewilderment, his father allowed Catherine to take his place, which she did. Then Sister got into the back seat with the boys and Malloy installed himself up front with Catherine, and they were off after good-byes all around and a last glance at the cemetery. It never occurred to Malloy to ask Catherine whether she could drive or not; he knew from the minute she put her hand to the ignition key that she could.

The party did not talk all the whole way back to Brooklyn, but strangely enough there did not seem to be silence from the driver's seat. To Sister Secret, anyway, the story of a life before she had known Catherine seemed to be unfolding, mile after dark mile, but it did not once occur to her that Catherine might now take it in her head to leave the Shelter.

"Matt," she said at the door of the Shelter, "you must have a truck, an old truck, something that still goes, and could pick up and deliver children? Have you anything like that, Mattie? It needn't be anything to look at, but it would be ever so helpful to us, wouldn't it, Catherine?"

Catherine said nothing. She looked as if she'd been dancing, swimming, sailing. She looked fresh, young.

"You're a pretty good driver," Malloy said to her, bringing a startled "Oh!" to the lips of the girl who had seen so much in too short a time, but tonight looked as if the world was all new to her again—new as a new moon.

"Well, Matt, think about it anyway. Anything with four wheels will do us. As for fixing it up, we'll find a way."

"Annie, it's been a wonderful day, even if it was a funeral. Say good-bye to my boys. You might have been their mother, you know."

"Good night, boys. Don't pay any heed to your father. Give my love to your mother. Better her than me, I always say, though don't quote me. I know one of you is Matt, but which I'm not sure. You? No, wrong again. Well, some other time. Don't forget the truck, Matt. Any old thing will do Catherine and me."

That night Sister Secret sat for a long time in her hideout up on the third floor of the Shelter. She was joined by Catherine, which was often the case. They had twenty-five children staying overnights counting Robert Devereaux, whose mother would not show up for weeks at a time. When she did, she'd threaten to take him "home" with her. It was when she was most adamant about getting Robert back that she would go away and stay away, causing the little boy to wake up nights and walk about the halls of the Shelter and even to wet the bed again, because when he thought of her, missed her, he tended to relive the life he lived with her over again in his imagination, crying and running up and down the stairs after he had wet the bed, which he had long gotten over doing at the Shelter, but it would happen when he was emotionally roused after his mother's visits.

Sister Secret and Catherine were talking about the truck Malloy was bound to give them when the sounds of bare feet on the stairs hushed them. They waited for the door to open, and when it did, inevitably, the little visitor turned out to be Robert Devereaux.

"Oh!" he said, in a high voice that contrasted sharply with the still way he held his face, "you're here, Sister Secret!"

"Of course I'm here, Robert. Come in. Come say hello properly to Catherine."

Robert stepped into Sister's hideout looking slyly this way and that, for it was rumored Sister kept treasures up here, goodies—that she even had a little stove and oven where she cooked and baked pies and puddings. If this was true, Robert could make out nothing.

"Good evening, Miss Catherine," he said, making a bow. "Good evening, Sister," and he made another bow. "You know why you're back, Sister? You're back because I dreamed you back. Don't cry, Sister Secret. Why are you crying? Why are you sad?"

"I'm not crying, and I'm not sad. Well, at any rate, I'm not sad. I'm very, very happy. And you know why, Robert? Because I'm remembering old times with a dear friend who has gone away today."

"Well, anyway, you're not sad about me, and you shouldn't

be, because I'm never going to wet the bed again, not at the Shelter, and especially not when I'm famous."

"What makes you want to be famous, Robert?"

"Oh! because I dream it all the time, Sister. And I tell it before breakfast. You know that if you tell a dream before breakfast, it is bound to come true. My mama says so, and it's not humbug, though lots she says is. That bicycle. Now we'll never see that. But dreams are for nothing. No money can buy dreams. A dream is naturally free. So when I dream a dream, it is all mine and nobody else's. And when I tell it before breakfast, it is certain to come true. Dreaming you are famous and becoming famous is all one if you tell it before breakfast, Sister."

No one was surprised when Father Synge did not go back to Brooklyn in Malloy's car, but opted to stay for a day or two in Restwell with Benito. Bishop Fashoda thought it an especially sound decision. Now that his old friend was underground, the bishop appeared to take a firm new lease on life—very unlike his conduct at the funeral, where he had to be nudged to go forward and yanked to a halt.

He had failed to respond to prayers and was unaware that he could bend his knees anymore. A sitting position was the best he was up to, and he fell asleep even then. He smiled at everything, but not as usual; it was as if he was determined to smile now. It was only after the ceremony that he came to and regained his old self. The truth was that he could not imagine Stephan Colfaxen dead, or anybody else for that matter, least of all himself, so the less thought about that the better!

"John, forget that bunk at the Shelter and stay here in Restwell with Benito and write. I'll get you the pastorship, John. Let Benito run the place. It's what you want, isn't it? To write? Time to write? Sure it is. Give up the Shelter, John. Bohemian Christianity isn't for you. Stay here. I'm glad to hear it."

"Hear what, Bishop Fashoda? I haven't said a word. Of course I'll stay if you say so, only..."

"John, you're spoiled. Most of us are afraid to go home again once we've left the seminary, but you'd be welcome, and you know it. Every boy wants to please his mother, especially boys who have become priests. If you left us, you'd be taken care of for the rest of your life, as your mother's sole beneficiary. Is that what you want? The easiest way?"

"I'm not thinking of a living. I have no economic fear that I know of. I can always make a living teaching."

"John, you don't want to be a priest. You don't see any use for us."

"We might give them more to do than light candles."

"Now what are you talking about?"

"Something that Benito said about the people who come to us."

"Don't tell me Benito's disaffected too? If he is, it's all your fault, John. Get out if you want to, but don't make everybody around you rotten. Everybody knows how unhappy you made Stephan Colfaxen when you left St. Roses for the Shelter. Then doesn't Sister Secret tell me you're no sooner there than you threaten to leave her as well. Go home to your mother. That old atheist. She's waiting for you with open arms. But go alone, for God's sake, man! What in Christ's name did the church ever do to you that you're so hell-bent to destroy her? Why am I talking to you as I am instead of giving you my back?"

"I don't know, I'm sure. I'll do whatever you tell me to do. Only tell me *something*. No one seems to know what to tell anyone, really. Father Colfaxen was more eloquent at the Metropolitan Museum of Art with me than he was in his study at St. Roses."

"He wasn't! He had such faith as rarely comes to a man. His love of pictures was an integral part of his faith, a sure sign to him of God's manifestation. I've looked at pictures with Stephan; those he liked and appreciated were like epiphanies to him. Art was one side of religion to Stephan, to him its brightest, most comforting aspect. Of course he did not say so. I do not think he could have said so had he wanted to. But great things moved him in a lasting way. He was a simple man, his needs were few."

22 July 1965

Precious JACK—

Rec'd. your sweet, very
amusing note just as I was leaving
the Athens hotel. That Tilletson!

Marella Agnelli's
father died suddenly and she had
to fly back to Italy. So I sailed
alone on the yacht with Kay
Graham. Imagine that!— having
a whole huge yacht to yourself.

However, the Agnellis, plus

other guests, are rejoining the boat

at Rhodes on the 26th. We

are going to bypass Istanbul and

go directly along the coast to Smyrna.

Spetsopoula is the private

island of Niarchos. Fantastic!

Beautiful! Have been here 2 days,

but leave this morning.

Hope all is well with Charlie

and Sister. I love you and miss my darlingest

T.

The bishop allowed himself a sidewise glance across the grass at the cemetery of St. Jude.

"We were very different," he said then, ever so humbly. "Stephan stopped at Notre Dame, loved it as a lover should, with all his heart and soul; I went on to other cathedrals, Chartres, Beauvais. I am faithful in my fashion, but Stephan Colfaxen once in love was always in love. I hope we don't lose you, John; but if we do, my consolation will be that Father Colfaxen won't be around to see it—not that he'd be surprised."

It had started to rain lightly. Someone ran to Bishop Fashoda with a raincoat, which he scrutinized for a minute most critically before pushing it aside, preferring to walk to his car as he was. Before getting into the car he looked back at the cemetery, frowned, waved, then suddenly doubled up as if he had been struck a blow. The last Father Synge saw of him was his handsome face incredibly grieving.

Chapter 35

Nearly everybody was wonderful to Truman at first, and he was stubborn about relinquishing the illusion that this was the whole story. Once when he was being a bit short talking to me about Harper Lee, he stopped himself with "Ah, but she was such a wonderful child!"

He was the same about places, and relished his guided tours. If his guided tour of Paris amounted to no more than a visit to Natalie Barney's house, or his tour of Venice began and ended at Harry's Bar, tant mieux! Natalie Barney may have been dumpy and plain at her last Friday afternoons in her house at 20 Rue Jacob, but she trailed a myth of loves from her past as well as set a good, full table in the present. Harry's Bar might have been unbearably talky and smokey, but one had arrived there in the rain, soaked through with the wet beauties of Venice.

Truman and I were never together-together people as

most couples are. Such proximity would have killed us. We were always dreaming away from wherever we were, thus repeating the pattern that had commenced in childhood, when one's need to escape from one's own kind was so savage, so burning in its intensity, that had either of us stayed home, he would certainly have perished.

When, after our long séjours abroad and following the publication of *In Cold Blood,* Truman started tripping with others, I was more or less relieved that someone had taken this new Truman off my hands once in awhile. He had given the houses at Sagaponack to me, and I settled down as much as I was ever meant to, which wasn't much, really, since I spent winters in Switzerland, where Truman did not follow us—Maggie, Diotima, and me—autumn and spring in New York, and only my summers on Long Island.

But his new friends seldom lasted, or they lasted too long. They were never a concern of mine unless I felt Truman had been duped by them. What I say about them will read like hearsay, and some of it is, though it was from Truman himself that I got it, half got it, guessed it, or it was intuited. It does not take God to tell you that your friend has been had. I seldom knew about these things until they were over, and even then I frequently had to guess what had happened, since I was too proud to ask.

"Sometimes," Truman said to me, "we like to be asked questions."

Essentially Truman was a brave person. He saved my kerry blue, Kelly, from certain death by coming between him and a high-strung boxer, and was seriously wounded in his hand as a result. Of course he made light of the thing, but it hurt me to see his bandaged hand, since I knew well enough he would not have come between the fighter-dogs had not one of them been beloved by me.

I never asked him but for one thing, and that was for my house in Sagaponack. He not only gave me the house, but his house as well, and all the ground. Few people give outright like that. When I asked him why he had given me his house as well as the one I lived in, he replied, "Oh! It was too much trouble to divide things. But I want you to make a will and leave them to me, hear?" He loved my house, and was more secure in it than he was anywhere, though not without me in it. He would look at it in a certain way sometimes as if he wondered at what it had become to him, since neither of us was a possession-ridden person. He insisted on its neatness and would not tolerate a scrap of paper on the floor, but would pick it up himself.

How often have I come from the beach in the dusk and seen him sitting in his chair by the window, having turned on all the lamps, waiting for me. He used to look so fearless, yet expectant, making me feel that I should always return to Truman, always keep him foremost in mind. Viewed from outside from amongst the dark trees, he was an extra light in my little house in Sagaponack—the light that counted most to me, and without which all others were dim and befogged.

If I felt, naively, perhaps, that Truman was better off with me than with others, good, bad, or indifferent as they might be, it was because chez nous he worked; he wrote, he was quiet, and, I'm sure, very frequently bored as well. But boredom after work, or even while working, is different from boredom when one has not worked at all. Then one's boredom (as a creative artist) is compounded with guilt. What's happening? Why am I here? I wish I were home. But he wasn't. It was not in our stars to be always together. Though close and loving, ever so comfortable in one another's company, we were both at the same time propelled by the compulsion to wander apart, even in our reading. We did not have the same tastes, and we did not try to have them. We had a taste for one another's company above all others, that's about all, but not always, nor for all the time. Once, after long hours looking at pictures in the Prado by myself, I found him seated on a big chair by the main entrance of the museum waiting for me.

"My dear Truman, why didn't you go back to the hotel? Have you been waiting long? I shouldn't have dragged you here."

"No, that's all right. I haven't been waiting long. I liked sitting here watching the people. It was interesting."

My heart never left Truman, but I had to have air, I had

to have room to think and work and play—and so did he. Domesticity was never our forte; we played at it, but it was more a costume than anything else, which we cast off and put on when occasion asked for that sort of show. With us home was where order was, whether a rented house in Spain, a purchased apartment in the Swiss Alps, or a state-room on a Norwegian freighter bound for Greece. We were exclusive enough there. We were happiest there. There we experienced our richest hours and they were many.

Chapter 36

"I don't see why you don't go with him, as you used to do, and as you should now," Father Synge said, when I told him I was not sure where Truman was at present, unless it was California. "You don't know whether he's there or not? How ridiculous. Is he living out there? He seems to be. Has he a house there?"

"I think so."

"My God! I don't see what you're doing together."

"Sometimes I wonder myself, Father, but it seems fated."

"Why wouldn't he have told you about the house out in California—if he has one?"

"Je ne sais pas. Shame, perhaps. We always tell one another how much we hate California. Maybe he's decided to live another life away from the one he lives with me."

"You're so passive about it all. Don't you care?"

"Yes, but it doesn't worry me, really. We're not a together-together pair. We're more friends than lovers."

"Well, that sounds all right, that sounds like an advancement of some sort."

"I'm glad you think so, Father."

He had found me out as I was sailing on Mecox Bay. He had asked around, and little by little he had found the road where my Mustang was parked with the trailer attached to it, and had come to the water's edge and stood there waiting for me, like a wounded heron. He was a pest, but my conscience, part of me now, someone I felt I could not order away, though I certainly felt like doing so, especially now, when I felt far from heeding anyone reminding me I was my brother's keeper.

I was thinking of Truman because it had occurred to me that the figure on shore might be him. If you are sailing awhile, and sometimes into the setting sun, you are liable to imagine you see anything. No one else was out, it was nice, the end of summer, the end of a day.

I did not know where my sometimes peace of mind came from unless it was from all this, but I really did not think so. I had sailed through the inlet to where the duck farm used to be (it's all houses now), and watched birds zooming from thicket to thicket. The goldenrod was drying up, though there were some bright yellow stalks still left. The feather-bannered tops of swamp grass bent seaward, like an army marching, as I sailed by in the opposite direction. Geese passed overhead, and ducks, and wayward gulls. Canary-like birds twittered about their affairs, and frogs croaked over theirs. Even I felt engaged just sitting in my boat twitching the sheet.

Years ago I might have had Truman for a passenger instead of beetles and grasshoppers and intricately gotten-up praying mantises. Now Truman belonged to everybody, to the whole world, like a god. He was transported abroad in yachts and private planes by people who listened as he told them of *Answered Prayers,* his book to be, never dreaming that they were to figure in it.

Thus sailing or flying, or else purring along in their Rolls-Royces, did Truman beguile their time away for them. And, never forget, he was a very good listener when they talked, which they did, it was only natural, frequently and voluminously, of themselves as well as others of their kind. Listening, Truman forged a sword that was to strike vital parts, uncover vanities, prides. Why did he do it? How could he see them so black when at the same time he loved them so much? I wish he had never written about them. The price he paid of alienation from them was too great for him. It was none of their business any more than it ever was what he wrote. Then, in letting it out piece by piece in magazines, he made the mistake of allowing them to make the story theirs. They took it, as they take everything they can lay their hands on, and made it theirs, perhaps knowing in their hearts that it would be the only thing they would leave behind them, besides their money, that would give them some of the éclat they had when making their short, smart splash through this world.

When the magazine pieces did appear and they lashed at him and closed ranks as well as doors, it was lonely for him—just as they desired it should be. Why he did it I do not yet know, unless he hated them, but I do not think he did hate them. What he did do was to *see* them, and seeing them, he wrote about them. They had become too much a part of him not to do so—the next biggest thing to the South of his upbringing, and the multiple murders. Since he loved Barbara Paley most of all of them, I called her from here in Sagaponack at their place in Manhasset. It was a Sunday afternoon. I had the feeling the house was full.

"Jack!"

"Babe, you must see Truman. Will you?"

"I don't know. I'll have to ask Bill."

"Babe, you're friends. It's none of our business, really, what Truman writes. It's not for us only. It's for everybody and for a very long time. What he writes is one thing, what he is to us is another. He's our friend, Babe. Talk to him. This thing between you that's given both of you such pleasure you made between you. Don't let it die, Babe. Don't destroy it."

"I'll ask Bill. I'll ask Bill."

Babe Paley never spoke to Truman again.

But today all that was in the offing and I knew none of it, thank goodness. Truman was different, but then so was I, so was this minute different compared to the last one. The wind was down with the sun, and the water looked smooth enough to skate on. I saw a hummingbird, a dragonfly, and thought I heard a jay as I sailed back through the inlet.

By the time I was ready to make one last tack into the beach, Father Synge had rolled up his pants and was in the water, ready to help us land. This annoyed me even more than the fact that he was there at all, since he obviously did

not know what he was doing. I was used to bringing in the
boat myself, and help was a hindrance to me. Because there
are only two things besides the head-board you should touch
on a sailboat—the tiller and the sheet—Father Synge only
got himself knocked over into the water when he attempted
to guide us in by taking hold of the sail!

It was a warm evening so it really did not matter, but I
wondered in a flash how he would handle himself, and
whether he would strip in front of me or not. I had to admit
he was more attractive to me wet than he was when dry.
His shirt stuck to him before he took it off in a graceful way,
and the water running in rivulets down his face and off the
ends of his nose and chin gave him a sheen, a shine. He
glistened as he perhaps had not done since he was a boy.

I did not allow myself any lengthy looks at him after he
had removed his wet pants but not his shorts, but occupied
myself with my boat. But as I cranked it out of the bay and
up on the trailer, I felt a sudden thrill at the sight of Father
Synge's bare back and its taut markings. By the back of him
I felt he was filthy angry with himself, there being no hu-
mility at all about him, to say nothing of humor, over his
tumble. That's what the bastard got for believing he could
guide and direct us, no matter what!

As was usual with me after sailing, I was experiencing a
terrific sense of calm. This happened to me even on days
when the waves would pitch my boat up on the pebble
beach. Today the calm I felt seemed to match and even su-
persede the peace I saw around me in all but Father Synge.
I felt myself undergoing a change in my feelings about his
looks. It was pointless to tell myself to look away from him
now. I could not. I waited to see how he shaped up without
his pants before I got into my car.

Desire and pity for him chased one another through my
head and body. My only hope for my sanity, since I did not
dream of gratification, was that he might be feeling something similar. He helped me hitch the trailer to my Mustang, then gathered his wet shirt, pants, and sneaks in a
bundle and came at me so precipitously that he took my
breath away. But, inevitably, he held tightly to his slimy bun-

dle of clothes and sneaks, beyond which neither of us ventured towards each other.

In the car I asked him how he had found me.

"A guy was cutting your grass. He said your boat was out, so you must be sailing. I left my car at your place and decided if I went too far trying to find you that I could always hitch a ride. Actually it's Father Colfaxen's car."

I recognized Colfaxen's car as soon as we drove into our driveway and got out of the Mustang.

"He's dead, you know. He died the night he left you. They gave me his job in the parish on the North Shore."

"I'm sorry to hear of his death, Father Synge, but I still don't think he had the right to act the way he did with me when he was here."

"I'm sure it was for your own good."

"It had nothing to do with us."

"Really?"

"No; and I think he had a nerve breaking into Truman's house the way he did, though I would never have told him so."

"I don't see why not, if you considered yourself in the right as much as you seem to do now."

"Well, I didn't."

"Then it's over."

"Not really. He left leaving me with the feeling that our lives were in ruins and that it was all my fault."

"It is largely your fault. You are the most mature of the two of you. Yet I find you out sailing."

"Well, why not? It's not as if sailing a boat is all I do. I've finished a novel this summer. But you don't care about that."

"No, I'm afraid I don't. Nor am I concerned about your friend, except as a sick man, bound to grow worse. Writers come a dime a dozen."

"Not good writers! What a stupid thing to say."

"And the night Father Colfaxen came here he said you'd been walking on the beach. Walking on the beach in the dark, and your friend ruining himself in California. One would think you would have taken heed and done something by now. Instead you talk to me of a book you finished.

What do I care about your books? Standing blithely by letting a soul go its way to burn in everlasting fire. It's true. And you know it's true. You believe it as much as I do, if not more than I do!"

"That old man came here for you."

"For me, when I was in Brooklyn."

"I don't care where you were. He came expecting you to be here, hoping you'd be here, blaming us, in a way, that you weren't here."

"Now what are you implying?"

"That he loved you."

"Of course he did. And I loved him. There's nothing curious or startling or dirty about that. It's people like you who made it startling and curious and dirty."

"If it's dirty it's dirty to you, Father Synge. What was lousy and underhanded was his blaming us for having come between you, for your going to Brooklyn, for your not coming out here to the parish on the North Shore with him. It was for that he berated me, needing a scapegoat as he did."

"He called you a lag, a former prisoner. There is something locked up and imprisoned about you in this lonely, godforsaken place, with that empty haunted house over there—you and your animals, your so-called work."

"Come, Father Synge, you don't mean that."

"I do."

"No, you don't. You're cold, you're shivering. You're like he was the night he came here looking for you."

"You believe he did, really?"

"Of course he did. He probably knew he was about to die."

"You think so?"

"Probably. At any rate he ended up quite forgiving. He seemed at peace when he left here."

"Yes, he seemed at peace when I talked to him over the phone. We laughed. We laughed about you, actually."

"You did?"

"Yes, I found myself telling him about how you used to be a ballet dancer, and what cloistered lives dancers live. We laughed. We agreed you were like monks for all your seeming worldliness. He had never seen a ballet. Nothing like that. I loved him."

His voice was low but nowhere near to breaking. He stood upright, firm and strong. He was more positive than I had ever seen him, both physically and in what he was saying. An overpowering desire swept me to reach him. It seemed so crude, though, so exploitive. Yet it struck me at the same time that it would be the kindest thing I could do for him, opportunistic or no. I wanted him, but I did not want to seduce him. I loathed that sort of thing and always have. He could have been somewhat experienced in erotic love, but I did not truthfully think so.

I felt he was waiting for me by Colfaxen's car, that if I touched him it would be as if it were Colfaxen doing so, doing what they both might have subconsciously yearned to do during the older man's days on earth. The thought was chilling, even disgusting, and brought me back to duties and pride in our way of life, no matter what. I ran to my house and fed Maggie and Diotima, hoping all the while that Father Synge would take himself off to his parish on the North Shore. Instead he appeared at the screen door, looking peaked and undesirable again.

"I'm sorry about what I said about your book."

"That's all right. Do you want to take a warm shower? Why don't you? I'll give you some dry things to change into."

He came in without a word and went upstairs, where I soon heard him showering. When I followed up there, I heard him singing softly to himself as I passed the closed bathroom door. I imagined him soaping himself luxuriously, and again I desired him. I put out clothes for him and went down and let Maggie and Diotima out, then waited. I felt cold myself but refrained from putting on a shirt. I lit the fire I had laid that morning, and Father Synge hurried downstairs in my clothes as if drawn by the sounds of crackling flames.

He smiled broadly, boyishly. I asked him about Brooklyn, the Shelter. "Oh, the Shelter! They've taken it away from me. I don't know that I'll ever go back, though I want to. I would like to have you and Truman come there and talk about your writing to the kids. Would you?" He was in a good humor, very constructive, altogether different from what he had been out by Colfaxen's car. I could see how beneficial he could be to boys and girls who had nothing in the way of material things—how he could enrich their lives, plant ideas home, uncover talent ashamed to show itself for fear of being laughed down, called different.

"I dream of Truman interesting himself in the Shelter," he said, lowering his head in a charming way, then covering his face with his hands. "Oh, I'm so silly!" he exclaimed. "This thing about Truman turning around some day, working again, just won't let me go." He looked at me through his parted hands. "Forgive me for talking the way I do to you sometimes. You must hate me then. I hate myself."

He sat down on the floor in front of the fire. I thought about asking him if he wanted a bite to eat, but I didn't bother. I got something for us. When I handed Father Synge his plate, he took it looking up at me. "Do you think he'll ever want to meet me?" he asked. "Really meet me, I mean? I suppose not after the things you've told him I said to you. I don't blame him."

Father Synge would never get it into his head that we did not talk about him, that Truman had no idea who he was. He made me feel that Truman was beyond curing, especially if it depended on people like Father Synge. But of course it did not depend on people like Father Synge. It did not depend on soul doctors or head doctors or any of the rest of the doctors, or on anybody but Truman himself. Yes, but if Father Synge had just a shadow of the effect on Truman that he had on me, I thought it might benefit him. Something about Father Synge had made me hold back from making a pass at him when I wanted to with everything in me. What had stopped me? It was more than shyness or fear of rejection. He had seemed mightily accessible. He had made me feel for seconds that I could mesmerize him, but I had not even tried. I tended to my boat. I drove the car. I boiled water for tea, made us onion sandwiches. What was it in him that had helped me resist trying to seduce him? Was it what he stood for? I was not sure what he stood for. He did not seem to be too sure himself what he represented.

I gave him a sweater to wear back to his parish and saw him out to the car. It was a hot, sexy night, every bush alive and buzzing. I had nothing on to speak of, yet I felt suffocated. My chest felt wet, more than just damp. When we reached the cars, they were covered with night-dew. Something crashed through the brush, Maggie after it, but in a halfhearted way. Diotima complained for us at my bedroom window screen. Father Synge had failed to comment on either animal. I guess he was a holy man, after all.

But when he took off the sweater I had lent him, protesting the heat, the simple action struck me as crucial, and I stepped towards him in the dark, half hoping he wanted me to and half knowing I was a fool. At that he opened his car door and, tossing the sweater on the front seat, said, "I always expect him to be there when I open this door. After all, it was his car. He was the last to drive it before me. I can't believe he's gone."

He was back with Colfaxen, and here I was buzzing around him like a moth around a flame. He got into the car. Maggie came back and tried to climb into the front seat with him. There are people who do not see animals, and Father Synge was one of them. "So long. Don't forget about coming and speaking to the kids at the Shelter, you and Truman." He wasn't even at the Shelter anymore, but I guess he felt he could always go back.

Chapter 37

Odd that Truman and I should have reached an undeclared but deeply felt estrangement of sorts. He did buy a house in California without telling me about it. That was the way we lived. There was always some kind of struggle of wills going on between us. I did not put the house down when I saw it, but rather it put me down. It was not for me. California is not for me. Thirst's End was blatantly not for me.

I did not realize this at first. At first sight I felt I could safely spend some time there. But I was wrong. My body would not let me stay in Thirst's End. My body couldn't take it. The deadly boredom of the place nailed me. There was nowhere to go and nothing to do. The heat. The dryness. The turdy little buildings. The crawly people emerging from their holes at sunset. The empty stores. The empty streets. The rotogravure mountains. The jailness of it all. The empty tennis courts. The belligerent Indians, the rightful owners, snarling in their simmering trailers. The creeping cars, the sticky traffic. The Saturday night raid of kids from Los Angeles splashing in the deadly water tanks at the rear of every house.

Thirst's End was another yacht, one that never took off, never would take off. It was a yacht in the desert. A desert yacht. The same sky nailed overhead, blue by day, black by night. The same frying sun. The same old, the same very old. The same packed doctors' offices. The same lines before restaurants.

It was so poor in amusement, so rich in boredom. A physician's paradise, a nurse's haven. But whatever Thirst's End was, our little part of it was worse. First, there were the servants, a black and a white. The black arrived on a beer high and grouched at my purchase of garlic. Whitey, an Irisher from County Skidoo, stayed all hours. Truman's bedroom had a glassed-in garden for a window, no other natural light but that, thus giving him the appearance of having chosen to sleep in an aquarium. I was treated as a guest, maybe because he did not feel any permanence about the house even for himself. Really, it was rather as if both of us were walking around the place, outside, not inside, far from the heart of it, if it had a heart. But it was not unattractive. It was a thick-walled, one-story affair with openings to rooms where there might have been doors. The difference between outdoors and indoors had been dismissed, rather than solved. And I liked it if Truman did. I did not think I could live there, or that I would be asked to do so. Actually, I rather dreaded being asked. The cul-de-sac it offered appalled me.

He played a recording of a song he had written for the new production of *House of Flowers*. It told me that he was debauched clear out of his mind. It made me feel that everything we had was breaking up, or already broken, and would break me if I did not get going.

But how? Anyway, I was probably wrong. I was sure I was wrong. I went for a walk and told Truman about it. "Don't walk in the desert," he said, "there are snakes there." Then where could I walk? The streets were stage sets in search of a play. The houses were all shaped like cubes, but there was nothing of the adobe houses about them. They were a half-assed version and lacked charm, just as the imprisoning mountains lacked vegetation. There were palm trees, there were oleander trees, there were eucalyptus trees, but the shade they cast was miniscule compared to the great encircling brown of the mountains.

People kept ringing the doorbell all day long, some of them had English accents and looked like more servants, and they were: servants with messages. Nights we went to restaurants and ate Polynesian food or Mexican food, but I was hungry all the same. And all the time the desert yacht remained glued to sand, surrounded by hostile Indians.

Truman saw people, I never spoke to a soul. The Saturday night jamboree of kids from L.A. sounded like the world again, the real world, the world I missed, but cops soon chased them. And anyway, the next day was Sunday. Oh God. Think of a town with everything Scotch-taped in place. That was Sunday a.m. in Thirst's End.

My crisis brought us together again, gave us an objective, a goal, something to look forward to and hope on, thus paring away our mutual impatience with each other and, inadvertently, solving the dilemma of the house. I felt he had bought it without asking himself if he could stand Thirst's End. I knew I could not.

"You'll be all right as soon as you get wheels rolling under you," he said generously, and the lot of us left the next day, never to return. It was one of the most generous acts of his life as far as I was concerned, and, as you can see, I am far from forgetting it.

The drive home took us through the Southwest, Willa Cather country, and I would have adored stopping at something else less dreary than motels on the ends of towns, where the views always seemed to be the same, but I could see that Truman, having given in to me, wanted his own way now, and I did not blame him. We took turns at the wheel.

He asked me if I was taking pills a doctor in Thirst's End had given me as antidotes to depression, and I replied that I was, but I wasn't. I no longer felt depressed and afraid I was going to die, which was how I felt in Thirst's End. The rolling wheels, the change of scene cured me of the dumps, but the memory of them filled me with awe. I really felt I was about to die out there in California, where everything had begun to depress me as I had not been depressed before. God knows what happened to me. I did not know myself, and still don't, not altogether. It must have been I had begun to feel our life together was over. If I felt so, or if Truman thought so, neither of us ever let on. What ailed me could not possibly have been solely due to the geography of that purloined oasis. The song Truman had written for the revised edition of his show came back to me, though not in words or music; all I remembered of it was the thud it gave me emotionally that Truman was losing himself in some lurid sensuality. That he was wanting to experiment farther than he should go gave me the feeling that we were in a house on fire.

Of course, underneath this overextending of himself may have been his boredom. The only thing that did not bore him, really, was his work—new work—though it was harder and harder for him to get down to. Thirst's End was no answer, intellectual swamp that it was. Nothing suited us better about it than the leaving it. We never said why we did leave it except to admit without words that I could not take it. Maybe what I could not take was Truman in it, intuiting, as I well might have, ruin for him if he stayed in that awful house with the aggressive help.

He thought his own thoughts about it on our way back home, handling me rather like an invalid. Who knows? He may have been thinking of dumping me if I did go bats, which I seemed to be on the verge of doing back on the yacht that foundered. He fled us in New York, not even giving me time to let him out in front of our building.

He hated sickness and death like poison, but felt dutybound to visit the one and bury the other, ofttimes in quick succession. "Thank God I went to the hospital!" were his words to me on hearing of the death of Bennett Cerf. He never got over the small size of Carson McCullers's coffin. And after attending a high requiem mass at St. Patrick's for somebody who happened to be a prince of the church, he rushed home to me filled with the spirit of revelation: "I know what the church is all about now. Glamour! Glamour from beginning to end. My God! What a show!"

I don't think he was ever taught to pray as a child. His family appears to have worshipped money. He was stoical about his illnesses and not one to complain, though bully-ing by power-mad persons temporarily over him could set him raging in self-defense. He reached his sense of wonder about life all by himself, no teacher, no preacher, just as he worked his art out all by himself and with a handful of books. For in the beginning, everything was wonderful to Truman.

He told me that when he first saw Harper Lee, he shit his pants. I wonder why. Was he scared of her? I think so. I think he was scared of Harper right off. Such a tomboy. Sure she was. And she must have made the first of her adorable, mean faces at him. Terrifying for a kid to whom the uni-verse is a wonder. Of course, no one saw Harper, really, until Truman did; nor was Sook ever really seen until Tru-man came running back from the drugstore with her mor-phine and *looked* at her!

Chapter 38

"John! Mrs. Wallop is here. She's hysterical. She says they put her out of her apartment. Where've you been, John? All in white, too. Was it a tennis party in Southampton?"

"Don't be silly, Benito. I fell into the water; someone was good enough to lend me these clothes."

"Fell into water, John? But you have been baptized. I must say that you do look born again, John. Are you sure you're not?"

"Not what? Where's Mrs. Wallop?"

"Over in the graveyard. She won't come into the rectory. She says people will talk if she does. They will, too. Especially here in Restwell. John, whatever you do, don't go sit in the church and die on me like Father Colfaxen did. You don't suppose Mrs. Wallop came out here to die on our hands, do you, John?"

"I don't know, Benito. I'm really awfully fed up with Mrs. Wallop."

"I know. She won't let us forget."

"Well, let's find her. Forget our past with her at St. Roses?"

"Not only St. Roses, John. Everything. All misery. She's forever stalking before a barefooted, raggedy hoard, people of all races, from all countries…"

"Oh, shush, Benito. You're raving."

"I am, John. I'll stop. Except she says she sees the guy you went out with the night your picture was taken for the *News*."

"She can't possibly. He's in California."

"That's what she says."

"How would she know whether he's in California or not? You're feeding her ideas, Benito, putting her on. Where is she, anyway? Really, she's an awful bore. Why doesn't she go somewhere where people will take care of her?"

"Don't talk so loud, John. She'll hear us."

"Oh! Let her. It's time she found out how we've always felt about her."

"She knows all about that, John. There's nothing Mrs. Wallop doesn't know about us. I'm glad she's on our side. There'd be hell to pay if she were of the other persuasion."

The young priests drew up at the freshly painted silver pipe fencing the cemetery where Monsignor Colfaxen lay buried. There was a racing moon in the sky and an end-of-summer feeling about the night. No sound of the surf here, as there was in Sagaponack. The air was still, stymied. Here and there grave markers showed in a sullen, grey way in the crisp, burned-out grass. A remnant of an American flag clung immobile to a thin, black, barely perceptible baton. Yet something moved. A piece of kite, it seemed, had hitched itself to a telegraph wire about their heads, its rag tail alone moving now. But no! It wasn't a kite at all. It was a little dead squirrel, clinging by its teeth to the wire that had electrocuted it. Its tail moved, but not with any starts and lovely stops anymore, but swinging as a lifeless piece of cloth might swing, back and forth beneath the rigid little body of its once animated owner.

"Look, John, it's a squirrel. It must have been crossing the wire. Why would it do that, unless it was being chased?"

"Or playing."

"It must have slipped, lost its footing, and bit into the wire and got electrocuted. How long will we have to look at it, John?"

"Why? What does it matter?"

"But it's so sad."

"Oh! Control yourself, Benito."

"I never thought I'd have to come away out here on Long Island to see anything so sad, John. I hope Mrs. Wallop doesn't see it. Maybe she can't see that far."

"Where do you think she is anyway?" Father Synge looked up at the squirrel again and frowned. It was sad. It occurred to him that he might be standing on the little squirrel's winter hoard, and he moved abruptly aside.

"Don't go back to the rectory without Mrs. Wallop, John."

"I'm not going back without her. Where can she be?"

"She's not at Colfaxen's grave, she can't be in the church."

"Why not?"

"Well, don't they keep it locked? John, answer. Don't they?"

"Not always, Ben. Sometimes I tell them to leave it open and I'll close it."

"And you don't?"

"No, not always."

"John! Why don't you tell me these things? Supposing she's dead in there?"

"Don't be silly, Benito, Mrs. Wallop's not going to die; she's going to live and live, reminding us how she's old and we're young, how she's afraid and we're not, how we feel we are going places, and how she feels she is going to die."

"On the street, John. John, she's changed. They've put her out. She was always clean, John."

"Why, what do you mean?"

"She says they didn't even want her over at the Shelter, that she would have done anything, cleaned toilets, just to be close to you."

"I told them she was difficult. She is difficult. They have enough to do at the Shelter without the likes of Mrs. Wallop being on their hands. There's all those kids. God knows the things she'd say to them. I heard the things she's already said to them, actually."

"Like what, John? You know how she was. She goes on, I know, but her heart's in the right place."

"Right place? Groveling in front of the kids for a job? They didn't know what to make of her."

"They didn't, John? Are you sure it wasn't you who didn't know what to make of her, and not those kids? Poor kids, kids from crazy homes, what's new to them?"

"Mrs. Wallop was new. They didn't expect the likes of Mrs. Wallop at the Shelter, where everything's clean and orderly."

"Why, what did they do, John?"

"The kids began begging for a job for her—a job at the Shelter. It was the strangest thing. For a minute things were quite out of hand. Even Sister Secret said so."

"So that was the last of Mrs. Wallop, huh?"

"Don't say it like that, Ben. She's turned up here, hasn't she? We'll give her refuge, won't we? Well, won't we?"

"If you say so, John."

"You won't at all!" a voice broke out from behind the two young priests. "Expecting me to die in church like he did, huh?"

Father Synge did not recall ever hearing Mrs. Wallop laugh in his presence before, but now she did, inordinately.

"Come into the rectory, Mrs. Wallop. Don't stay out here in the damp."

Mrs. Wallop looked up at the squirrel but made no comment, for which the young priests appeared grateful.

"Father Scarpia was afraid to take me in for fear he'd cross you," she told Father Synge.

"Why would he cross me for doing something I would have done and will do?"

"Because," said Mrs. Wallop.

"Because is no reason, Mrs. Wallop. Because what?"

"Because that is what you've become."

They led her into the rectory. She did not look so bad to Father Synge, but Benito ran a tub for her, which she failed to use.

"I thought you might like a warm bath, Mrs. Wallop."

"I don't. Why?"

"To help you sleep better."

"Sleep? Oh Jesus! Sleep? I'm afraid to sleep. But don't tell him. Don't let on to Father Synge. He won't understand."

"Understand what, Mrs. Wallop?"

"Understand. You know, understand."

She winked at Benito and rubbed her hands together.

"That's right," she said. "But he'll go far. Mark me, he will."

"If you say so, Mrs. Wallop."

This, an expression Benito had often used with the former cook, roused a look of remembrance to her face. "Huh?" she said. "You can't deny we had good times at old St. Roses, can you, now?"

The next morning she was gone. Father Scarpia took daily mass. There were a few women, that's all. The young priest wished he had their faith. His mind kept wandering after Mrs. Wallop until he was startled to see she was one of the women in the church.

SAGAPONACK, 11 JULY, 1981

I took a swim and a walk on the beach, but my heart was not in it. The moon was in half and shining bright. His house was dark when I passed it. No lamp lit to read by. Sometimes when I look at him, I think to myself, now I have seen everything. I know, though, that's not true. The end will be something I have not dreamed of. My heart breaks and mends as often as I draw breath. I take heart constantly, and lose it constantly.

> *Mais, nous ne bougeons où nous sommes,*
> *Plutôt souffrir que mourir,*
> *C'est là la devise des hommes.*

SAGAPONACK, 12 JULY, 1981

Truman asked me, as I left him last night after getting him to eat something, to give him a "forever kiss." I never heard him say that before. He has been dipping into my manuscript, where Peach (Joan McCracken) demands a forever kiss from me, and I tell her that there is no such thing!

SAGAPONACK, 7 SEPTEMBER, 1981

Sometimes I think Truman would die for me. What an extraordinary thing to say! I'm not bragging either. It hurts me to say it, hurts me to believe it—which I do. He gives me all the childlike side of himself. If I close my eyes, I see him running at me with a bunch of lilies-of-the-valley. We once picked lilies-of-the-valley somewhere together. I remember Truman snatching them up, one after another, intent on what he was doing, as usual. They did not last. They would not be tame. And they had a wild smell, not sweet or flowery at all, but uncouth, and meant to put us off in a wonderful sort of way. Maybe they weren't lilies-of-the-valley after all, but jack-in-the-pulpits.

Chapter 39

"We already have a housekeeper, Benito. Besides, Mrs. Wallop is troublesome. It's bad enough..."

The two young priests were in the dining room of the rectory of the church of St. Jude in Restwell, Long Island, and they were eating their lunch. Mrs. Wallop was the cause of the interruption of their conversation.

"There's no need to stop talking because I came into the dining room, and you both know it," she said.

There was a sigh from the kitchen as she spoke. Mrs. Wallop turned and gave it her attention.

"Your housekeeper's put out about me being here. Well, I don't mean t'stay."

"We're sorry to hear that, Mrs. Wallop," said Benito.

Mrs. Wallop looked at him. "You know something," she said, "I think you are."

Her arrivals and departures had always been sudden and swift, and today was no exception; she was off back in the kitchen before either young man had a chance to reply to her.

"John, you were saying it was bad enough. You mean Restwell?"

"I didn't say that, Benito. I just said it was bad enough period."

"You mean the threat of nuclear war, all that?"

"That's right, Benito."

"John, I don't think we're ever going to get rid of Mrs. Wallop unless you get her a job in the Shelter. She's our charge, you know."

Father Synge put his hands to his ears. "I'm sick of that word charge. It haunts me."

"That's because it makes us feel so uncomfortable, John, so helpless. And, besides, John, you hate it here in Restwell."

"I don't. I love it. We both do. They'll be sending someone out to be over us soon, then we'll really realize how we've liked it, Benito. Think of that."

"You've been wonderful, John. Before I run away and join the Peace Corps, I feel I should tell you that, John. How much I appreciate your patience. I must be awful to live with."

"Oh! You are, Benito."

"I drove Colfaxen crazy, John. I killed him. I'm sure he'd be alive today if he'd had you with him, John."

There was a terrible racket from out in front of the rectory. The two young priests rushed up from the table and into the parlor.

"It's probably only the guy who came to take down the screens," Father Scarpia wailed. "Nothing happens here."

A beat-up old van had parked before the rectory, and out of it poured nearly half a hundred children, all sizes, shapes, and colors, the quickest moving of whom scooped himself up an armful of autumn leaves from the gutter. "I got me my leaves!" he cried to the other kids, who rushed to imitate him. "Robert was first, but I'm second!" a little girl in a yellow plaid skirt and bright white cotton stockings announced to her comrades, all of whom were also busy gathering leaves.

"Why," said Father Synge, "there's Robert Devereaux, my little pal from the Shelter."

"John! Did you know they were coming? Did Mrs. Wallop?"

"Of course she did, the witch, but I didn't, Benito."

Benito stared pop-eyed at the emergence of a nun—dressed in the old-fashioned way—from the van. "There's your Sister Secret, John. John, I can't meet her."

"Why not, Benito? Besides, you already have met her. Maybe she's come to take us away, to rescue us. Think, Ben, to be back where everything's at."

"She'd never take me, John. I can see by her face she wouldn't. She reminds me of Miss Jowett I had in grammar school. Miss Jowett said I'd never grow up, and I believed her. I still believe her."

"Sister Secret's not like that at all, Ben. She's the most positive person I know. She's come to save us. Pray that she'll take us away, won't you?"

"Don't ask me to pray, John. You know I can't."

"Think a prayer, then, Ben."

Father Scarpia closed his big, wet, bulging black eyes while Father Synge regarded him credulously, with a smile. Father Colfaxen, he thought, had tried to be a good priest, but Benito Scarpia really was one. For a minute the round-faced boyish young man before him appeared to gleam to Father Synge, but when Benito opened his big eyes, the peaceful expression on his face fragmented and he burst out in a voice full of the pain of desolation, "Can't say I didn't try, John!"

At that point Sister Secret entered the parlor and Benito fled.

"Why," exclaimed Sister Secret, "you'd think nobody lived here, it's that clean and neat. A regular doll's house. John..." She held Father Synge's hand and looked at him quietly for a long time, as if she had all the time in the world, which was the way she nearly always behaved, and with nearly everybody. "Come back, John," she said. "This," with a look around at the "doll's house," "is no place for you. We need you at the Shelter, but we won't keep you there, John. I see you back at Harvard someday, John. Teaching where you once were taught."

"Teaching, Sister? Why, for heaven's sake! Teaching what?"

"The Lord will provide, John."

But the children, having left their leaves outside, wandered piously about the rooms ohhing and ahhing at every little polished thing. There was no need to tell them not to touch anything. They didn't. Or not to scrape the floors. They didn't. There was a piousness in the way they lifted their little feet. For it was a grand house grandly kept. Their smooth young faces regarded even the unmarked parlor walls of the rectory of St. Jude with awe. About the only thing that made them raise their voices was the sight of Mrs. Wallop, who enlightened them soon enough as to her standing in the world. No, she replied to their anxious questions, she was no more employed and earning money from it than they were. They knew all about Social Security and unemployment insurance. The little girl with the yellow skirt and white stockings boarded Mrs. Wallop's bony lap and threw her plump arms around the old cook's neck and told her she was never going to let her go. Mrs. Wallop appeared to be very surprised at the little girl's behavior, which made the other children laugh and declare they would never let her go either. "I've found a place at last," was Mrs. Wallop's dry comment.

"No, we mean to give yawl a real job, Mrs. Trollop," Robert Devereaux told her. "A real job for Mrs. Shallop!" the kids yelled. Sister Secret came on the lot of them in the kitchen of the rectory, with the regular housekeeper, a staid Long Islander named Iris Iseminger, looking on as if she was wondering what in the world the little white Republican village of Restwell had come to, flooded as it was with New Yorkers, to say nothing of the hoard of small fry from

Brooklyn. "Now, I'm sure Mrs. Iseminger has work to do," said Sister, who seemed to know everybody's name, "so let's all out on the front porch into the blessed sunshine."

"Into the blessed sunshine," the kids sang.

Father Synge felt he must go outside as well and say hello to Catherine Lepore, since she would not leave the van long enough to come say hello to him.

"Father Synge," said Catherine, "we miss you."

Father Synge had never seen Catherine look so happy as she did seated in the driver's seat at the wheel of the old van.

"Mr. Malloy gave it to us," she replied to Father Synge when he questioned her about the vehicle. "Now we can pick up some of the children and save their mothers the trouble of going out of their way on their way to work."

"Do you like to drive, Catherine?"

A look of surprise came into the eyes of the girl who had seen too much too soon. "Oh!" she said, "you bet I do. Who wouldn't?"

"Would you like to drive me across the island to the South Shore?"

"Sure I will. And don't worry about the time. There'll be plenty of that. The kids have brought their lunches, and we planned to make a day of it out here. We'll give them time to eat, then gather leaves to take home. Hop in, Father."

Father Synge opened the door of the old van just as little Robert Devereaux rushed out into the quiet street to him from the rectory of St. Jude. "You still here, Father Sing?" the beautiful little black boy sang out anxiously. "I thought you'd gone. Oh, I'm so glad!"

"Sure I'm here, fiery stallion. What's all the excitement?"

Robert perked up at the sound of his nickname, though he had been close on to tears only a moment ago.

"Nobody calls me that since you left the Shelter, Father Sing. I 'most forgot it myself. Don't you leave us now. Promise."

Father Synge took the boy up in his arms. He felt he could never tell a lie to a child.

"You sad now, Father?" the knowing little boy wanted to know.

"Not really, Robert. I just thought…would you like to go on a drive with Catherine and me?"

"Would I? Sure I would. I'd go anywhere with you. You know that."

As they got up into the van, Robert said, "This is our first trip together, Father Sing. When I'm big and famous, I'll take you with us everywhere. You'll see."

When they drove into the overgrown driveway to the two houses in Sagaponack, Robert rolled his eyes, convinced that all was enchanted here, here amongst the tall pines and wild cherry trees and by the two still houses, both of them locked up, both with their owners away.

"Are you sorry nobody's home, Father Sing?"

"Yes, but I didn't expect anybody to be here, Robert."

"Maybe next time."

"Yes, that's true, Robert."

"What are they like, the people who live here?"

"Well, they are both writers, Robert."

"Oh yes. Writers. That's what I'm going to be."

"And not a tap dancer or famous ice skater you told me about? What happened to those plans, Robert?"

"Why, those plans of mine, they have gone with the wind, Father Sing. I've growed a whole half-inch since I made those plans."

Robert looked into the windows of one of the houses. He looked and looked, Catherine and Father Synge watching him sympathetically.

"Now what in the world are you up to, Robert?" Catherine finally asked him.

"Oh!" Robert replied, shading his eyes and continuing to regard the interior of the small, vine-covered house, "I'm seeing myself in there, like it was mine, the whole house, and you know something, I'm all by myself, but I'm not afraid. Yes, all by myself and not afraid because I'm waiting for somebody I'm sure is coming. So even when he's not there I feel safe, safer than I have ever been in my life…"

"What is this profound difference I feel between the North Shore, where we've come from, and the South Shore, where we are now?" Catherine asked Father Synge.

"Where you are now is the sea, Catherine. It's the sea you feel and sometimes hear on the South Shore."

"Why don't I hear it now?"

"Because the wind's from the land today, from the north."

"What a pity! And I did so hope we'd at least hear the surf today."

As they turned back to the van, they felt the air against their faces in a caressing way.

"It feels fresh suddenly," said Catherine. "Now I realize I'm by the sea. Why didn't I before?"

"The wind has changed in the interim, Catherine. Soon we'll hear the surf. There you go. Hear it?"

"Now I do. You mean to say it changed just as we were standing here? I can hardly believe it."

"It's true, though. It has to change sometime, turn around. Actually it's never still. It's always changing, as everything is, as everything must."

Father Synge looked wistfully back up the driveway as they left the two silent houses.

"Where do you think they are?" Catherine asked.

"God knows. Not with one another, you can bet."

Chapter 40

Truman did not have it in him to learn much, except what he taught himself, which was plenty. Places like Hazelden dried him up to near death. Institutions cannot give love, their caring is too spread out and for too many to amount to much when it comes to separate cases.

At Hazelden there was this Sam, a lady doctor, Samantha. She called me from out there in Minnesota, trying to get nearer to an understanding of Truman, I guess. He liked her. It may even have been because of Sam that he went back to Hazelden, hoping against hopelessness that it might do something for him.

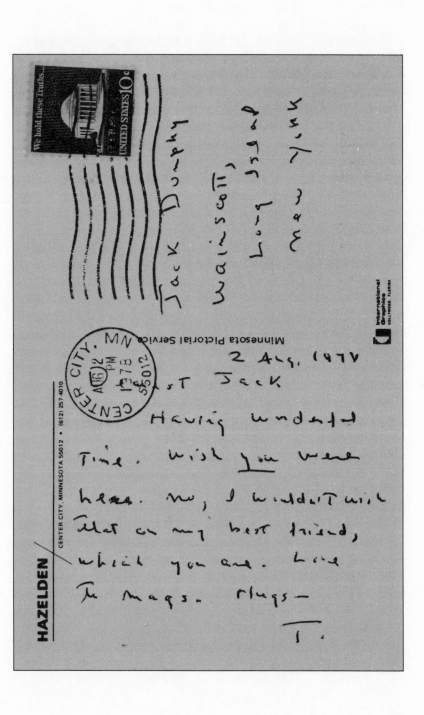

Jack Dunphy
Wainscott,
Long Island
New York

2 Aug, 1974

Dear Jack

Having wonderful
Time. Wish *you* were
here. No, I wouldn't wish
that on my best friend,
which you are. Love
the mags. plugs —

T.

People came from everywhere to be cured at Hazelden. Europe, China, everywhere. A priest who had kicked the habit for fifty years, then tripped and fallen back into his bad old ways. Truman wanted to write a story about him and call it "Altar Wine."

As Truman was going into Hazelden for the second time, Dr. Samantha, or Sam as everybody out there called her, was driving home. She did not stop her car when she saw him, but passed him by. He told me very little about Hazelden, feeling it would bore me, as it did him, but this he did say: Sam passed him on his way in without speaking to him. Was she too busy, did she black out, or was it that she suddenly remembered her *position?* Truman made no further comment to me about it. He did not have to. I knew the encounter had hardened him, so that his visit could not have possibly come to fruition. It was an instance of one of those recurring scenes in his life, throwing him back emotionally to other times, when his expectancy rushed him to the edge of what turned out to be one more abyss, where he stood alone and trembling, instead of being swept up into the arms of somebody who cared. Truman never met anyone who gave him as much as he gave them.

15 Feb 1980

Dearest Jack

I will not bore
you with the agonies of the
voyage. No matter — it was
pure joy to see you and
maggie. You are both so
beautiful!

I love you, Jack.
Hurry home, and bring me
a big hug —

T

Chapter 41

His arrival in Switzerland was sweetness itself, full of charm and wit. "Dr. Livingston, I presume?" were his first words to me when I opened the apartment door to him.

He was wearing a checked overcoat he had given me and which he always referred to as "your Sherlock Holmes coat": "Can I wear your Sherlock Holmes coat?"

We were glad to see him. Maggie and Diotima treated him as if he had only been out to the store and back. In no time at all they were in bed with him, Diotima purring on his chest. As I was leaving to buy us a chicken for supper he asked me would I get him a bottle of vodka. It was lonely for him to drink alone, and not as of old, when we did so much together and cocktail time was a ritual with us, when we would tell our doings and thoughts to one another while supper was readying on the stove.

He did not eat much and he slept even less, waking up every once in a while and turning on the light as if he was unsure of his whereabouts. He did not look bad, which is not to say he looked good. Towards morning he woke up asking me what we were going to do about the party we were giving, the people who had been invited, etc. His anxiety was great and painful to witness. He held my hand beseechingly, as if he was seeking the answer to this obviously painful fantasy. When he came to, realizing where he was and that there was no party, he announced his intention to go to the clinique in town, a few steps away from where we lived, but light years from his former behavior in the Alps, when he shopped with a pack on his back, hardy and uncomplaining, and worked with a pad on his knees and a pencil in his hand, as if he could never come to harm, surely not by his own hand, he looked so wise then, so in control of himself, even if he was imagination's child.

The clinique, a three-storied affair over a restaurant, a jeweler's, and a drugstore, looks across Verbier's main road at more restaurants. Since it is the ski station's sole hospital and the one place you can get a doctor, it is always crowded and noisy. Verbier's clinique does not even share its single blessedness with ambulances; you come and go as you can, and at your own expense. Truman fell out of his bed his first day there, so when I visited him, he was surrounded by workmen caging him in as if he was a wild thing.

"I'm getting out tomorrow," he told me.

He always said that when I visited him in hospitals. This time he was as true as his word. I arrived down from the mountain at about five o'clock on the following afternoon to see Truman standing at the front door of our chalet as if he did not know where he was. His shoes were untied, he was hatless, and he was wearing the Sherlock Holmes coat, buttoned cockeyed. It was dark and gloomy and quite cold; paths were slippery. I was glad someone had given him a ski stick to support himself, but wondered how he managed to carry it without gloves.

Verbier was no place for Truman now. Every road is either up or down, and even with his luck and physical dexterity he was bound to fall and hurt himself. Not that he wasn't used to falling; he was as used to falling as an apprentice acrobat. I took the baton away from him and got him back to the clinique, where we were joined by the director, Dr. Gas, a man I was so far from trusting that I could not bring myself to look into his dodgy dark eyes. Never have I seen a face so nearly covered by a beard—to such an extent, indeed, that the doctor appeared to me at times to have no mouth at all. The voice was a surprise, as if a bush had spoken, or hay had laughed.

"What have we here?" he asked in English.

Truman was in bed all dressed up, undone shoes, Sherlock Holmes overcoat. He complained that the nurse had failed to give him sufficient medicament. He did not have to come all the way to Switzerland to say that; he complained of that everywhere, in no matter what hospital. That evening there was a bottle of whiskey in his room to which neither of us made any reference. I expected him to come home after a few days at the clinique, but then I began to feel he was better off where he was.

The next time Truman jumped the hospital wall in Verbier he was led by a child, the both of them as bewildered
looking as could be, but charming all the same. I felt they
both knew so much more than I did. They were enormously
touching, the boy balancing his skis on his shoulders, while
Truman kept dropping his sticks, which the kid had obviously lent him to help himself along.

I had just skied down from the mountain at my usual time,
five o'clock or so, the hour Truman used to expect me in
the old days, and when I came in he would always say how
he could not get over the way Diotima knew it was me on
the stairs. He would be sitting in bed fully dressed, wearing
a sweater, a neat pair of trousers, socks, pantoufles, a writing pad on his knees. In the beginning, when we first came
to Verbier and he wasn't used to me skiing, he would come
searching for me around this time, asking ski instructors if
they had seen me or not. "The staircase is busy at this time,
the elevator bulging with returning skiers, but Diotima
doesn't budge till you come into the chalet. How does she
know it's you? Why does she go to the door only when you
come to it?" he used to say.

"Truman! What in the world are you doing out of the clinique again?"

"You don't want me home."

"I do. I do more than anything, but not if you're going to
carry on."

All the while the little boy who had helped him home was
staring from one to the other of us.

"Merci bien," I told him finally, taking his sticks from
Truman and handing them to him. "Que tu es gentil," I
said.

"Mais non, Monsieur," he begged to differ with me. "C'est
normal. Au revoir, Monsieur."

Upstairs Diotima met us at the door as she had done
through the years. Really, everything was the same. Some
of Truman's old self-assertiveness showed in the way he
took off my Sherlock Holmes overcoat and hung it up himself in the closet. I walked Maggie smack into a pale new
moon, barely perceptible in the twilight, as alone in the sky

as I'd ever seen her, not a star. Leaving Maggie to roll herself clean in the snow, I rushed upstairs to Truman.

"There's a new moon, Truman. Come wish on it. Aren't we lucky not to have seen it through a window first?"

"Oh! seeing a new moon through glass is the worst luck," he said, taking my hand and letting me guide him downstairs and out of doors where he stood looking up into the sky at the new moon with a pleading expression on his face, as if he were praying to something somewhere, the moon, the mountain, the sky, the world itself and all it held to help him to aspire again; give him back the man he was, aid and strengthen him. The stars came out as we stood there, at least the evening star was now visible. Lights appeared in the windows of chalets. The tops of the mountains gleamed like the backs of polar bears. More stars showed. Maggie cried on account of the length of our ritual, not dreaming how serious it was.

I will never forget our walk back to the clinique that night, Mags trailing us faithfully though dismally. It was as if we were turning our backs on all we loved, all we were, and all that had been; it was as though our futures were so unwell that they had to be hospitalized even before they arrived. And, despite his pain, his disappointment, knowing I would not return to the States with him as he secretly wished, but would finish out the season here in the mountains, Truman displayed the beauty of character to think of Maggie, grumbling behind us.

"Maggie shouldn't be out without a leash," he said.

After he left Verbier, I had the two little girls in from next door to show them a toy Barbara Paley sent him a long time ago. It is a wind-up toy, and it represents a white rabbit who lives in a head of cabbage. When you wind him up, he appears ears first to the sound of music box music and chomps on what was once a carrot, but is now only a part of a green leaf. The kids liked the show, and as they were saying goodbye, the eldest bid me say bon soir au petit lapin.

Chapter 42

No one used to tell me what to do with my life; now everybody prescribes sacrifice, and no one does so more forcefully than Father Synge. "You must stay with him, no matter what." My only company after Truman's departure from Verbier was two flies. Winter flies appear this way to me in the Alps, so do spiders. They are company, but not so satisfying as I could wish.

I wrote early to Madame Trollat for a room at her hotel on the Quai Voltaire, Paris. Madame informed me on our arrival that I had already received a telephone call from the States—two calls, in fact. She smoked and pored over her ledgers as if to tell me she had done with me, so I went upstairs with Diotima and Maggie, heavier in heart than I had been on our arrival. Not for the first time did I look on the telephone as a monster.

It was three o'clock of a sunny afternoon. When a barge went by on the Seine outside my window, I stepped out on the balcony and saluted its wash strung out on a clothesline stretching from one end of the flat-bottomed boat to the other. In my anxiety over the phone calls from the States I forgot to check the bridges over the Seine near the hotel, something I always do on my arrival in Paris, not only to see that they are still there, but what's happening on them, if anything. They are the Pont Royal and the Pont du Carrousel, and my hotel is between the two of them. Directly across the Seine is the Louvre, sedate as ever. The Pont des Arts, which used to take us from the Institute to the Louvre, is closed for reconstruction. Beneath me, on the quai directly before the hotel, is the motor traffic, consisting of trucks, cars, buses, cycles, and police vans—roaring, sputtering, rattling, and shrieking, except when momentarily brought to loudly protested halts by the light at the next corner from us, up near the Rue de Bac. I like it. I like everything about Paris but its telephones. It was Father Synge who had been trying to reach me.

"Where in the name of God have you been?"

"On my way to Paris. How did you know?"

"I guessed it. I wanted you to be on your way home."

"Why? What's the matter?"

"I can't find him."

"Have him paged in California," I almost said, but did not. Instead, I told Father Synge that I would be home in a week.

"I don't trust you. I'm coming over to get you."

It was only after I hung up the phone that I began to suspect he had something terrible to tell me but was reserving it for when we met. He was so baroque. It had never occurred to me that he might be a Jesuit. Whatever he was, his devilment of me was a masterpiece. He arrived at the hotel next morning without baggage.

"Are you staying at the hotel, Father Synge?"

"I'm not staying at any hotel. I'm going back today, and you're coming with me."

He did not always talk like this. He was not really a rude man. I hoped travel fatigue accounted for his present misbehavior. Or was he the carrier of bad news?

I looked bereft enough, standing in my bare feet in the lobby, but Madame Trollat, knowing me, took it well enough. "Voilà, Monsieur. Vous êtes bien habillé pour le temps qu'il fait. Il fait chaud aujourd'hui, heureusement."

I asked Madame if there was a chamber available for my friend. She dove into her ledgers without even looking at Father Synge, who, I was glad to see, had no idea what we were talking about. When Madame handed me a key and I in turn offered it to Father Synge, he took it with a smile. "I'm dead," he said, "I really am." I liked him better this way. Did he have to be knocked out for me to love him, as when he fell into the water of Mecox Bay? I crossed the quai when I took Maggie out and looked up at his room; it was directly over us, and gave me a surprising sense of gratification for Father Synge's presence in Paris.

They had put terrible new things in the Tuileries: great big bucket-assed women kicking their bronze legs in the air. The old green statuary across the way, with its air of patience no matter the weather, was more sympathetic.

The sun was setting beyond the Gare d'Orsay. Maggie groused in the grass. I thought of Baudelaire passing here while the Petit Carrousel was being constructed. Men turned up the flower beds for spring planting; the perfumes of the suddenly liberated earth permeated the evening air. We went back to the hotel by way of the Pont Royal. I bought a pot of primroses in the Rue du Bac for Madame Trollat.

Father Synge was out on his balcony when we came up the quai. He waved to us. The idea of intimacy with him, that could never be consummated, broke into my just-achieved sense of peace and smashed and scattered it until it was as if it had never existed at all, and I wished I was alone again, really, and knew almost no one in Paris—the best way to see the city itself, I felt, and leave it inexplicably refreshed.

I put Maggie upstairs and came down again. The primroses I had given Madame Trollat were purple, and though she had failed to thank me for them, they were on her counter, and they made me feel I belonged. It was raining outside; already the branches of the trees hanging over the closed bookshelves across the quai were wet and black. I pulled the hood of my windbreaker over my head and made a dash for it. The marché in the Rue des Saints Pères was going strong when I reached it.

The fish store extends out over the sidewalk into the street, as do other shops in the Rue des Saints Pères. There is no smell of dead fish. What you do smell is the sea. Three huge skate took up a whole slimy table, and quite a crowd had gathered to admire them. The young salesman in black boots and blood-splotched apron replied to questions concerning the skate with a very knowing air, though he could scarcely have achieved thirteen years of age.

"What in the name of God are we asking him for?" demanded a fat woman with a basket of new potatoes which she was obviously trying to sell; she was annoyed with the boy and his skate, since no one was paying attention to her or her new potatoes. "Potatoes! Potatoes!" she cried. "New and just born—like him," she said, pointing a dirty, blunt finger at the little fishmonger.

"I'll have you know, Madame, that I'm older than you think," was the kid's reply to her sarcasm. "I'll have you know I'm a father."

"God bless the boy for a little liar! Potatoes! New potatoes!" the fat woman cried.

"Come, little father," said a man with the air of a pilgrim about him, what with his backpack and his short brown beard, "give me one of your skate before the rain comes down with a vengeance and washes us all away, saints and sinners alike."

"You're a fine one to talk of saints and sinners in this nuclear age," the potato vendor scolded him. "We have more things to concern us than that."

"Maybe so, Madame," the pilgrim replied in a hushed and humble sort of way, stepping out of the path of the potato lady and on my feet. "Oh! pardon, Monsieur," he said, looking at me keenly. He must have once been handsome and had superb eyes still. His upright way of carrying himself, as well as talking, appealed to me. I found myself longing to speak to him, but the rain was coming down for good and all now, and he hurried off with his skate with a long look at me that seemed to say we will meet again. He was a romantic-looking sort of chap and had probably been sowing that look of his throughout his fifty-odd years with pretty good results.

The rain was joined by the wind and soon the Rue des Saints Pères was empty of all but stragglers like myself. People arrived in doorways stamping their feet and cursing the springtime. Only lovers were still, or slow, or careless of all but one another. They kissed in doorways or crawled along under one umbrella. They raced hatless down the middle of streets or leaned lips to lips across moist cafe tables. "Potatoes! New potatoes!" I bought four from her for fun and presented them, wet and muddy, but parfumée, to Madame Trollat with instructions to cut them up and plant them at her little place in Meudon outside Paris. "Oh! I know, I know. Je le sais bien quoi que faire. You don't think I have always been trapped here in this wretched Paris? Pas de tout."

Father Synge was descending the red-carpeted staircase

into the lobby. He stopped and watched us. He possessed the gift of looking different at different times. I could see Madame Trollat was more impressed with his appearance now than she had been on his arrival this morning. It amused me to think of what her reaction would be if I told her he was a priest. I decided not to. Besides, the way he stepped towards me went to my head. I was glad for the presence of Madame Trollat or else I do not know what I might have done. My eyes must have showed up a pretty hot blue, for Father Synge made a mouth, a faint expression enough, but it pulled his whole face down for an instant, so that in a flash I saw him old and withered and saying nay to all but God, though he would be no surer of Him then than he was now. The look passed and so did my sense of being alone with him in Paris, far from the restraints of the hierarchy of the American Roman Catholic Church.

Someone came into the hotel with some flowers—more primroses! Paris is full of them in springtime. "Let's go out," I said to Father Synge. He looked startled, as if I'd suggested we jump into the cold water of the Seine together. "Don't you have to walk your dog?" "Yes I do." He mentioned Maggie in such a way as to make her out all duty. I rushed upstairs and kissed her, hoping he would be gone when we got down, but he wasn't. "Don't bother to come with us, Father Synge," I cried, flaring up at him. "I know you hate dogs and consider walking them a chore." He appeared utterly baffled by my outburst. He looked pitiful as well. "I'll see you when we get back," I told him.

After a rain is a good time to walk in Paris, but then there are so many good times to do that: in the dead middle of a hot summer night to climb through Montmartre and look down on the city burning electrically below; or down to Les Halles before they circused it up; I like the dinner-hour walk along the Seine to Tom Curtiss's apartment in the Rue Cardinale Lemoine. I hug the Seine and feel lost in Paris when it is not nearby. But after a rain, when the chestnuts drip secrets as well as last raindrops, is best. Everything's wet but not runny wet. The world's on wheels, on foot, at windows, everywhere. One's heart misses a beat: it's Paris.

After telling Father Synge to stay where he was, I crossed the quai and the Pont du Carrousel with Maggie to the Tuileries Gardens, where the wet grass smelled fresh-cut and the newly plowed flower beds filled me with a longing for Sagaponack and the spring plowing in the potato fields around us there. Sagaponack seemed so free, while this strictly regarded space, esthetically free of banalities, tended to give me the smothers. Yet I love it. Paris is my refuge. Faith, it is said, is a belief in order. In Paris one can stand, say in the Tuileries, enclosed on three sides by the palaces of the Louvre, and know with a feeling of the greatest assurance that beyond one's left and right, all around in fact, are areas of such beauty that one has only to think of them— of the arches in the Rue de Rivoli, the galleried apartments of the Palais Royal, the Institute, Notre Dame de Paris, l'Isle St. Louis—to achieve peace of mind for a time. For a time is enough. More than that, I thought, recalling my bête noire waiting for us back at the hotel, would be too much of a good thing.

But he wasn't waiting. I wondered if he would call while I was feeding Diotima. I went out again, following the little streets to Notre Dame, where I knew I'd find him, and I did. Paris is small if you particularize over it. Both of us wanted its past, and rather begrudged the fact that it was past and not present. To me, it made the two of us look like spooks, leaning as we did towards other times when wars were playthings for knights to fight and kings to gain by, when religious crusades moved vast populations eastward, burning and killing in the name of the cross.

Now, despite incessant movement, all activity seemed to have died with the past, and the whole world waited to murder and destroy when the time was ripe. As we looked at Notre Dame de Paris in the dark, it seemed to be a reminder to us of a time when people did things, for better or for worse, and did not play the waiting game.

A figure stirred in the dark behind the grille of the main portal. I was dumbfounded to recognize the "pilgrim" who had bought the skate from the fishmonger in the Rue des Saints Pères. His eyes, which I had found startling enough earlier, now burned in a troubled way. "I've been locked in," he said. He spoke French, but all the same I was not surprised when he broke out into English: "How absolutely awful! What am I to do? Stay the night. What else can I do? I'd be afraid to rouse the gendarmes. They'd suspect me of terrorism. Here," he said with sudden urgency, at the same time struggling with his backpack, "take this fish, won't you? I don't want it. It will only rot on my back if I keep it. Give it to somebody along the street. That should be easy enough to do."

"I wouldn't, if I were you," Father Synge warned me as the clammy package was pushed at us between the iron bars of the grille. "Who knows what might be in it?"

"Your friend seems suspicious," said the man who I thought had tried to pick me up earlier in the Rue des Saints Pères. "What's the matter with him? Doesn't he trust anybody?"

He moved close to the grille and fixed me with his wonderful eyes.

"You trust me, don't you?"

A thrill went through me because of the look he gave me and our proximity to each other also. There was something holy and at the same time madly sensuous about him. His lips were red, though very dark red—they looked black, really—but his teeth were extraordinarily white, and certainly his own, every one of them.

"Well...don't you?" he insisted, since I took so long to answer him. "Don't you trust me? I bet you do."

"Yes I do," I said. "It's easy enough to trust a caged man."

"Yes, I suppose," he said indifferently. "Damned if I know why I got locked in here."

"You sure you don't want us to call somebody?"

"Absolutely."

"I know," I said. "I'll get you some coffee—or wine."

"Wine."

"And a sandwich."

"Sandwiches."

He offered us money, but Father Synge restrained me from taking it from him.

"He's not poor, you know," I said while crossing the bridge

to buy food and drink for the captive. "He bought this fish in the Rue des Saints Pères. I saw him."

Father Synge was silent, but his silence was acquiescent, not negative and restrictive. He followed me into a Greek bistro over on the Left Bank with light feet. He was enjoying himself. "We have to assume, of course, that he was locked in by accident," he said after I had bartered the pilgrim's skate for chicken sandwiches. Then when I attempted to pay for a bottle of red wine, Father Synge stopped me, offering to pay for it himself.

"You don't care how you spend your mother's money," I said, making a joke.

"No, I don't. Not really. Actually, I spend far less of it than she would have me do. She'd enjoy this, though."

"About the guy caught in Notre Dame for the night."

"Yes, she'd say that it served him right for going to church in the first place."

"Goodness. Really? Is she that way?"

"All the way. She hates it that I'm a priest."

"And you? How do you feel about it, Father?"

"I feel driven, if you want to know—driven to right wrongs, driven to try and stop destruction. But I'm not always a priest, of course. No, when I teach the kids at the Shelter, for example, I'm just what I'm supposed to be, a teacher. I'm good at it, I'm liked, I'm happy, and most of all, I feel there's a future in it for me. Whereas this..." We were back in the parvis of Notre Dame. He raised his arms. "All this overwhelms me. I feel imprisoned in it, like this guy we're helping. Only with me, especially now that Colfaxen's gone, there's no communication anymore. Yet, you know something, I believe. Yes, I believe more than I disbelieve."

"What do you mean?"

"Well, why did Truman call me Father the night I saw him home from Rajah's Bar?"

"Because he saw you were a priest."

"How, when I wasn't wearing my collar?"

"Truman's liable to call anybody Father under certain circumstances."

"No, it's my miracle. Let me keep it."

He looked very touching and young. I wondered if he slept in his skin. He moved back from me as if guessing my thoughts, as usual.

"Come," he said, "the poor man's waiting."

At first we could not make him out in the dark and thought he'd gone after all—or been kicked out. When he emerged out of the obscurity, he replied to our questions in a grouchy voice. "You woke me up," he said. "That's probably the only sleep I'll get tonight. Do you think I'm some sort of religious nut? I'm not, you know. I have no interest in the subject. It's true that before leaving the cathedral tonight, I decided to confess. So I did. Can you imagine?"

"Aren't you going to eat?" I asked him.

"After, after," was his laconic reply. "Actually, you know, I don't feel hungry. I don't feel anything—except different. Yes, totally different from what I was when I bought the fish I gave you. How did you get rid of it, by the way? Was it easy? I'll bet it was."

"They were willing to give us two chicken sandwiches for it. I saw you buy it in the Rue des Saints Pères."

"Oh, yes, that was before I confessed. Can you imagine? I never did it before. Yes, and the priest said, 'What's on your mind?' and we started to talk. Is this confession? I kept thinking. We talked and talked. We went on forever. No wonder I'm locked in here. Well, it was so on my mind I felt I had to ask him, else I'd go crazy. So I did. 'Is this confession?' It didn't phase him a bit, but the way he looked at me reminded me of an old hunting dog I had. She used to lick the palms of my hands, taking care of me as if I were one of her own, washing me clean. The priest was a good-looking man. I don't know why I should have seen Hannah in him. What's going to happen to me, do you think? When I bought that fish....Say! I remember you now," he said to me. He gave me his old look, or tried to, but all that had changed. He said himself he felt different. "All my life I've done things for the hell of it, too," he said. "Who would have dreamed that I'd end up this way? Tomorrow I'll go to the bank. I'll feel the way I used to. Or at least I hope I will. I must seem very eccentric to you two, do I?"

"No," I said, "you seem quite ordinary to me, if you don't mind my saying."

"Oh thank you! Thank God! I don't mind at all. Matter of fact I wanted you to say that. But...what happened to me just now wasn't ordinary, was it? You don't think I'm mad, do you?"

"No, not at all," I said.

He didn't seem to care much about Father Synge or to be able to take him in, but now he did.

"How about you, do you think I'm mad?"

Father Synge seemed to me to have been waiting all through the man's harangue to say what he did now.

"Bad, not mad!" he shouted, startling the both of us, maybe himself as well.

"Why, what's got into you?" the man behind the bars wanted to know. He obviously felt he was innocent, and he said as much. "What's bad about it?" he asked. He sounded more than innocent. He sounded hurt. "I haven't done anything," he said, "but I feel something's been done to me. I was only having a bit of fun. What's wrong with that? You don't believe in curses, do you? You don't think a curse has been laid on me?"

Father Synge murmured something indistinct which the man failed to catch.

"What was that you said?" he asked Father Synge. "What was it he said?" he then asked me.

"What do you care what I said or not?" Father Synge burst out.

"Oh but I do! I do! There has to be an answer to the way I feel, the strange way I feel. Why, I can't imagine I was light-hearted enough to buy a skate, a silly skate, only a short while ago. What's happened to me?" He reached for me through the grille. "You saw me then, have I changed to you? Look at me. Have I?"

The feel of him was repugnant to me, though I never dreamed it would be. I felt sorry for him and repulsed by him.

"Take your hands off me," I said. "You haven't bought me, you know. I'm not a skate."

"Don't talk that way to him," Father Synge said to me. "He's only asked you a question. Has he changed to you or not? Or don't you know?"

"Of course I don't know. How would I remember what he looked like before?"

"Before he confessed."

"Whatever it was he did that he feels changed him. All that's the matter with him is that he's locked up and can't get out until morning."

"I daresay," Father Synge said.

"That's right!" the man behind the grille cried. "That's all's the matter with me. I'm locked in and want out. Who wouldn't? Wouldn't you? Sure you would. You both would. There! That's better. I feel better already. Of all the ridiculous things. It reminds me of a cook I had in Spain. She said she went to the circus, and when the clown said, 'Oh, if my poor mother could see how ridiculous I am now,' it made her cry. Here, have a swallow before you go." But we did not. We refused him. "Maybe you're right," he said. "I'll need all the wine I can get tonight."

On our way back to the hotel we stopped at a Greek restaurant only because Father Synge desired it. Plastic vine leaves were tacked to the walls, and the clients, most of them northern Europeans, appeared to think they were more hardy, hearty, and healthy than the rest of us. Father Synge heeded them no more than he did Diotima or Maggie. He said he liked liver, brains, sweetbreads when I refused everything but rice. Outside he bought a single ticket to an old Louise Brooks movie and disappeared out of my life, but not for long. Louise Brooks will never say die in Paris. She's more than a fad there; she's a cult. Father Synge was far too young to have ever seen her in American films. He did not stay a minute at the movie. I heard him upstairs at the Quai Voltaire moving about in his bare feet, then silence. The last thing I wanted was to go home with him on the same plane, so I let him sneak out of the hotel next morning as if I was not perfectly cognizant of every move he made.

I was restless after he left. I did not miss him, far from it, but I thought about Truman and wanted to know what he was up to and where he was. I hastened my departure from Paris, and we left the next day. Truman was fine when we arrived at 870 United Nations Plaza, not penitent, just fine. I was tempted to ask him to write a foreword to my book *First Wine* as the publisher wanted me to do, but I did not. I asked only one thing from him, and that was to be OK. He was so proud of himself when he did not drink. We got so we never talked about it, but all the same it was as if we were secretly holding our breaths, the two of us. The simplest thing, like saying "What time is it, Truman?" and him being able to answer, was a triumph for us, both of us. The sound of his footsteps, steady and firm as of old, was music to me.

When *First Wine* came out and he read it, he said, "You're a great artist." He was very emotional, crying, laughing. "I know you say I cry because of drinking," he told me, adding that it was not always true. "Beautiful things make me cry too."

I asked him if he remembered the number of the house on Lexington Avenue where we met.

"Yes," he said, "I remember the number perfectly well. There are some numbers I remember, but most I forget. I don't know why. The number of the house was 1453."

Chapter 43

The house, a decrepit brownstone, with creepy, dark halls and no furniture to speak of, was...heated, that I will say for it. And though there were lots of books, it was a readily admitted fact that our host was not much of a reader. You felt that if he did not have another thing in the world to do and did pick up a book, he would skip mostly, saved inevitably by the bell—of the telephone. You can imagine the conversation:

Person on the Telephone: What are you up to?
Leo: Reading.
Pott: Reading? Really? Reading what?
Leo: Ouida. She's marvelous.

To say that I had been dragged to 1453 Lexington Avenue is no lie, no exaggeration either, nothing but the truth. The evening was mild outside, no rain, no snow. I was living at the time in a cold water flat on East Seventy-Sixth Street, no heat, so I was wary of cold. About two years before, on my return from the war in Europe, my wife had run away, and Harpers had published *John Fury,* my first novel. *Harper's Bazaar* bought a story from me. *Story* magazine printed "Death of a Carrot," notes of things I saw of wartime France and Germany from the open door of a Forty-and-Eight. I had seven hundred dollars in the bank, my apartment was sixteen dollars a month, and I ate most of my meals with Todd Bolender.

Whether Todd has forgiven himself for dragging me out that night I do not know, but I do know he did not forgive himself then. For I was soon seeing more of Truman than Todd thought I should, though I was no more social then than I am now. What happened was that after dinner Todd suggested we visit Leo Lerman and Gray Foy up on Lexington Avenue. Todd lived on Second Avenue, also in a cold water flat, but it wasn't as though we were looking for someplace warm to go. Anyway, as I have already noted, the weather was mild.

We were in good health, good spirits, and had just spent a very pleasant summer in P'town together, mostly at Todd's expense. (I went halves with him on the food bills, he paid the rent.) Was I doomed to break someone else's heart because my own heart had been broken when Peach left when I came home to her after the war? I don't know. I'm not sure. It's terrible to hurt people. I believe I will pay for having made people cry over me. En revanche, I do not feel that people are going to pay for having hurt me.

Sometimes I feel we can never be hurt again as we were as children, perhaps mostly because we don't depend on people heart and soul as we do as kids; then we ask everything of others, heaven on earth, and expect to get it. Childhood is terrible in its dependence on others. It is beautiful too, of course. Could it be that the part of us remaining vulnerable all our lives is the most childlike part of us? Is that the part that loves deeply, faithfully, trustfully? I think it was the believing boy in me, the boy who had found his love at last, that Peach hurt (though she failed to kill him) when she ran away from me after the war.

Why, Todd and I were not in that house at 1453 Lexington Avenue ten minutes before our host was on the phone: "Jack Dunphy's here." Poor Todd! He looked at me, brightening his eyes, as if to say, "See, you're being talked about." As if that was anything, to be talked about. Soon the front doorbell rang, and I heard Truman for the first time.

He was wearing a smart, well-cut little sheep-lined suede jacket, Knize grey flannel trousers, sturdy, rubber-soled shoes, and a cap. He only had eyes for me, and I was flattered. He was markedly rude to Todd, but that did not bother me. Soon nothing would do but that we go to Truman's place, also on Second Avenue but overlooking Queensboro Bridge. That was November. By February Truman and I were on the high seas bound for Italy. "To follow the spring down through Italy," he said. We went to Paris first and stayed at the Hotel Pont Royal on the Rue du Bac. People Truman knew began pouring into my life. Here are some of them: Pearl Kazin, Andrew Lyndon, Phoebe Pierce, Mary Louise Aswell, Cecil Beaton, Frankie Merlo, Tennessee Williams; and there were many, many more.

I'd known Frankie before, but it was a different Frankie I met in Florence with Tennessee, a Frankie already showing the strains of the burden of living with and for a celebrity. The four of us drove down to Naples and took a boat to Ischia, where Auden and Chester Kallman had a house, but I rarely saw them. They snubbed Tennessee, though they had not a thing against him but his success. Auden liked best to have sycophants surrounding him. Once we all went to take baths in some bathhouse on Ischia, everybody in separate tubs in separate compartments. It smelled very bad,

I must say. I never saw any of that crowd in swimming. The only two who talked (and there may have been seven or eight of us) during that bathhouse teaparty were Auden and Chester. I never felt more cringey in my life. Truman told me he knocked Chester down in front of Maria's Cafe on Ischia. This was a revelation to me. It seems that Chester slurred me to Truman's face. Chester kept house for Auden on Ischia. There was usually a pot of meat rotting away under their kitchen sink, and this day I commented on it.

"What's that pot doing walking around under the sink without a lid, Chester?"

"Don't be funny. That's my sauerbrauten."

Best about Ischia were its cliffs, its few fields, its vineyards. I liked to walk to and from the cove where I swam every afternoon. The light would be golden as I faced back into town, everything would be etched against the superb blue of the sky—a proud, cruel blue if you had no shelter against it. The late afternoon shade of the narrow streets felt soothing as I walked to the pensione where Truman and I had rooms. Bougainvillea flopped over balconies everywhere. The floors of our rooms were paved with blue and yellow tiles. Boys lazied on the seawall in the evening as we drank martinis. Soon the white shirts of their uncles and fathers would gleam like lamps in the dusk. We had little red fish almost every night for dinner. Truman was writing a novel called *Summer Crossing* that came to nothing. I wrote a short story that has disappeared in the wash of time. The truth was we were too new to each other, and perhaps too happy, to do anything about writing except to keep our hand in.

This rustic experience was interrupted by the appearance on Ischia of a couple Truman found fascinating. It marked the first time I was to see him carried away by the frenzy of an enthusiasm. Nothing would do but that we should trail these two strangers to Africa! I can see us to this day arriving by boat at Tangiers, and on the dock, gathered to meet us, looking like vultures awaiting the wash-up after a hurricane, are Paul Bowles, Gore Vidal, and Jane Bowles. The Bowleses told us they lived in a wonderful pension, which turned out to be a dump, depressing beyond words. That evening we had our first of those awful couscous dinners, Jane moping over her food, Paul malnutritious-looking unto death, no matter what he ate. A pity we left Ischia for North Africa. For the quiet island we exchanged a dusty coast blaring with Ramadan nights.

Yet for all the people we met in North Africa, the Arab world remained unintroduced to us, and this bothered me. It made me feel left out of the biggest thing about North Africa, its people. Of course one could always simplify the whole thing, as the British seemed to do, and look on most of the citizens of Tangiers as servants. But this was sad and made one feel more of an outsider than ever. I could not stand the feeling. There are people who feel they are inside no matter where they are, in on everything, but I'm not like that. The colony of expatriates saw too much of one another and inevitably quarreled when they did. Cecil Beaton came down with the heel of his slipper on David Herbert's instep on the dance floor at a party. The Second World War was fought over by those who had served their country and those who had served their own personal interests. David limped everywhere afterwards.

Truman ran around a little, which was always his tendency, but we dined together with the Bowleses at the pension from a table covered with cracked oilcloth nearly every night and sometimes had drinks in the bar, a small, damp place presided over by a grouchy man with a granite-grey face. When he played his little radio, it sounded exactly like an iron poor box as you drop a penny in it.

It was a sad bar, and there was something universal about it. Here's why. Mostly it was empty, but you never knew who might come in, or what color they would be, or what language they would speak. The people who owned the pension had three handsome teenage daughters and a superb eight-year-old boy, not one of whom ever looked your way except under the greatest pressure, but the little boy never. "Hotel child," Truman called him. The Arabs ran the place, but the bartender was not one of them. He was from Erewhon for sure. He was all right, really, except he seemed to

wear, stitched like a war-wound to his forehead, the admo-
nition THOU SHALT NOT BE GLAD. He was a change from
the crowd of expatriates we knew, stomping one another in
their fury to show they were having a better time than those
they had left at home.

When Truman told me we were invited to a masquerade
party, I thought it would be fun for us to go as Topsy and
Eva, but no one else was amused. When we arrived at the
party, more than backs turned against us. We seemed to
smell bad to the people there too. Never was the difference
between us and others more manifest. Our costumes were
simple but perhaps rough. Instead we were given drapes to
wear, and the festivities soon came to an end for us. We
said nothing about it, and never did, but it brought us closer
together.

Afterwards we sought refuge in the bar of our pension,
assuming it would be empty. It wasn't. An ordinary-look-
ing, middle-aged woman without jewels sat alone at a table
across the room from us with a glass of untouched stout on
the table before her. The bartender was there of course. He
was always there. We had nothing to drink, but were content to sit at an empty table and make plans for the future.
There was no common sitting-room at the pension, and our
rooms were too cold and uncomfortable to do anything but
sleep in them. Ramadan being over, the night outside was
quiet. The Arabs, their feast ended, were asleep for a change.
No longer did the restless wail of their rietas wind up to us
out of the casbah. Our only music was the barely perceptible jingle of the bartender's "poor box."

Truman wondered if we shouldn't leave Tangiers tomorrow. There was a boat for Marseilles. Good. Let's book passage on it if we can and go. Great. I drew out of my pocket
a ham sandwich I had lifted from the party, and we shared
it. Suddenly the woman across the way sang "Galway Bay"
from beginning to end, looking out of the open door of the
bar as she did so, as if she could see everything she sang
about, while beating time with her open-toed, black patent
leather shoes on the stone floor.

Afterwards, except for the sucking sound she made drain-

ing her glass of stout, the silence was exceptional. For one
thing, the bartender had turned off his radio.

"That was well sung, after all," he said to the woman.

If I had not heard her sing English just now, I would have
sworn she did not know what the bartender was talking
about. She did not look his way when she got up and walked
out of the bar without the slightest bend in her knees that
I could see. The next a.m. we gave our Topsy and Eva costumes to the Arab cleaning women and prepared for our
journey to France. In Aix-en-Provence we drank new wine
from stands on the street. It was good to be back.

The two straight years we spent together in Taormina seem
sometimes never to have happened to us. Even the name of
the house we lived in there escapes me, as it does now, actually, and all I can recall are heaps of summer visitors,
though not necessarily their names or nationalities. Winters were quiet, for of course we were there in winter. Spring
was noisy, but not with visitors. It was noisy with the sounds
of goats and sheep, the songs of the people passing along
the little path behind Fontana Vecchia. There's the name of
our house! Isn't it lovely? Fontana Vecchia would vibrate
with the passage of the flocks as though it felt the spring
warming its old joints and longed to bleat and to bellow as
well.

Built at the head of a ravine, Fontana looked across the
Strait of Messina at Calabria. All summer there were fire-
works on saints' days, and the dark blue sky would be tap-
estried with gushing chrysanthemums and leaping stars
above the quiet gleam of fishing boats tirelessly working
while we played. There was nearly always some town cel-
ebrating something in that lava-enriched coastline domi-
nated by Mount Etna. Once we arrived at a village, after a
perfumed ride up the mountain between groves of flower-
ing orange trees, to discover people in a frenzy of expec-
tation before the open doorway of an unpretentious little
brown church. Suddenly a gang of sweating young men appeared carrying on their shoulders the heavy bust of a black

saint between them. They had brought him from a church higher up in the mountain as they did every year at this time, but it was always exciting, apparently, and as if for the first time, like Christmas. Afterwards there was a procession followed by dancing in the square. Musicians showed up encumbered by their horns and an accordion. Lights had been strung up all along between the trees, but as if in secret, since there was a roar of surprised delight when they came on and the music played. Still we worked. Truman wrote *The Grass Harp* at Fontana, and I wrote *Friends and Vague Lovers.* But we did not let on much about it. We were awfully unassuming, really.

SICILIAN WAKE

It was the wily little owner of Fontana, our landlord, Mr. Cacopado, who suggested we go. I think he needed us as a buffer against the family of the dead child whose wake it was. The brother of Graziella, our cook, had run over the baby with his Vespa and killed it. The tiny white coffin, like cake icing wrapped in mosquito netting, the flies, the child's father bent over the coffin as if he would embrace it if he could, coffin and all, sobbing, moaning, crying out. The rest of us seated on chairs against the stone walls, while their beasts bellowed and brayed to be watered and milked. No other child present. No greetings, no words, no food, no drink. No sounds but those of the young father and the beasts in their stable next door. No conversation except the savage monologue of sorrow and vindictiveness of the young father howling his need for revenge.

The baby was dead, but its family were peasants and they wanted recompense, they wanted to be paid, they wanted money, land, they wanted blood. And yet it was plain the young father could not get over his grief. He seemed to be the victim of a recurrent dream where the child was alive and running to him, only to go dead in his arms. He would look at its face, still as a stone now, its little closed mouth, its sealed eyes, and he would howl afresh in disbelief.

I think he fell asleep a lot. He would then raise his head from the edge of the coffin and stare at us, blinking his sharp, black, little red-rimmed eyes that somehow could not look sad or elicit pity, they were so hard and mean and calculating. All seemed a dream to him until he looked at his child. Then the storm broke from him again under the vicious enlightenment of memory.

This went on for all the time we sat there with Mr. Cacopado, easily more than an hour. Nothing happened but that and the begging of the beasts to be milked and watered. They banged and howled, too, in their way. The whole farmhouse smelled of the stable, a rich, wet smell, pungent and piss-ridden. A bundle of snow-white kittens played in a square of sunlight in the doorway of the room in which we were seated like putti in a holy picture.

Graziella's brother, the one who had to do with the actual death, was not present; it was as if he was in hiding after having run over the little thing with his Vespa. Graziella and his other sister had come, but not his mother. His father, a poor, footloose wanderer on the town, did not count and was not there. The old lady took in wash. Graziella was only a girl herself. She sat staring silently in front of her. The sister did the same. Mr. Cacopado, our landlord, was acting like a lawyer, except that he was silent as well. One felt that the time for negotiations, for settlement, was still far away. The young father had to howl and hack and bring up phlegm and spit it out on the stone floor for hours yet, maybe days; the hot sun would sink as it was sinking now, and rise again, and sink again, before he would listen to reason, if he ever did. It was hard to see how he could do anything but grieve while his child, his firstborn, mind you, lay before him under the tireless buzzing of the flies, who, despite him and the netting, found their way to the corners of the baby's mouth. Then the young father would look up as if he felt he had been tricked. He'd done all he could in the way of behaving himself, yet here he was, way down under, like any bum. Listen to his beasts clamoring for care. Look at his brothers, all four younger than himself, more's the pity, waiting in the chairs against the wall for him to tell

them when to move, what to do, to go kill or not to go kill.
He was ashamed to look at them. They were used to him
leading. Now what could he lead them to but a baby's grave?
He stood up, wiped his face with his brown hands until it
was a smear and made him look dirty and unkempt, when
actually, he was clean; they all were, all the brothers in
gleaming white shirts, dark pants, even shoes.

"Go tend to the beasts. Can't you hear they are crying?
What is this to you that you sit doing nothing, making things
worse for me than they already are?"

The brothers plodded out of the room as he cursed them
and crossed the patio to the beasts, whose furry heads jut-
ted from their stalls in a mystified way. At the sound of their
silence the young father fell over the coffin again. For everything was different from what it used to be to him now.
Everything had meaning. Things he had given no thought
to before, he thought about now, as they would be without
his child.

The gateway to the farmyard was a ghastly thing to pass
through to us, so think what it would be to the young father,
since it was by that path the baby had run out of the house
into the path of the motorized scooter of Graziella's brother. The boy had fallen off the vehicle, breaking his wristwatch, and that was all his mother would talk about, his
watch and how he had broken it and it was no good for
nothing now. Such was their life. It was rude, it was hard,
and it made them hard on themselves and one another.

Cacopado, because he had been to America, was generally considered to know a thing or two. He knew better than
to open his mouth now. A vendetta was being nursed where
words would have been an indiscretion. It would have been
different had Graziella's family had anything. Had her
brother looked forward to an inheritance, that in itself would
have been grounds to parley. As it was, there was nothing
to talk about or think about, when the time came, but revenge.

It was boring sitting there in the hot room with the men
of the family sharing none of the action with us. It was embarrassing to feel we were no more important to them than

their women, none of whom seemed to count, now that the
young father and his brothers did not want sex or food. Truman was pale with boredom and fatigue, to say nothing of
the heat, to which he was always sensitive. But he would
never have budged until Cacopado gave the signal to part.

In a way we were part of the bargaining; that is why Cacopado had brought us along, wily little man. Yet he had
nothing to gain by making peace between the parties that
we knew of. He appeared to be doing it for something to do.
Maybe he meant to run for mayor of Taormina. He seemed
fussy compared to the men of the farm. He was undoubt-
edly thinking of getting back to Fontana as much as we were.
We had come in a taxi, too, and that was waiting. But the
taxi gave our being there more weight than if we had arrived on foot like mendicants.

It was easy to see from the beginning that nothing was to
be done, nothing said. We were all part of the ritual of the
wake, which was as it should be. The thought may have
been as comforting to the others as it was to me, but I
doubted it. Just when I decided I did not much mind sitting
there, hardly being able to breathe because of the stinging
smell of the stable, Mr. Cacopado stood up as if he did not
have anything to do with it, as if he had been compelled to
rise, motivated by forces outside himself, or from somewhere so deeply buried within him that it was a secret even
to himself.

Anyway, he stood up. Then Truman did, with an expression on his face of total disbelief that our agony was about
to end. On our way home Mr. Cacopado allowed his hand
to slip from the thigh of Graziella's sister into her crotch; it
was hastily plucked out by Graziella, who acted as if she
was the elder of the two girls, which was not so. She just
had more sense. We did not talk about the case at the farmhouse or about anything else. Mr. Cacopado's left hand continued its researches for as long as the journey to Fontana
lasted. It was a wonder we ever got out of the farmhouse.
For when, following Mr. Cacopado, who appeared to be motivated in his rising by celestial wires, the rest of us also
stood up, even the women of the farm, who until then were

as if nailed to their chairs against the white stone walls, the four brothers of the young father came back from tending to the animals and, without exactly meaning to, I'm sure, barricaded the open doorway against us with their lean, upright bodies. It was plain that they dreaded our leaving, since that would signal the time of decision had arrived, and they would have to go forth, as the decent men they were, and procure blood for blood whether they wanted to or not, and I did not think they wanted to. I felt they wanted us to stay.

Time stood still for them as it seems to do in all ritual deeply felt and sincerely participated in. What difference did it make to us, Americans on a perpetual holiday, if we stayed or not? None as far as they were concerned. Besides, it was a grand thing, this wake. Their brother must be stood by. He must be urged by our presence to go ahead with everything up to the point of actually killing Graziella's brother. That he might do someday when convenience would have connived to make murder less noticeable than it would be just now. There must be time for hatred to flower. Let Graziella's brother go into hiding for a few months and emerge pale and jobless. He might even die of shame and terror and would not have to be blood-revenged after all. He had lost his watch, his Vespa. His good name was gone. It was terrible to think of them on our way back to Fontana. They had moved aside; it was as if in going by them and out the farmhouse door we had been afraid we would tear our clothes on them, they were so sharp, so vindictive, and so hard.

The whole thing affected Mr. Cacopado monstrously. No matter how efficiently Graziella worked keeping his hand away from her sister our landlord persisted as if he could not help himself, which he probably could not. They are easily unnerved, Sicilians, particularly the men.

Graziella's mother was waiting for us at Fontana with our wash. She showed us the boy's broken watch and complained about his motorcycle, also damaged. But when Graziella talked to her about the wake, she turned away with her arms raised and made fists of her hands which she shook in the direction of Calabria. Below us the trees in the olive grove marched down the ravine in front of our house in their snarled way, the silver-green coloring and gentle undulations of their leaves contrasting heartbreakingly with the stark, dark bodies of Graziella and her family. Kelly did not want to go down to the beach with me, but I made him. I have always regretted that. He wanted to stay with Graziella, and she wanted him to.

Is that how it was? Well, it was harder. It was like the rocks and the cactuses of Sicily and its long, bright summers. It was dramatic to us rather than pathetic. We were not moved by the suffering of the peasants at the farmhouse as we would be if we were there today. Then nothing deeply concerned us but ourselves, our work, and Kelly. Mount Etna's eruptions did not phase us. We watched the flaming cinders trip down the mountain as if they could never amount to anything much anymore. But the Sicilians were worse than us. They held picnics on Etna so as to enjoy the spectacle of the mountain's eruptions in the company of their families and friends, eating and drinking, with their automobiles parked nearby, which they assured us would take us to safety if necessary.

We cried when we left Fontana. I remember we went down the path single file following a boy pulling our luggage in a cart, and how Kelly would not come. No, he would not. But since it was his nature to see to it that we stayed together, he stood torn between us and the house, his sun-rusted coat now blue, now black, now orange. Graziella hung over the balcony rail off her kitchen, crying and waving to him: "Kelly! Kelly!" He wanted to go back to her, but he could not bring himself to leave us. He did not know what to do. It had been so long since he had worn a leash that he did not seem to recognize his old collar when I fixed it on him.

At Fontana we used to go down to the water after lunch to a small beach covered with white pebbles that were so hot that Kelly could not bear it until he had reached the water, nor could we. We swam from an old rowboat, each of us taking the oars while the other swam, Kelly barking all the time. But he was quiet in caves that were dark, green, and full of the musical sound of gurgling sea water. There we snorkled, and all he could see of us was the pipe through which we breathed. We took turns with the mask, since we only had one between us. Truman did not like me to stay underwater long. He said it bothered Kelly. "Imagine thinking someone you love has turned into a fish," he said.

Chapter 44

Father Synge telephoned the rectory of St. Jude's from Kennedy Airport and a strange voice answered, making him feel like a runaway, which he was, of course, but he had not felt he was, the reality of it as well as its possible consequences, until now.

"This is Father Curler. You aren't Father Synge, by any chance, are you?"

"...Yes, I am."

"Ah, good. We're expecting you, Father Synge. May I ask where you are?"

"Sure. That's all right. I'm at Kennedy Airport. Is Father Scarpia around?"

"Ah yes. I thought you'd like to speak to Father Scarpia. I'll get him right away. Hold on. By the way, how was your trip? Where were you, anyway?"

"Paris. A friend..."

"Ah yes. That friend. I understand. You needn't explain. Why, here's Father Scarpia now. I'll give him to you."

Benito made sure that Father Curler took himself off before he spoke on the phone.

"John? Where are you, John? John, I didn't think you hated me. That makes two of you now who did."

"Did what, Benito? What are you talking about?"

"You and Father Colfaxen. He hated me. He died to get rid of me. You run away. Where are you, John?"

"Kennedy."

"Don't move. I'll come get you. Where'll I find you?"

"I don't know. It all looks alike to me. Really, Benito, I'm not sure if I ever left Paris when I look around. It seems as if I'm still there."

"Arrivals from Paris. I'll meet you there. Don't move."

"Father Synge asked an airport guard where the arrivals from Paris would be, and the guard told him it was right where they were. He bought a *New York Times* and settled down to read it when he heard his name coming over the loudspeaker inviting him to call at the correspondence desk. At the correspondence desk he was given instructions to contact his mother, which he did. Maria answered the telephone.

"Father Synge, we were so worried about you."

"Hello, Maria. There's no need to worry about me. How's the baby? How's Esperanzo?"

"Esperanzo is fine, Father Synge. But let me give you your mother. We have put an extension on the telephone for her."

"You baby her, Maria. You and Juan. You'll make an old woman of her before her time."

"She's very worried about you, Father Synge. Everybody is except Sister Secret. Did Sister Secret know where you were? She acted as if she did. Here, let me give you your mother. She's calling."

Nora Synge did not sound like herself at all.

"Why, what's the matter, Mother? You don't sound like yourself. What's up?"

"Don't say that, John. I'll be all right now that you're back. I had the strangest feelings that you were not coming back; that you'd gone. I'll never forgive Annie Bushnell for that. Never. No matter what you say. Don't defend her."

"Defend her for what?"

"Sister Secret kept her secret all right, and it almost killed me."

"What secret?"

"The secret of your whereabouts, John. Don't tell me she didn't know where you were, because she did."

"Oh God! I suppose there's no talking to you the mood you're in."

"No, there isn't. I know what I know and that's that. There goes your call. Don't waste any more money. Come see me."

Father Synge called her back anyway. Maria answered the phone. He heard her baby in the background. Everything had changed in the house on Willow Street.

"Yes, I know it is you, Father Synge. Didn't your mother tell you not to call? She doesn't like the telephone any more."

"Why, what's come over her, Maria? She sounds so changed. Is she?"

"You'll see for yourself, Father Synge. She has lost interest. Now I must go tend to her and Esperanzo. Father Synge, I hoped you would go to Mexico and see my people there."

"How would I see your people when I don't know where they are, what they look like, or anything else about them?"

"Oh! It would be a miracle, Father Synge. It could happen, no? I see you don't think so, but I do."

Father Synge found it unbearable that his mother was changing for the worst and that he could do nothing about it. He had not been much of a help to her. Everything he did disappointed her. She would have preferred a worldlier son. The father used to feel that they were close and even alike in ways that counted most, and Father Synge had let him think so. Actually, he was very split in his character and favored the mother more than he did the father, but when he acted, it was as Harry Synge wanted him to do and not Nora. For all that, he was closer to Nora and did not want her to break with her past and crumble out of all recognition before his eyes. What he felt about her, really, was that all his life she had been telling him not to conform, even though the word had yet to cross her lips in his hearing; even though he had never heard her say it, it was as if she had, and repeatedly; it was always echoing from somewhere where she was or had been.

All this time Father Synge held the *New York Times* before him as if he was reading it. He stared at a photograph on the sports page of basketball players, one black, one white, their arms raised, their bodies stretched, their eyes surprised, as if they were passing one another down through the air in a fall from a cloud. Suddenly, still another head fell with them. Father Synge drew back as if he intended to get up and run.

"Excuse me, but may I have your *New York Times* if you're done with it?"

"Oh! sure."

"Thank you. I'll give it right back."

Father Synge was about to protest that he had no more use for the newspaper when he caught sight of Father Scarpia searching every face, even faces of people who did not remotely resemble himself. What's he think I look like now, for God's sake? Has he forgotten me to the extent that he's not sure anymore if I'm black or white? I haven't been away that long. It must be fun to exaggerate the way Benito does. Look at him! He's having the time of his life. Looking for me, and I'm standing right in front of him.

"John! what're you doing hiding from me? You can see I'm looking all over the place for you."

"I hope that awful Father Curler didn't come with you, Ben."

"He wanted to. But who would mind the store? How'd you know he was awful, John? He's come to kill us, murder us both, and send our hearts to Rome."

"Where's your car? Is he really so bad?"

"Who, Father Curler? I hope I can find the car. It's really your car, John, remember?"

When they reached the car in the parking lot Benito asked Father Synge if he would like to drive.

"Yes, I would, actually, Benito. Thank you."

"You surprise me, John."

"I do? I surprise myself a lot of the times, Benito. I'm awfully glad to see you, you know. I can't tell you how I appreciate you coming in for me. Except..."

"Except what, John?"

"I don't want to go back to the North Shore. I never want to see the North Shore again."

"John! You can't. What would Father Curler say?"

"Fuck Father Curler."

As always when there occurred a terrific declaration of

feeling other than his own, Benito was quiet. He got into the car, and Father Synge drove them to the North Shore, though not without some coaching.

"North Shore, John," Father Scarpia would remind him every once in awhile. "John, North Shore," and Father Synge would go left when he obviously wanted to go right. Finally, after what might have been an inner struggle with himself, Father Synge kept to the way to Peconic. "There's nobody out there anyway," he said, as if to himself.

"Out where, John? What are you talking about?"

"Sagaponack."

"Oh! Is that where they live?"

Father Synge laughed.

"You make them sound like villains," he said.

"I do, John? Then I must sound like Father Colfaxen. Father Colfaxen felt they were wrecking your life. One of the few people I know with a vocation, and you let him take it away from you."

"I threw it away before I ever met the guy, Benito."

"You quit? I can't believe that, John."

"There's a lot you can't believe, Benito."

"I know that, John. I'm not like you. Pentecost and all that. I can't swallow Pentecost. But you do, John. It's like I say, and Colfaxen said, you have a vocation."

"If you say so, Benito."

"I do say so. In spite of everything you're a priest. Even your own mother didn't want you to be a priest. That shocks me, John. You know I can hardly bear looking at her because of that. I hate people to talk about sin, but I guess I consider her a sinner, even if she is your mother, John. Now I overstepped myself as usual, haven't I, John?"

"You're sweet, Benito."

"John! Don't talk like that. I'm serious."

"Mother's all cut up about me having taken off for Paris without telling her. I can't stand the idea of losing her. I'm an awful sissy, really. All I've ever done is take from her."

"You've given her a lot, John. It's not your fault that she fails to realize it."

"No, she'll die unrequited."

"She has you, John. I don't see how you can say that. You're already a pastor. You realize how long it takes some guys to become pastors? Forever, John. Until they don't care. Until they don't want it."

"Like me."

The town of Restwell did not greet them as they drove into its main street. It did not have the habit of greeting anyone. You rarely saw people shake hands on the sidewalks. Sometimes, way out of town, a pair of pick-up trucks would pull up alongside one another and their drivers would parley provided no one was looking. Father Synge felt only despair when he thought of facing Sunday mass crowds, though crowds was hardly the word. There were no crowds in Restwell unless one counted the summer people, and one did not, not really, except in terms of economic gain. It was twilight, but the windows did not blaze with light, nor would they later on. They were black as the branches of trees. There was a face at the rectory window of St. Jude's, but it was not Mrs. Wallop's face, though Father Synge had hoped it would be.

"Where is she, anyway?"

"Where's who, John?"

"Mrs. Wallop."

"Why, she's gone to work in the Shelter. You knew that."

"Then...that must be Father Curler."

"I've waited supper. I call it supper rather than dinner. It's more homey. Besides, it makes the food taste better. So you're Father Synge, are you? You're younger than I thought you would be, though I knew you were young." Everything was cold, and the cook had been let go. "I sent her to the movies. I don't think she has much of a life. Well, Father Synge, here I am talking when it's you who have been places and seen things. Do you mind taking 7:30 mass tomorrow morning?"

"I'll take it. I don't mind," Father Scarpia butted in. "John's tired. Or should be. Are you, John—tired?"

Father Synge offered to say mass. No, he was no more tired than usual.

When the phone rang in the hall, Father Curler took it.

"There's the phone," he said, before leaving the dining room. "I thought we might talk. I hope it's not a mother."

"He meant your mother or my mother, John. Not the mothers of Restwell," Benito whispered before the new pastor of St. Jude's got back, which was soon enough.

"It's for you, Father Synge."

As Father Synge failed to stir himself, Benito cried, "John! it's for you," which seemed to startle Father Synge, who confessed to having been thinking of something else.

"Yes? What?" Father Curler asked.

"Why, of Mrs. Wallop."

"How extraordinary. Don't tell me you're psychic, Father Synge. Mrs. Wallop is the person on the phone."

Father Synge said mass the next morning, a weekday, as he felt he had been instructed to do. He had never really considered himself pastor of St. Jude's and was more relieved than not that now the directorship of the small parish was definitely set in the hands of Father Curler.

After mass Father Synge sat alone with Benito in the dining room of the rectory of St. Jude. The cook, having served them their breakfast, left the house to go shopping. Father Curler called in to them from the hallway that he was off for the morning, but they did not trust him. They waited, listening to his car start up and depart before they talked.

"Tons of people visit him, John, and he says they're all family. I can't make him out. He's not the only one."

"Who's the other one you can't make out, Benito? Me I expect."

"That's right, John. How come you don't say anything about what Mrs. Wallop had to say to you on the horn?"

"That's because there just doesn't seem any place to tell you."

"You mean Father Curler?"

"I don't think he'd be interested in hearing about what Mrs. Wallop had to say, do you, Benito?"

"John, you realize he was at mass this a.m., don't you?"

"Was he? I didn't notice."

"John! Six people out front, one of them Father Curler, and you didn't notice?"

"Well, actually I did. You must have been there yourself."

"I peeked in."

"To see if he was there."

"That's right. To see if he was there. And he was. John, he's everywhere. You noticed how he jumped up to get the phone when Mrs. Wallop called you. What did Mrs. Wallop say anyway?"

"Oh! you know Mrs. Wallop."

"Besides, Curler says he's from Dobbs Ferry. I wouldn't trust anybody who says they're from Dobbs Ferry. Just the sound of it."

"Benito! everybody can't be from Brooklyn or the Bronx. You're awfully provincial. Don't be so provincial. You get more provincial by the day."

"Well, I'd rather be provincial than Parisian—or whatever it is you've become."

"Not Parisian. What makes you think I'm Parisian?"

"Foreign then. You're beginning to act foreign. You use your hands more than you used to. You gesticulate."

"I do? I hadn't noticed."

"Watch yourself sometime, and you'll see you do."

"I don't see where I could have picked it up, if I do. Am I doing it now?"

"What?"

"Gesticulating."

"No, you're more yourself now."

"If that is so, then I wish Mrs. Wallop was here to see me. Mrs. Wallop says I've lost all track of myself. She says I'm drifting."

"Mrs. Wallop wants us to be all together again, the way we were at old St. Roses, John. You know that."

"Oh! that was lovely. I loved all that. So much happened. I suppose it was Colfaxen. Colfaxen was great. There's nobody like Colfaxen."

"He loved you, John. It killed him that you were taken up with that guy on First Avenue. Of course I don't mean that literally. I'm amazed you're still at it after all the bad luck it's brought you. Nobody knows what to do with you, least of all yourself. Mrs. Wallop's right. You're drifting."

"I know. It's the most wonderful thing."

"John! you talk like a hop-head. You're not into anything, are you? I bet you never read him. He comes at you out of the blue on First Avenue and you take him for the Holy Ghost, but you haven't read him. I have. Look, here's his book *Music for Chameleons*. He confesses to everything in it."

"I know. He lays it all out on the line. He's like Blake. Blake said the trouble is that we see with our eyes instead of through our eyes. That's what Truman did the night he helped me cross the street."

"He didn't help you, John. You helped him."

"He called me Father. I know it's childish to go on about it, but he did. He saw through me because he was looking at me with everything he had, which is an awful lot. I've never been the same since. Why should I? He knocked me out. Of course I'm drifting. Mrs. Wallop's right as usual."

"Don't talk with your hands, John. It's very un-American."

"That's what I am, un-American."

"John! not with this Pope."

"I didn't say I was anti-American."

"I don't care what you said, John. With this Pope you have to be very nationalistic, jingoistic, and…provincial, what you say I am."

"You're a darling."

"Now where'd you pick up an expression like that, John? It's gay talk. You haven't given in to them, have you, John? Your inclinations."

"Probably."

Suddenly Father Synge began to cry. He cried steadily and he didn't grimace much, matter of fact he smiled. Benito was confounded. His pop-eyes seemed to stand out an inch from his smooth, round face. His thick, black hair en brosse seemed to rise. He was the picture of dismay. He looked ten or eleven but big for his age. "I believe you when you say he brought you to grace, John. Satisfied? Are you satisfied that you have turned into the biggest influence in my life? That you have shattered all I held dear into glittering pieces that I will never be able to put back together again, but like

a boy with an impossible jigsaw puzzle I'll never stop trying
to make the picture the same that's on the lid of the box the
puzzle came in?"

After that, Father Synge sat listening to Benito banging
around in his room upstairs. He sounded like a boy packing
to go away to summer camp. Father Synge went up to him.
It was a lovely room. Life-size pictures of Willie Mays and
Joe DiMaggio hung on the walls. There was a picture of
Charles Lindbergh and his airplane *The Spirit of St. Louis.*
Stuck in the mirror over the wash basin was a reproduction
of Piero della Francesca's painting of Our Lord climbing
from his tomb with the air of a returning soldier. There were
pennants and sweaters and a basketball.

"Where are you going, Ben?"

"Home. I don't know. Home, I guess."

"Here, let me help you."

"Thanks."

"I'm not really very good at packing."

"That's all right."

Compared to Benito's room, Father Synge's was bare. It
made him wish he was a boy again. He thought about boys,
how there are boys and boys, and how Ben had been an
ideal boy and still was. Father Synge was rather ashamed
of himself for having talked the way he had to Ben about
seeing, because Ben really saw. Ben's talk was all obfusca-
tion. It was word-play. Benito employed talk to camouflage
what he had seen through his eyes.

Father Curler had returned from deviling the poor parishioners of Restwell. He had the sort of voice that made
things jump in the china closet. It was resonant and resounding. It sounded like a recording. It sounded as if Father
Curler had studied voice himself and was thoroughly cognizant of its effect, and it was effective. Father Curler's voice
was so impressive that it almost made you forget the man
behind it. Father Curler was not the man his voice was; nothing about him could possibly live up to it. When Father
Curler spoke, one listened, but afterwards it was sometimes
hard to remember what he had said.

"What is going on here?" he demanded, knocking on

doors and opening them without permission. "I have been sent to restore order in case you two don't know it, and order is what I'm going to get. Your parishioners themselves are a bereaved lot since you came here. They say so themselves. They feel let down. They have no confidence in us. What's all this packing? There's to be no more travel unless I say so. Certainly there is to be none without my permission. If it weren't for the shortage of priests, I'd ask for the removal of the two of you. Your Peck's Bad Boys days are over. Please remember that I am not speaking personally. It is not a matter of personalities. We are priests, priests first of all, priests above and beyond all. Come, I like you both; not that that has anything to do with it, really, but I do. Father Synge, you are a kind of star, but don't let it go to your head. Work in the confines of your appointed parish under your pastor. You've heard all that before. You heard it from Father Colfaxen. I knew Stephan. We were seminarians together. I'm younger than he was. I was always in awe of him. Now, here in Restwell, where he died, I feel reunited with him, with all that was best in him. Come, help me. I'm not Colfaxen and I know it. Give me credit for admitting it."

As an appeal it wasn't bad. He made a good pitch. God knows what he was thinking, really. When the voice stopped, the emotion stopped, and Curler took off; so did the boys. "I don't know how you got all your stuff into one bag, Ben, but you did, didn't you?" "I don't see why you felt you had to come along, but I'm impressed all the same that you have, John. Are you sure you know where you're going?" "Sure I am." "The Shelter?" "That's right, Ben." "It was Mrs. Wallop, wasn't it? I knew she'd get you, John. She says you'll be running the Shelter yourself someday. By that time it'll be a school maybe. Mrs. Wallop says it will be. For kids from broken homes. Sometimes they're brilliant, kids like that, who had nothing but trouble and misery. I believe in miracles, but especially in people who make them. As when there occurs in one person a renaissance. You know what it means, John? It means that seeds have existed and do exist, seeds that need the right time and place to open. When they do open and this person appears and is remarkable in every way, it is no accident, John. The world needs light; without it, it would not be the world. These children, these remarkable people, are the children of light. You might almost call any one of them lightning's child. Some burn long, some burn hardly at all; some are dim, some are bright; but no matter for how long or the intensity of their illumination, they all bring light. Or am I crazy? You think I'm crazy, John?"

"You're a darling, Ben."

"I think that's what the Shelter of the Sacred Heart of Jesus should be about, John. Of course they won't take me. What would I teach? I don't know anything. Not well enough to teach it. Besides, it's not a school yet. When it is, you'll probably be back at Harvard teaching."

"Teaching? Teaching what, Ben?"

"I don't know, John. You know how you go on."

Mrs. Wallop let them in. "I knew it! No, don't touch me. I'm all over grease. I knew it'ud be you. What made me drop me pots and pans, will you tell me? Because I knew it'ud be you. You, Father Synge, and not him. Not Father Scarpia."

"You're right as usual, Mrs. Wallop. I don't intend to stay," Benito hastened to agree with their old cook from St. Roses. "I'm on my way home."

Mrs. Wallop gave Benito a look. "Come in a minute, anyway, the two of you," she said in her knowing way. "It's quite a scandal you've created, the two of you, leavin' that guy out there all alone, so that he'll have to work for a change, and not just shoot off his gub Sundays."

"Scandal, Mrs. Wallop?" Father Synge asked.

"Why, you're runaways, you know. It'll probably be in the papers. Not for the first time, huh, Father Synge?"

"Well, Mrs. Wallop," Father Synge replied to all that, "we're together again; least the three of us are."

"You'll find me quieter, I suspect, Father Synge."

As if to prove just that, Mrs. Wallop slipped back downstairs to the kitchen of the Shelter without another word. Father Synge soon saw why. Sister Secret stood before him.

"Old friends are sad friends, John," she said. "You'll find that out as you grow older."

"Sister Secret, you've met Father Scarpia."

"How are you, Father? Have you come to help us out?"

"I don't think there's room, Sister. Besides, what would I do? Anyway, since we've been told by Mrs. Wallop that we are runaways, and since Mrs. Wallop has always been right in our experience—right, John?—maybe I better keep going. My family might treat me to a trip abroad. Who knows?" Here Father Scarpia looked crestfallen as anything. "Of course they'll be awfully disappointed I've come home. You know how families are, Sister?"

"Don't I though? Why shouldn't you go home, if you want? God's ways are not our ways. Who knows what He has in store for all of us?"

"A good bawling out is what's in store for you if you don't get back upstairs to your visitor," Catherine Lepore called down to her boss from the top of the big old house, which had quieted enough for Catherine to hear (eavesdrop) but now echoed with the cries of freshly liberated children making a playground of the halls as they changed classes. Here and there, parties of two little girls walked arm in arm exchanging confidences. Suddenly Father Synge heard his name called out from all sides; faces peered down at him from over the banisters of the second and third floors. And as Sister Secret broke free of him and Benito, Robert Devereaux appeared in the crowd of children at the top of the stairs. He was wearing a light yellow cap and a bright green suit and looked like a flower for sure. He was all dressed up and he knew it. As he came downstairs (nothing could have stopped him), Sister Secret told him he did not have but a minute to talk to Father Synge.

He's grown up! Father Synge thought with a pang of regret as the brown-skinned beauty advanced towards him. He'll never be so beautiful again, nor so pure!

"Hello, fiery stallion."

Father Synge extended his hand, but Robert lunged past it and threw his arms around his friend's slim waist. Father Synge took away Robert's yellow cap and put it on his own bright head and squatted down on the floor, thus meeting Robert eye to eye. And what eyes. They were like green violets, if there are such things, and the surrounding whites were like light on a pool of dark, shadowed water. His hands were like leaves, smooth, tan. He did not have black hair, as do most colored children. His hair was blond, not yellow at all, but the color of very dry, sparkling sand. His lips were the color of purple plums. His teeth were perfect.

Sister and Catherine watched him from above.

"I dread what will happen to that boy if his highly passionate nature is not channeled. What a priest he would make!" said Sister.

"Priest, Sister?" Catherine retorted. "Why, all he talks is fame."

"There's nothing intrinsically wrong in that, Catherine. Men dream of fame and always will. Robert is just an early starter. They are precocious, these unwanted ones, you know."

"Unwanted? Robert Devereaux unwanted? Why, he's everybody's favorite. Look down there at Father Synge on his knees to him, as if he was a little god—the god Pan."

"Yes, call him back up for his class, Catherine. He causes panic enough. All the little girls are in love with him, especially in his new Easter outfit."

"Oh Sister, how shameful of us to complain of him. Think what he was when we found him? Don't begrudge him his fine clothes. He had nothing on then."

"You found him, my intrepid Catherine. There would be no Shelter without you."

An elegantly clad figure of a smiling man descended the staircase above them. "My heart is with you, but my head says no," he said. "Which should I follow? Tell me, Sister. You know everything. Tell me what to do about those two scallywag priests below in your vestibule."

"Forgive me for keeping you waiting, Bishop Fashoda. Did you find anything to amuse you in my hideaway up on the third floor?"

"What, for God's sake? It's as bare as a cave in an uninhabited island. You're a shipwreck, I'm sure, washed up on us in poor old Brooklyn with no more to your name than a tenacious will to get your way."

"There is nothing I will not do if you say I should do it, Bishop Fashoda."

"Oh yes, there's nothing you won't do to get your own way."

"It's not my way."

"I know. It's the will of God. You're only an instrument. What can't a man or woman do, if they use God as an excuse? It's a wonder to me that you've stopped here in these stuffy old houses, when God knows what you could not have if you wanted it."

Catherine Lepore went downstairs and took Robert Devereaux away from Father Synge. They were passing Bishop Fashoda and Sister Secret at the top of the stairs when Sister stopped them and drew the little boy in his yellow cap to her.

"One of these is enough to make me feel I live in a palace, my bishop," she said.

The worldly, well-got-up prelate moved back from Sister as if he had been slapped. Sister herself was dressed in a faded gown in the old-fashioned way, which failed to conceal the fact that she herself was finely made, good bones and skin, green eyes, and her own teeth. Sister Secret was good to look at, interesting to hear talk, and always challenging. She was a willful, ambitious, predatory woman, a nun who carried on a love affair with an aplomb a queen might envy. But she was dictatorial, she was narrow-minded, really, she was provincial. She never went anywhere, nor did she read anything. She was everything but boring. The most fascinating woman in the Catholic Church, wasting her time in a dump like this, trying to save kids who were lost anyway, for the most part, but were jewels to her. In a way she was a sort of miser, polishing and perfecting, protecting her loot of little prols against the day when she would be forced to give them back to the world they came from—yawning, black tenement doorways, the worst of their kind sprawled across the front steps, windows bawling music, men on street corners in their underwear drinking from cans of beer wrapped in brown paper bags. The cynic of the neighborhood never off his front step in summer or away from his open window in winter, talking endless poison, chomping ambition in the bud, sneering down beauty, hugging his transistor radio, coughing, spitting, smoking, drinking. Hope?

How could you have any hope for kids who went back from the Shelter each night to all that, carefully divesting themselves of all they had been all day, putting on disorder for order? The return of the little natives. Yet this brazen nun claiming in the name of God to be able to win souls away from that....*One of these is enough to make me feel I live in a palace.* That's what she said. The bishop felt he did not understand holiness, and that he would not like it if he knew it when he met it anyway.

At least she wasn't boring. Still, there was always the possibility that the whole thing could be blown up before her eyes, taken away from her before she knew it. Now how do you like that? Then where would she be? Her and her old lover Malloy with their houses empty and the kids scattered back to where they came from. All, all, all of it as if it had never happened. How would she like that?

"Bishop Fashoda, you're not listening to me." No, he was not. "I know I'm taking up your valuable time, asking you here to consider the case of these two young men. How did I know they would turn up here? Oh, that was easy, my bishop. Everybody winds up at the Shelter. Look at yourself." Clichés. She was full of baloney. So was Joan of Arc full of baloney. Yet down through the ages, right down to the present, Jeanne d'Arc has transmitted her belief in God to me and I am absolutely powerless against it—as I am before this powerful woman.

"It would be a shame to let them go. Are there so many of them? Not so many seem to be coming in as before."

Below her the two young priests were acting as if they were taking leave of one another, one protesting the other's going, as is often the case when friends depart from each other. They were too young yet to know departures can be final.

The bishop did not pity their air of bewilderment. He could only think of how they made him feel old without even trying, perhaps not even being aware of his presence at the top of the stairs, so taken up were they with one another, also characteristic of the young and the cause of their seeming blindness to others. "There's a place for them here, Bishop Fashoda. Why send them home, where so many of them wind up wrecks? Not all, of course. But why let one go?" What power she attributes to herself! Of course she says it all comes from God. "Let me keep them. What good are they to the world half priests, half laymen? Divided till they die. I'm not going to be here forever. The more I leave behind, the better. My cause is little, but my feeling for it is big. I was nothing till I came across Catherine and she led me to these children. Now they flock to us. There's hardly room. But that there should be no room at all one day wounds me, wounds all of us, if we would only *see*. See, Bishop Fashoda, they want to stay, but they are young and brazen and ashamed yet to listen to the sweetest side of their natures, that side that tells us to give up all we have and to stand on our own two feet. That's all Joan of Arc ever did— stand on her own two feet, and tell her king and country to do the same. That's all saints ever do."

"If I were an ambitious man, I would sweep all of you before me," was Bishop Fashoda's reply to Sister Secret, who regarded him in her steadfast way, as if, in her thoughts, she had one foot here and one foot in eternity. In her green eyes he saw green fields of waving wheat and rye, and beyond the wheat and rye the sea, where he dreamed from Brooklyn Bridge of sailing as a boy before God got him and so he never saw Genoa as a sailor or passed Gibraltar; all places, all things were seen from windows, never as he had hoped as a boy, from the top of the topsail. He had conformed instead, and was therefore wary of unfulfilled dreams, there being nothing quite so wounding. "Stay," he said, passing the two young men on his way out of the Shelter, but at the door he stopped and spoke his last words up to Sister Secret: "You see," he said, "I'm not an ambitious man."

Chapter 45

I am sitting here by the window in the library waiting for him to appear or call. There is nothing to watch on the river but a now-and-then gull. No boat traffic. If it were a sunny day, at least the old Circle Line sightseeing boats might be going by. I remember a day, the alley of the St. James Theater, when Agnes De Mille passed me on her way into a rehearsal from which I had been excused. Agnes asked me where I was headed. When I told her I was about to take a boat ride around Manhattan, she appeared to be astonished at what she obviously considered a waste of time. There goes the telephone!

"Hey there, honey!"

"Truman! How glad I am to hear from you! Where are you? Are you all right?"

"Sure I'm all right. Why wouldn't I be all right?"

He was calling from a hospital in Montgomery, Alabama.

"Why Montgomery, Truman?"

"That," he said, "is a saga."

It seemed he left here and boarded a plane for Montgomery because he was sore at me and the world, not that he would admit that now, if he even remembered, which I strongly doubted. Anyhow, he sounded great, and I was relieved to hear from him.

"It's very wholesome here," says he. "And that is why," he adds, with his old kick, "you'll be seeing me soon."

He called me again before he left the hospital and said his room was full of flowers. He cried. He had gone down there to be back home with his beloved Aunt Mary Ida, but, as usual with him now, he fell by the wayside and woke up in the hospital in Montgomery. He never did get to see Mary Ida after all. But in its way it was a homecoming, since Truman, like Blanche DuBois in Tennessee's play, always expected kindness from strangers, and received just that in Montgomery, Alabama.

He is adamant about not going away for a long cure somewhere, telling me that he intends to behave himself from now on. Well, I doubt if I could ever send anyone away without his consent, especially not Truman. A doctor from the hospital in the South called me. A decent enough man, I suppose, but credulous and parochial. Truman's plane gets in at 2:30 this afternoon. I woke up at dawn this morning feeling cold and clammy at the thought of his homecoming and the turbulence he brings with him wherever he goes.

Of course he looked wonderful when he came in, but he was home no more than five days before he had himself driven out through the snow and rain to Southampton Hospital. Rain came down in torrents in New York. I know, since I walked over to Lincoln Center for ballet tickets, then to my tiff with Tiffany's, after I walked around the wristwatch counter three times scrutinizing watches (and, in turn, being scrutinized by the house dick himself) without once obtaining the attention of one of the three salesmen in attendance.

One of the *three* salesmen had heaven on the phone, so I can hardly blame him for paying no attention to me. Another was determined to find nothing that might please his customer. "We don't want that. We don't want this," he kept saying. The third salesman was doing push-ups between the counters, so help me God!

I might have been more disgruntled, though I don't take stores or their help any more seriously today than they do me, had not a familiar face amongst the gawking tourists caught my attention.

"Why, for God's sake, Father Synge," I said. "What are you doing in Tiffany's? For that matter, what am I doing here? Let's get out, anyway, no more questions asked."

Father Synge was with an adorable-looking guy with pop-eyes and straight, standing-up black hair. I took him for a priest too, though both were in mufti, on the ragamuffin side.

"You look like hoods, the two of you," I said, feeling sort of swell myself, having put down Tiffany's.

"We've just come back from our parish on the North Shore and we wanted to make sure that everything that makes

New York tick, even Tiffany's, was still here," Father Synge told me. "This is Father Scarpia," he added, nudging the eager-looking young man at his side with his elbow.

"You've probably heard of me," Father Scarpia pleased me by saying, without the slightest hint of vanity in his voice. I didn't say I had. I didn't think he needed it. I was happy Father Synge had him. I didn't mind terribly when Father Synge drew me aside and asked me about Truman loud enough for Father Scarpia to hear.

"The trouble with Truman lies in his poverty of ideals," Father Synge said. "He was born to lead a mundane life, and when an affliction befell him, in his case addiction to drugs, he had no means of coping with it. Especially so since the peacocks abandoned him, which they did, in his misery; all the worldlings he'd entertained and sweated to keep awake after dinner fled him, or ignored him, or grieved that he had to all intents and purposes died to them and their world."

All that sounded pompous, pretentious, pushy, as well as unanswerable. I looked to nice Father Scarpia to help me out with this Savonarola.

"Do you live in New York?" he asked me.

I replied that I did but not always.

"Change is the best thing, even a necessity," said Father Scarpia.

"Yes," I said, "I feel that I could never stay in one place for the rest of my life."

"I agree, but all the same I feel I'll never leave this area."

"That's too bad, especially if you want to. Do you want to?"

Father Synge regarded us as if he felt we did not make sense to him at all. I was pleased to note that his attitude did not phase Father Scarpia in the least. "We just wanted to make sure it was all still here before we came over tomorrow to hear Dan Berrigan," he said, adding by way of an invitation that perhaps I might like to come along with them.

The idea of attending a talk against nuclear war by Father Daniel Berrigan struck me as naive, but I was curious about him. At the same time Father Synge seemed to be waiting for me to make some reply to what he had said about Truman and his friends. I tried to do this, if only to prevent him from thinking I had agreed with everything he had said. The rain had stopped, but the wind was up, and Fifty-seventh Street was busy, so half of what I said was lost anyway.

"Truman is indifferent to everything. There is no sense in blaming those he used to know for abandoning him. It was a two-way thing. Little by little invitations piled up, grew dusty, went unanswered. The telephone was turned off. What interest he shows is a mere faint echo of his former vibrant curiosity. He seems to care for nothing and nobody socially. His indifference is contagious. I feel indifferent too."

"If you are, I've seen no signs of it. See you tomorrow," Father Synge said, and away they went to catch their subway train to Brooklyn, talking enthusiastically to one another as they made their way through the indifferent crowd. I envied them, remembering, as I did so, Jennie Bradley's praise of envy and how I had appreciated it that day when the agent had given us lunch in her Paris apartment, where all was so ordered and well appointed. To arrange one's life to one's taste—to where it has some sheen, some sparkle to it—seemed best to me as I stood in the springtime gloom of New York remembering Paris with its primroses everywhere. Then, to envy would have been all right, because I was young and could do something about it without appearing indecent and tasteless. Now envy should be out of the question. Envy was a mean-spirited thing to me now, now when I was perhaps closer to it than ever before in my life, with all my troubles, because no troubles had come near exceeding these I suffered today with the boy I likened to lightning's child when I first met him, whose faithfulness to me had always been monumental, and who had kept me out of making an acquaintance with envy, since with him I was able as Edith Hamilton wrote, "to pursue vital interests along lines of excellence in a life affording them scope"— which was happiness.

Chapter 46

I was curious about Berrigan, and the next day being a Sunday, May 1st, matter of fact, I walked down through the warm, empty streets to the Community Church on Thirty-sixth Street. They say, in Paris, that springtime is a time of revolt. The American bishops had backtracked on their stand against nuclear arms. I thought Father Berrigan's followers would be wild, but they weren't, and there were mighty few of them. This was the eighties; the people of the sixties were now raising children in the usual order of things. Many felt they'd been taken; few would admit their attention span had snapped. La vie biologique had claimed them as it had most of their fathers and grandfathers. Berrigan was the sort who would carry the ideals of his youth with him to his grave. He was a poet, and poets are always young.

He's a well-made little man, with a thick head of greying hair, rather heavily lined face, a florid complexion, expressive hands, and when he puts on eyeglasses, which he only very seldom does, a lot of him disappears behind them, especially the pixie side. He was once fat, I presume, but is now slimmish. He wore a low-toned checked shirt, jeans, and, disconcertingly, a pair of grey shoes. He speaks in broken phrases, rolling his eyes, blowing out his cheeks, etc.— a very mobile face for a priest, though the body is quiet enough.

Father Berrigan spoke against nuclear arms, his theme, his life. He does not speak with passion, and I do not know how passionate his poetry is, if at all, but he gathers his followers with every word. Most winning is his conversational way of conducting himself on the platform, his air of not being quite sure of his next word, giving you a string of them, as if he was talking to himself while in the act of writing. Looking at him, I wondered which came first, the poet or the priest. Is he more priest than poet, or more poet than priest? People stood up and applauded for a long time after he sat down. He was generous with his time later on, when answering questions, some of which I thought were batty.

Father Synge and Father Scarpia were outside in the sparse crowd afterwards. I felt the last thing they wanted to do was to discuss the goings on in Community Church. Father Synge surprised me by suggesting we attend mass together. "There's an old church nearby you might be interested in. Unless you've been there, have you?" I had, but I did not let on. It was an old church for this country, probably built in 1884, and made of brick that recalled the more primitive times of capitalism, when the highest things built to heaven were smokestacks. It seemed to want to serve more as a fortress than anything else. Of course it was hideous. It was not meant for great crowds as were the great cathedrals of France, but for small clumps of immigrants, refugees, who found nothing here of what they had left behind them and furthermore did not seem to want it, demanding only that things be new now, new and utilitarian.

"We like it because it reminds us of St. Roses, our old parish in New York," nice Father Scarpia burst out as soon as we were inside the church.

"Yes," I said, "it is rather like. Do you miss St. Roses, Father?"

"Oh yes! We didn't think much of it when we had it, but now it's gone, it has taken on an importance all out of proportion to what it really was, hasn't it, John?" As Father Synge failed to answer, but seemed to be off in a world of his own, Father Scarpia continued, though rather apologetically, "Well, it has for me. Did you know Father Colfaxen?"

"I met Father Colfaxen right before he died."

"Yes, I remember now. He went over to your place in Sagaponack, didn't he? Say, that's interesting. How did you find him?"

Father Synge winced and moved away from us, afraid, I guess, of what I might say.

"Well, I found him very concerned about Father Synge."

"Oh, yes. They were close. You felt that, did you? You know, he didn't like me a bit, but he was stuck with me. John's stuck with me too, I guess. I'm not sure John's crazy about me being with him at the Shelter."

"You're both at the Shelter in Brooklyn? How do you like it?"

"Oh, well, you know, it's very far out. Every day you feel they'll close us down. We don't live in very innovative times, do we? Not that we're political or anything like that, though we care. We used to worship Dan Berrigan. So, really, it was sort of sad today for both of us, seeing him in that empty hall."

"It wasn't empty."

Father Scarpia surprised me. His eyes filled with tears.

"For us it was," he said. "That's why John couldn't talk after. It was a little bit like Gethsemane to us. Dan still carrying the flame, and so few followers. He's a real hero, you know. Don't you think so?"

"Father Berrigan?"

"Yes, sure, Dan."

I thought Father Scarpia was lovely.

A short, stout, pigeon-toed priest, whose name, I believe he said, was Father Haight, conducted the rites of the mass with a vengeance. He did not let us forget it was May 1st, but brought it up with the vengeful vigor he considered necessary. Father Berrigan fights war, Father Haight fights for one. He can't wait, because he does not know. He reminded me of the English priest in *Saint Joan,* who, having pleaded throughout the play for the saint's death, rushes on stage horrified clear out of his mind after witnessing her actually burning at the stake. Father Berrigan was soft-spoken, Father Haight talked in a loud voice directly into an electric sound amplifier placed under his chin like a bib. One sophisticated, the other naive. Haight preached against simplistic thinking while practicing it, while Father Berrigan, Johnny One Note though he may be, blew his horn in a devious, interesting way that beguiled many and interested everybody. Father Synge and Father Scarpia fled the place after mass as if they smelled fire. I envied their involvement in things, knowing at the same time that their way was not mine. I felt that soon I would not see Father Synge again, that he would have played out his part in our lives and gone on to other things.

Chapter 47

"I would never have given you the houses if I knew you were going to fill them with young men, Annie."

"Why, Matt, don't tell me you're jealous of a pair of priests."

"I don't like it. It doesn't seem respectable. Remember, the world thinks of you as a nun, even if you prefer most of the time to have forgotten it."

"Well, Matt, you're probably right. I'll try to do better."

"Now don't give me that, Annie. Humble pie was never your dish. Why, I don't open a newspaper today without your name in it. You realize that in the eyes of ordinary people you're a success. You might as well have gone on the stage for all the publicity you receive."

"I know, Matt, everything's become too big. You're right, we are a success."

"Well, I don't mean you to feel so bad about it."

"But I do feel bad. I know far better than you do what you are talking about. I'm beginning to feel cramped on all sides, cramped in a spiritual sense. I hardly have time to pray anymore. Oh, Mattie, they have robbed me of my religion!"

"Who? Tell me who they are and I'll smash them. I'll... I'll...splatter them!"

"It's not 'it,' or 'them,' or 'those,' Matt. It's everything and everywhere, insidious and corrosive, seeming to give everything at first, everything you've ever wanted, but taking, really, taking from you much more than it ever gave you back or could give you back, for all your effort, all your prayers. It's success, Matt. I'll move underground and grant no more interviews. I'll let the men run the Shelter. Catherine and I are tired. Yes, Father Synge and Father Scarpia will face the world for us from now on with a low profile."

"Not with my help they won't, Annie."

"Now what are you talking about?"

"Why, it's you I give to, not the Shelter; without you the thing would not exist for me."

"I understand that, Matt."

"You mean you'd go on without me?"

"With God's help we would, Matt."

Malloy stepped towards the painting of the Last Supper before which the two old friends stood talking in their old combative way. As happened before, he seemed to be a part of the picture when he stood closer to it. It seemed to influence everything he did while near it and to shape everything he said, though he had never once referred to it in an open, bargaining way until now.

"I've always threatened you, and I suppose I always will, Annie. Remember I used to say I'd destroy myself if you would not have me?" He chuckled, but it was not a cynical chuckle, it was more derisive than cynical. "Then I married and had children. I repeated myself. I multiplied, rather than destroyed myself. Sometimes, you know, there seems to me to be a number of Matt Malloys. One of them just now, for example, thought of taking this painting away from you."

Sister Secret turned away at that, and in so doing faced Father Synge and Benito, whom she seemed to ignore or at most count as part of her fold, two left behind, perhaps, forgotten by mothers seeking weekend pleasure, which happened. There seemed to be others; for from above there sounded the noise of running footsteps, which turned out to be one pair only, actually, those of Robert Devereaux, the bright little black boy, who descended the staircase simultaneously with the ringing of the front doorbell, which he forthrightly answered, as if the Shelter was his own house, which in a way it was—all the home he had, anyway, though the way the caller acted with him you would have thought Robert had another, and with her, which was only common and to be expected, it being his mother.

Robert was all eyes for her. Both were dressed like bright flowers. "Now, you know you love yoh mama an' yoh mama best, Robert. Tell Sistuh who yawl love, Robert. G'wan talk, boy. 'Les yawl don' wanna go out wif me no ways. Say somethin', boy!"

"See you later!" said Robert to the assembled company, which is not what his mother wanted him to say at all.

"Now, thad ain' no way t'talk. Ain' whad I tole you t'say,

Robert. Ah ain' takin' no boy walkin' wif me who cain't even tell hisself whad Ah jus' done said to him."

Mrs. Devereaux was a stout woman and evidently sweltering in her tight clothes, and suffering from the pain her tight shoes must have given her. And she was in fact often too busy for Robert.

"Ah ain' scacely got time t'put up wif a boy lak yawl, Robert."

She made as if to go without him; the boy lunged at her, nearly knocking her over. He tore her dress where it would show the most, but he would not let her go. He was not the bright, attentive boy the Shelter had made of what it had found of him sitting on the wet mattress in a cold, empty room. He seemed not to have learned anything worthwhile since then. When he faced the civilizing side of his life, Sister Secret was a stranger, a hostile stranger, someone who had no say over him after all, no legal right to him. All that was behind him as he struggled at the Shelter door to be taken for a walk through Brooklyn's downtown streets and worse.

"Take me to Forty-second Street, Mama. I'll be good. I'll say whatever you want me to. Only take me to Forty-second Street."

He wanted the tawdry, the cheap; he wanted the boardwalk side of life, not the other things, things they talked about at the Shelter. He wanted to sing and dance and see and hear all that was near and at hand. He cried as if his heart was breaking that his mother was playing with him, like a cat with a little mouse, in front of all these people, who talked so swell and were so kind and never rough, but never talked of anything but the future, never of today, always of tomorrow, while his mother was fun and fast-food and he loved her best and was ashamed that he was ashamed he did.

All day long Sunday he had been waiting for the big, brightly dressed good-timer to come walk him out amongst the fun and fast-swinging crowds, where people were concerned with this minute, now, the day they were in and were part of and sure of, and not no tomorrow that might never come.

"I'll be good, Mama," he sobbed. "I promise I'll do all you tell me and to love you most. I do love you most, better than anybody, only take me with you, take me to the picture show like you said you would. Don' leave me, Mama. I promise. I promise anything."

Sister Secret, her days at the University of Cuernevaca behind her, was startled by the return to her mind of certain stone images she had seen stored in Mexican museums—stern, gaping stones crying for sacrifice; dumb, worshipped things that once tasted the blood of the young and beautiful, since nothing was thought too good for these blocks of granite from which so much was expected. It was sullen images such as those that Sister Secret was reminded of by the Sunday appearance of Mrs. Devereaux, with her wide nose and ear-to-ear mouth, her short legs and barrel torso.

It was hard to believe that the physically stunning boy, willing to sacrifice himself to her for a night's outing, was her son. Sometimes Sister and Catherine thought the hideous woman with her unappeasable vanity had stolen Robert. It was hard to tell. It was a mystery. He loved her, but of course he feared her too; he always played her against Sister Secret and Catherine, for he was devious as well as clever, and not without guile.

Catherine Lepore had appeared on the staircase, drawn by the tumult of Robert's tantrum. She sank down on a step and regarded their little protégé as if she felt he was leaving them for good. Malloy had put on his hat in his consternation and had taken Sister by the arm protectively, as though he meant to see her through this, though it was obvious that he had not the faintest notion of how to go about it. Father Synge and Benito looked sad and disconcerted. Nothing in their pasts gave them footage to deal with the situation before them. Sister Secret, constrained by the presence of Malloy, seemed to await its dénouement. Catherine alone watched the Devereaux' as if she felt she could handle them if need be. The mothers who brought their children to the Shelter looked down on Catherine, but they preferred to deal with her rather than with Sister. They were a little in awe of Catherine, but at the same time they knew she had been bad, and they felt that sooner or later she was bound to return to her old ways. This was because they did not know how wasteful Catherine Lepore felt she had been with herself in the past; that was her strength; that was her great step-up into this present.

"Ah don' want yawl lookin' at me lak hit's all mah fault, Miss Catherine, when it is really the fault of the Sheltah, thaz whut it is, thad mah lil' boy's turned to tantrums and bad ways so thad Ah'm mos' 'shamed to walk out wif him. Ah don' rec'nize him. D'yawl rec'nize yoh mothah, boy?"

"Yes, Mama. Please let's go, Mama. 1 recognize you."

What could they say? Not even Catherine felt free to retort to Mrs. Devereaux, so great was the fear of all at the Shelter that she could disappear with Robert one day and neither of them be found again. It was not as if you could advertise for him on milk containers and supermarket bags as a missing child when he was with his mother, was it? It was with heavy hearts they watched them go, the little boy in his yellow cap and green suit, and his wide mother in shoes that hurt her because she refused to wear her rightful size.

"I have an awful feeling that we might not see that kid again," Catherine Lepore burst out from the stairs, causing the company to move for the first time since Mrs. Devereaux had come and gone, so frightening was the black woman's power—backed by all the laws of state and country—over Robert.

"Catherine," said Sister, "you know things you say sometimes have a way of reaching me that nobody else's words have, even when you don't mean what you say. This is serious. Be thoughtful, dear Catherine."

Catherine looked through the bars of the stairs at the company as if she felt herself to be in prison. She said nothing more but continued to sit there.

"Don't mope, Catherine," Sister Secret told her.

"If," said Malloy, remembering his hat and taking it off his head, "if I thought I could do anything about getting that boy away from that terrible woman, I'd go to court in a minute."

"No, don't, Mattie. It's not worth the pain. She'd only come out the winner. She doesn't want him, and she doesn't want us to have him."

"I don't mean you. I'm speaking of myself. I'd adopt the child. If all you've told me about him is true, it would be quite an investment."

"Dear Matt, what about your family? I'm sure they have had quite enough of the Shelter. No, Robert will come through. Mark me if he doesn't. His mother's only one of the bridges he must cross. Of course he is meant to suffer, and he seems to know it already. I would like to live to see him reach his first plateau."

"And what will that be, Annie? This plateau you speak of."

"Why, when he publishes."

"Publishes, Annie? I'd be surprised if he can write his name. He's only a little nigger, God help him, on his way back to the ghetto where you first picked him up."

"Ah, yes. That was Catherine's work. That we know he's going to be a writer is John's work."

"Well, Annie, he's only a little nigger to me."

"Why, Matt, that's all he is to himself yet. He doesn't know he's a writer, a born writer, does he, John?"

Times like these Father Synge wondered how anything ever got done at the Shelter. The atmosphere struck him at times like this like those moments in a Russian play when the whole action may hang for a poignant instant on a girl harassed by the fact that the Italian word for window has escaped her. The old buildings, the people themselves, seemed to be the end of an epoch, a world. They felt too much, and thought too much, they considered things too finely. They were aghast, and even somewhat helpless, before people like Mrs. Devereaux, who, with the law in back of her, seemed sometimes to represent the future, when people like Catherine and Sister, Mrs. Wallop, Matt Malloy, Benito, his mother, and himself would be washed away. The thought gave him the smothers. He moved towards the front door, feeling the need for such fresh air as Flatbush Avenue had to offer.

Chapter 48

Outside, Father Synge felt better. He felt hope. He did not feel he was in a fin de siècle play about fin de siècle people. He saw where Robert Devereaux had every right to want to go out with his mother back to familiar things, however tawdry. They were rich things to him and might make him rich in feeling later on in his life. To a child a toy can be an object of beauty and a walk down Main Street on a holiday night heaven.

Father Synge thought of his own mother and how he had abandoned her to become a priest. She had never gotten over it, actually. Till then they'd been friends. She considered the whole thing something the father and son had cooked up between them to get her goat, and for a long time she played it for laughs. But she had missed him. She liked family life and Father Synge's absence put a dent in hers. She felt she had nothing to look forward to, not even holidays, to say nothing of grandchildren. Bitterly she relinquished all hopes of continuity, and best proved this by giving her house away to the Shelter of the Sacred Heart while she was still alive, though she did reserve the right to live in it as she wished with Maria and Juan and their baby until she died.

Father Synge found himself before Brooklyn's City Hall. He walked down Montague Street past the library where he had gone as a boy. Willow Street looked the same as it had then—fewer private houses, but there was still the air of a propertied class about the neighborhood. His mother was at her window holding on her lap a brown-faced baby with crow-black hair. It hurt Father Synge that Nora did not appear to recognize him. For seconds that's all he thought of, irrational though he knew it was, that Nora did not know him. He remembered when she used to recognize him as soon as he had turned the corner on Pineapple Street and how he had liked it when she waved, though he had never let on. Now he could have been anybody to her. Yet when he entered the house and Nora petulantly demanded of Maria to take the baby away, Father Synge objected.

"No, let him stay, Maria. I want to see him. Has he been baptized? Father Colfaxen should have been his godfather, don't you agree?"

"Father Colfaxen was too strict, especially on us, Juan and me, because we are Mexicans. I would not like him around Esperanzo, bossing him, trying to make a priest out of him. Right, Mrs. Synge? No, I do not want a son with an inferiority complex. Esperanzo is an American boy, a Yankee. We are through with Mexico and Mexicans. Remember Juan's uncle in Tasco would not take us in when we were poor and Esperanzo was on the way?"

Nora seemed to approve of everything Maria said. Father Synge could see they were close. There was no place for him here. It was wonderful in a way, considering that Esperanzo was lucky even to have been born. He was a sturdy child and could already walk.

"I hope he's tall when he grows up," said Maria. "Perhaps if I feed him in the American way, he will be tall. Don't you think he will be tall, Father Synge? Tall as you would be enough. I'm going to send him to you at the Shelter as soon as possible. I want Esperanzo to be like you, Father Synge."

"Well, Maria, what makes you think you do? Isn't Esperanzo going to be like his father? Most babies are. Or aren't they?"

"You aren't, John," Nora broke in. "You're not like me, either, not really. You're more like your great-uncle Stanislaus. He played the fiddle and went to China. You're like him."

"Whatever happened to him? I forget."

"You never saw him, John. I did, but I was too young to remember him. He was my father's youngest brother. He went to China and married there. Can you imagine? Got a job and never came home. Yes, she was a Chinese girl. Pretty. He sent us pictures of her, but none of their children. They had children. I don't know how many. Anyway, their name's Synge, like Sing, so it could be a Chinese name. It makes the world so small, doesn't it, John?"

Father Synge was swept with love for his mother. He loved her when she was this way, talking of the world as if she liked it and wished she had seen more of it than she had.

"I wish I'd known Stanislaus. I really do. I feel I do, anyway. You may have been alike, Mother. Uncle Stanislaus sounds as independent as you are."

"John! I never budge. I dream, though. Yes, I dream. I dream myself far away from Willow Street, somewhere where I forgive everybody, even my enemies. Don't ask me where it is, John. I don't know myself. I probably wouldn't recognize it if I were taken there."

"Why, you talk as if it's a real place, Mother."

"It is to me, John. Not that I could describe it to you. I couldn't."

"Maybe it's just a state of mind. Are you happy there, Mother?"

"No, John. But I'm not unhappy. It's an inevitable-feeling sort of place. A place much like another. It's me that's different."

"How, Mother? How are you different?"

"How, John? Well, I'm relieved. Perhaps I'm indifferent. It's only a dream, John. Don't look so serious. Nor you either, Maria. I've told you about it time out of mind. Esperanzo will know it before his ABCs."

"I'm teaching him his ABCs," Maria quickly put in. "You'll see, Father Synge, Esperanzo will be ready for you before you know it."

Father Synge did not seem to think so, and Maria was quick to take him up on it.

"You don't think so, Father Synge?"

"No, no, of course you're right, Maria. I can't wait to have Esperanzo in my class at the Shelter."

"You don't sound convincing, Father Synge. I'm taking your mind off other things. Don't worry about your mother. She often talks like this now."

Mrs. Synge stirred unhappily under the young peoples' scrutiny.

"I'm sorry I ever brought it up," she said.

"Oh! I'm not, Mother," Father Synge burst out. "Especially so since, if you forgive everybody, you must forgive me too."

"Forgive you, John? Forgive you for what, for God's sake?"

"Why, for having become a priest, Mother. Don't tell me you've forgotten?"

"You know something, John? I think I have. It doesn't interest me anymore. I've told you that I might be indifferent as well as forgiving in this dream place of mine."

"Well, I must say, you take it lightly enough."

"Yes I do, John. My burden's light. I don't even own my house anymore. That witch Annie Bushnell has it. Hasn't she wound up with everything, though? I'll say she has. She's welcome to them; it's all a nuisance, as she'll find out someday if she doesn't know it now."

"Oh! she does, Mother. She knows everything."

Nora looked at him steadily, even somewhat grimly. "Yes," she said then, "I used to think that way about Stanislaus: that he knew everything. Well, maybe he did know what he wanted. Maybe that's what we mean when we say people know everything. To know what you want early in life *is* everything. Didn't Annie Bushnell turn to me one night and tell me she was going to be a nun? I can still see the shoes she had on then. They were grey satin, and they had champagne stains on them. I kept looking at them because Annie had embarrassed me so. She hadn't had all that much to drink. Matt Malloy came running up to us. 'In the car, you two.' Treating us like cattle, as he did all women. Then he saw something was up. 'What's the matter with Annie?' 'Ask her yourself,' I said. 'Why should I? What's there to know that I don't know about her? Into the car, I say, and be quick about it.' "

Nora was silent. She smiled. The baby climbed back into her lap. That's all. But it was the last Father Synge was to see his mother alive, and he seemed to know it. At least that is what he would tell himself in the years ahead.

He had enough to think about when he got back to the Shelter, where he found all the lights on and Mrs. Wallop at her reassuring best, which had a tendency to terrify one, really. There was no one else in the houses, an unusual occurrence even though it was a holiday; not a child; not even Sister Secret and Catherine.

"I guess they couldn't stand the suspense no longer, so took off in the van after him."

"After whom?"

"Why, after the boy with the awful mother."

"Mrs. Devereaux?"

"It's kidnapping what it is, but what are you gonna do when it's her own kid she kidnapped? It's a case for a dozen lawyers, and her winnin' hands down against them without half tryin'. Motherhood ain't all it's cracked up to be, nor fatherhood, nor all the other hoods. That Robert Deviler's gone and took all our hopes for him with him. What I mean is, was he worth it in the beginning?"

"Of course he was."

"Of course he was, but does he think so? Will he ever think so?"

"He already thinks so."

"Then why ain't he here? Why's he back where he came from? Why'd he beg and kick and scream for her to take him back? You're fightin' a losin' battle if you think you can ever get him away from her for good. He offered his guts to go with her. He sobbed. He cried. He snarled. He was a little wild animal kept away from its kind it longs to be back with heart and soul."

"Well, Mrs. Wallop, there's no use sitting up all night."

"There is. There's somethin' to watching and waiting."

"I daresay. Do as you please, Mrs. Wallop. I'm off to bed."

"I'll watch for you. I'll do your share. You've got a life to live, a future to tend to. Guard against people like the Devilers, with their troubles and trials, who can turn you off your rightful path."

"Good night, Mrs. Wallop."

"Good night, Father."

But Father Synge did not leave the room after all. He stopped at the doorway and came and seated himself alongside the cook. "You're right as usual, Mrs. Wallop," he said. "I'll wait up with you." "There you go," said Mrs. Wallop.

Chapter 49

"Catherine, there's the Apollo where we used to see the best foreign movies in the old days. Imagine what it's become. This street's hell, Catherine; hell on earth. Don't tell me Robert's out there somewhere."

"Sister," said Catherine. "I'm afraid we'll have to leave the van and get out and walk. Do you think you can take Forty-second Street?"

"Park, Catherine. Find a place to park, and don't ask silly questions."

It was between one and two a.m., the day after May 1st. Above the lights of the movie houses there were stars, but none seemed to shine. The night was mild, but it did not seem to matter what it was; it did not even seem to be outdoors. The smell of food was everywhere. Food and cheap perfume. Stink enough to cut the appetite of the hungriest and sexiest of men. Everything was for sale and everybody, with the sole exceptions yet of Georgie Mathews and Rick Sanbrucci, two rookie cops, pounding the beat together on Forty-second Street. It wasn't a bad night. Even with their limited experience they'd known worse. A first warm day had made people tired. They weren't as likely to go for one another's throats as they usually were. Lost kids, runaway kids, kids as like to bite your hand off if you touched them were beginning to show with the promise of more warm days like yesterday likely to follow. The cops' radios, which they turned on from time to time, never stopped reporting disaster. To hear them, you'd believe everything you ever heard about Forty-second Street was true. Actually, there was a strolling air about the street this morning. Flamboyant characters, like fallen birds of paradise, stalked mutely by with an air that warned they were no different from anybody else. People wore summer clothes already, but people wore furs, too. That's Forty-second Street for you. You never know when a knife might come at you because somebody didn't like the color of your hair—or that you had hair.

Not that Georgie Mathews and Rick Sanbrucci were talking about the street, or even thinking about it. They were
talking baseball, football, then family, which was dangerous, so they went back to sports, because Georgie Mathews
had a son and a daughter, while Rick Sanbrucci had two
daughters and was beginning to feel he couldn't "make" a
son.

"Rick," said Georgie, "do you see what I see? Tell me to
control myself if you do."

"Control yourself, Georgie. Impersonation is no crime."

"It should be in this case. I'd take her for real anywhere
but on Forty-second Street."

"How about the other one? What's she impersonating,
Georgie?"

"His mother, probably."

"You think it's a guy? The nun, too? You think they're both
guys?"

"Sure they're guys. What's a nun doing on Forty-second
Street, and tomorrow Monday?"

"Yeh, washday."

"Nuns don't do the wash no more, Rick. I mean school. I
got two kids in Catholic school. Suppose she was one of the
nuns that taught my kids. I mean, even if she ain't, it's sa-
croligious."

"She isn't for real, Georgie. Cool it."

"I can't. I mean, I don't know. Even if she's a guy and
masquerading like a nun, I don't like it. There ought to be
a law."

"Well, there ain't. There's too many laws as there is."

"Let's follow them."

"I thought that's what we've been doing all along, Georgie. You sure we oughtn't to let them alone? They're only
gays, Georgie. Who cares how they're dressed?"

Suddenly Sister Secret and Catherine stopped and turned
directly in the path of the two rookie cops and began questioning them.

"Officers," said Sister, "have you had a report of a missing boy wearing a yellow cap and a green suit?"

"No, not that we know of," Georgie Mathews replied, after nearly a whole minute's hesitation.

"Turn on your radios, please. The two of them," Catherine ordered.

The cops did as they were told, their young mouths hanging open.

"I can't make a thing out of all that noise," Sister complained. "Can't you make it clearer? The reception is terrible."

"It's the traffic, Sister," Rick Sanbrucci replied in an apologetic sort of way, which brought a smile to his lips when he realized how he was acting. He was acting as if he was back in school again. "What's the boy look like, Sister?" he asked.

"An angel," Sister replied without a hint of a smile, and as if Forty-second Street was pasture land and the stars overhead could be seen shining. "A black angel," Sister continued. "You'd remember him if you saw him. Everybody does. You see...he's a genius."

"A genius, a black angel. That shouldn't be hard to find on Forty-second Street," said Georgie. "We're always meetin' geniuses, ain't we, Rick?"

Rick Sanbrucci shook his head reluctantly no.

"No, we don't, Sister," Rick said. "It's like you say: if we did, we'd know him right off."

"Turn on your radios," Catherine commanded. "He might come up on your radios. We've got to get back to our van. We're parked bad."

"You got a van too?" Georgie asked in a taunting way that was wasted on the nun and her companion.

"Take our address, and take our telephone," the nun ordered, and the rookies wrote.

"We can't stay where we are. We're parked bad," Catherine repeated, hurrying her companion away towards Eighth Avenue past the old Apollo Theatre.

"I know what we saw there. It was called *Les Enfants du Paradis,* and it was about actors, how childish and flamboyant they are. Just think, Catherine, that was years ago, and now I'm back on Forty-second Street again. Do you think we'll find him, Catherine? I do. I know. He'll find us."

"That's it," said Catherine. "He'll find us. He'd never let us down. That's Robert's trouble. He can't seem to let anybody go, Robert, not even his awful mother."

"But he has let her go, only he doesn't know he has, Catherine."

He was asleep in Father Synge's lap and Mrs. Wallop sat beside them, all three enjoying the air on the top step of the Shelter, when Catherine and Sister Secret drove up.

"He came home himself. God knows how he did it," said Mrs. Wallop.

"Why," said Sister, "because he wanted to, Mrs. Wallop."

They were about to go indoors when still another car drove up and came to a halt before the Shelter, only from this one it was Mrs. Devereaux who emerged, shouting. When Robert heard his mother he stirred unhappily in Father Synge's arms.

"I'm coming, Mama. Don't shout. There's no reason to shout."

"Hark to 'im fine talkin'. Don' yawl fine talk me, niggah! Get yoh ass in this cah, yawl heah?"

"Well, John, I guess she's got him from us for sure this time," said Sister.

"No, she hasn't," was Father Synge's reply to that.

"John, give him up. It's a losing battle. She's stronger than we are. Besides, she has the law on her side."

"I knew this would happen!" Catherine Lepore cried, stamping her feet on the brownstone step of the Shelter. "I knew she'd win. The bad always do."

Father Synge rose with the boy in his arms and went down the steps of the Shelter, Robert clutching him desperately around his neck.

"Father Sing, don't give me up. But if you have to, don't forget me. Promise," the boy whispered, adding that when he grew up, he'd be back. "I'll be big enough then to do what I want and learn all I have to. I'll take you everywhere with me. Let me down now."

"Never."

Father Synge stopped before Mrs. Devereaux, who backed away from him. "You're not getting Robert, Mrs. Devereaux," he said. "What would you do with him if we did give him up to you, but leave him night after night, and beat him when you'd been drinking? You only want Robert some

of the time, not all of the time, as we do at the Shelter. Go
to court, if you like. I'm willing to fight you there. And fight
you I shall. Don't try to answer me. Go home and sober up.
Robert will soon be of an age where he himself will decide
between us, what kind of a life he wants for himself. He is
learning-hungry. He has been stung with the itch to know.
You can't beat that. Why do you think he made his way from
you and your lover tonight? He knows of something better,
of another country than Forty-second Street."

"Who's talkin' Forty-second Street? You is talkin' that
street, not me," the big woman managed to reply at last.
"I'se tired of yawl," she cried, turning her back and waving
the Shelter and everything it represented away from her,
"tired of mah boy. Jus' tired. Gawd knows Ah did not mean
to do wrong."

"I'm comin'. Don' cry, Mama," Robert said to her from
Father Synge's arms, but he remained where he was all the
same, and so did Mrs. Devereaux. They were joined in a
way that nothing either would ever do would put them asun-
der. They were not to see one another again for a long time.
Robert would always be divided in his loyalties about her.
He would grow, she would rot. It was either that or the boy
rotting with her.

Chapter 50

The weather began to be burning hot in New York even though it was still only May, and I felt I was smothering in it. Two houses in Sagaponack where we could have doors open and hear birds and the singing surf, instead of this confounded noise of air-conditioners. Hoping to give me a good night's sleep, Truman slept in the narrow bed in the next room under a huge parrot hanging in the window overlooking the United Nations Park. I slept well, but was awakened at six a.m. by the night concierge holding Truman, bare-legged, barefooted, by the hand. He had wandered out of the apartment and twenty-two floors downstairs into the lobby in just his shorts. Later on he said something about me going to Ireland for ten days. This was because I'd said I might go to Galway. His attitude set me back—as if my every move depended on him, and I guess it does. He suggested we take the Hampton Jitney to Sagaponack. He will make the arrangements. *The Murderous McLaughlins,* my new book, would benefit from a trip to Ireland: "the kindest place I've never been/the greenest place I've never seen." Besides, I'm restless from the top of my head to the tips of my toes. My life is held together by chocolate bars.

No reservations were made for seats on the Jitney, Truman being bombed on pills. I've changed his shorts three times, washed out three pairs of them. At early mass at the Holy Family we were told that we all have a vocation to help others. The priest, a cadaverous-looking fellow (Lon Chaney in *Phantom of the Opera*), said how in walking through the Upper East Side he looks up at the high rises and wonders "what people must be wanting up there." Well, I could have told him what Truman wanted: two eggs. I had prepared them for him before going to mass. The East River was blue and unmarked. Lights gleamed in the dawn like yellow diamonds. A bus stole up First Avenue like a toy under a Christmas tree. The buildings had a whispering air about them, like ruins.

Later on in the day, after the Presbyterian Hospital took Truman in, I went out to Sagaponack by train with a heavy heart. He called me as soon as I reached the house, which was sometime in the late afternoon, promising to be out of the hospital by tomorrow (he always said that) and vowing to quit drugs (that too).

Chapter 51

I was happy to be on time for the lilac. I remembered what Truman had said about lilac one wet May day when every bush dripped and birds were cranky. I remember remarking that this was the end of the lilac, and how I liked everything about it—the shape of its leaves, its color, its scent. "Especially its name," Truman had said. The house was clean, my Mustang worked, the wind was coming from the sea, and I could still smell the lilac.

The light on the water was so proud the next morning that I sang out at the sight, as I quite frequently do on coming to the beach, the opening notes of the aria made famous by Caruso from Meyerbeer's opera *L'Africaine*, "O paradiso...," the opening notes being all I know. And though the water was still cold, I went in. Few people swim in the ocean nowadays. In, out. Dip, dry, the towel being an indispensable accessory in this accessory-ridden age. I have never carried towels to the beach, maybe because I learned to swim in the swimmies, where a towel would have been considered outré.

The swimmies let you in every hour for half an hour, the price of admission being your own desire to wallow in sweet water with a hoard of your own kind. Municipally owned and run, the swimmies were surrounded by a high brick wall and were roofless. Bathing trunks were required of us, though I don't see why, since there was a boys' day and girls' day at the swimmies. After lining up outside in the street,

we were let into a long shed before being permitted a rush
to lockers. These were closed wooden stalls inviting intimacy. The pool was packed. Everybody's aim being to swim
in deep water, it was in eight feet that congestion was fierc-
est. Few knew how to swim. What one did was to leap into
deep water and die a minute before surfacing and grabbing
for the wall.

But there is so much more to swimming in the ocean. No
matter how far you go, there's always the horizon miles and
miles ahead of you. In today's morbid search for security,
pools naturally take precedence over the sea and its un-
predictability. But perhaps men were never meant to go to
sea, since everything about it puts a sensible man off—its
storms, its mountainous waves, its rock and roll, the way it
pitches, its floods; even its calms are often sinister, especially after it has gorged itself on miles of innocent shore-
line. I love it, but I'm afraid of it. It calls me in spite of myself. What's more, I feel I need it, that I'd die without it,
having been born two steps from it. So that when the wind
changes and gives me the fumes of petrol instead of the
mackerel smell of the sea, the whine of motor cars instead
of the chug of fishing boats, the clink and stink of cultiva-
tion in lieu of the wash of pebbles on the beach—then I feel
captive and must make a run for it, back down to the sea.

I was glad to see a light in Truman's house when I came
home from a walk one evening. He was in good condition
and told me he never wanted to see the inside of a hospital
again.

"Come have supper with me, Truman."

"No, I have these assignments, deadlines on both of them,
and I want to go to bed and get up early and work."

He left early next morning and was not home by evening.
And even though it was still light, I worried because he was
out in the Mustang and the Fourth was a few days away,
which meant that cops and storekeepers were revving up
for arrests and profits.

He called me at last, but from a police station in Hampton
Bays, telling me the police had the keys to my Mustang. They
kept Truman in jail all night and were rude to me when I

tried to get him out. He was freed next a.m. on his own re-
cognizance, trial set two weeks from then. Truman was
charged with drunken driving, driving without a license,
driving on the wrong side of the road. I picked him up outside Saks in Southampton after the court let him go. He was
relieved to see the old Mustang ('68) still by the side of the
road outside the Bridgehampton golf course where the cops
made him leave it the night before.

He was pretty upset and asked me to drive him to Southampton Hospital. Unhappy with my constant berating of him,
he indicated a manuscript on the front seat between us. "You
say I don't work," he announced with premeditated sud-
denness. "Look what I've done." I had not seen the manuscript before and doubted it was, though I certainly wished
to God that it was. He then confessed that it wasn't his, but
that it had been given him to read. I was hurt that he lied
about his work. I thought we shared things like that, that
we helped one another, advised and confided in no one else,
really, but one another. So I blasted him. I said I was glad
I had not asked him to write an introduction to *First Wine.*
I said I did not want to read another word of his, that I didn't
care if he read what I wrote or not. After I left him off at the
Southampton Hospital and came home, I kicked the phone
off the hook, not wanting to hear from him or his curious
friends.

Torrents of rain fell. I felt everything was being taken from
me. I was reminded of when I came home from the war
and realized Peach had cheated as soon as I saw her, and
that she was mortally afraid of my return, perhaps even
wishing me dead, who knows?

"Don't be afraid, Peach," were the first words I spoke to
her.

I had not planned them as I went backstage to see her
after being more than three years away. She was starring
in a New York musical show on Broadway. I caught the show
before I went back. She looked the same. I was in uniform.
More than anything I longed to reassure her that we would
work out together again, but she was too proud of her in-
fidelity to me to desire that.

"Don't be afraid."

I knew more about her than I realized I did. It would be baloney to deny we had idealized one another; all young lovers do, of any intelligence and ambition, and both of us were ambitious, she more than I, perhaps.

PEACH

I saw you this morning. I was still in bed. You looked like a Renoir that had run, under a hat full of poppies John Fredericks made for you. That was a happy time, at least on the surface. Underneath you may have been thinking of quitting me; if you were, I'm glad you waited, since it's given me more time to look back on. If only I could get some of the happiness into the story of my return. Maybe if I went up to the Cape? But we weren't happy there, not the last time. The last time we were up on the Cape I thought of killing you. Something outside of me, but close to me, wanted me to pick up a hammer that was there in a closet in the room on the wharf we rented and kill you. I was outraged at the "thing" telling me what to do, yet I saw myself carrying out its orders.

"Don't be afraid," I had said. I might have added, "I will die easy," as Keats did to his friend Severn as he lay dying. But I did not die except for a little, maybe. Something went out of me that was not to come back—an implicit trust, perhaps, an openness. I would *act* more now, giving cause for Truman's description of me in the years ahead as a great actor.

Chapter 52

Truman was in and out of Southampton Hospital most of that summer. I worked. I swam. I sailed on Mecox Bay. The rock pools in the jetties down beyond Georgica Pond reminded me of when we used to snorkle in Sicily. They are full of life, but superficially seen they appear to consist of nothing but rocks imbedded in sand over which sea waves break. The rocks are so camouflaged that sometimes gulls and sandpipers who light on them are able to conceal themselves. Barnacles, mussels, and sea-moss cover parts of the rocks. The mussels are particularly enchanting the way they gleam, making of their habitation one big dark blue jewel. This world of rock, shellfish, and vegetation is a predator's paradise. While they cling rent-free to the rocks, devouring what comes their way, the barnacles, the mussels, and the sea-moss and other vegetation go unharmed for the most part until the rock pools dry up. Without the help of salt water the scant roots of the vegetation embracing the rocks shrivel and die; life within the barnacles withers, and the little shells crumble into powder; mussels lose their oily-looking deep blue color. But while they are washed by the sea and warmed by the sun, the rock pools thrive. Even on grey days they are vivid, the sea-moss being particularly green then, and the rocks extra black.

One morning I grew so lost in studying the rock pools that when I thought of Truman, it was as if someone had shouted in my ear, *"How is he?"* Nothing would do but that I must beg the use of the telephone of strangers who had a beach house nearby. They were two men, brothers I guess, and both had short beards. I forgot them when upon calling Southampton Hospital I was told that Truman was not there. This was astounding news, and it upset me dreadfully, especially so since I could get no more information than the barest sort from the telephone operator at the hospital.

My obviously reluctant hosts surveyed me from a doorway so I would not steal anything. Relatives watched me as

well, gibbeted from the walls, their likenesses done in to-
matoes, mud, and cantaloupe seeds, it seemed to me. A pair
of cracked china cats watched me too. I was in bare feet
and wore only my ragged red shorts. "I would like to pay
you for this call," I said.

"No," the littler man of the pair told me, wanting more
than anything to get rid of me, "that's perfectly all right.
Now, we're going somewhere, and we're sure you have
things you must do, so...."

Once they got me out they waved and carried on like mad,
almost as if they were close to tears at my departure. Somehow their craziness made me feel Truman was all right and
that he probably would be home when I got there. But he
wasn't. I called Southampton Hospital again to make sure
they had not made a mistake. No, Mr. Capote had left. When?
Why, early this morning. Finally Truman called me from
the apartment in New York to tell me he had run away from
the hospital after a nurse, having given him a mauvaise pi-
qûre, refused him a pain killer.

"Happy birthday, Truman," I told him, after commiser-
ating with him.

"Oh yes," he said, "what with all that's happened, I forgot
it's your birthday. Happy birthday."

I had almost forgotten myself.

"How's the weather out there?" he asked.

"Wonderful, Truman. I've already been in the water this
morning."

"Take a swim for me."

"I will. When are you coming out?"

"In a few days. I have to be in Southampton for my trial.
What a bore."

"I know it is, Truman. But behave yourself and see that
you make it."

"Why wouldn't I make it? Of course I'll make it."

I went into the water I don't know how many times that
day. The wind had shifted from southwest to southeast, because I heard the builders over by Town Line Road, one of
whom, a kid, removed his bathing suit this morning quite
close to people and took a short swim before either going to

work or returning to it. He dried himself with the inevitable towel, slipped back into his trunks, zipped up, and was off, combing his hair as he went. Just before he disappeared over the summit of the dune he looked over his right shoulder at me.

Truman telephoned after he stood trial in Southampton. He said he had been put on probation, and that the judge gave him a bawling out for appearing in court in shorts. Now he says he's a prisoner over in his house here in Sagaponack. "I want to go home," says he. Well, he hates it over there, everything about it, and he used to like it so much. Now he cannot bear to live in it and scarcely does, except with the tips of his fingers. He caught a ride from Sagaponack into New York the next day and called me from the apartment to complain of depression.

"It's not good for me to be in town by myself."

The next I heard from him he was in California. I was in bed reading Somerset Maugham stories Truman had given me when he called. We talked about them, the stories mainly, one we both liked, about an opera singer, called "The Voice of the Turtle."

"It made me think of what Willa Cather did with her singer in *The Song of the Lark*, Truman."

"I don't like *Song of the Lark*," he said.

We agreed that Maugham was an entertaining writer.

"Underrated," I thought.

"Very underrated. I agree with you."

The call—the conversation, the way I felt about it, the way Truman sounded—was like an echo of our past. In talking about writing in our old way, we opened doors to apartments that I could have sworn were shut and locked to us now; I discovered that they had always been open, the doors unlocked, all we had to do was try them. I was pleased when the telephone rang again much later on, but when I got downstairs it stopped ringing, and I heard a car outside. It was Father Synge.

"I thought it was Truman," I blurted out to him, not thinking.

"You thought I was Truman?"

"No, I mean on the telephone just now. But when I got downstairs it stopped ringing. I don't suppose it was him. He never calls late. People often call here in the middle of the night wanting someplace called Kismet."

"Kismet is the Arabic word for fate."

"I know it is. It's probably a social club up on the island with a number rather like mine."

"Don't you have a radio?"

"No. Why? Should I?"

Father Synge got out of his car and went before me to my house without answering. He sniffed loudly as he passed under the heavily laden trellis.

"They are grapes you smell, Father."

"I remember you have a Concord grapevine."

"Raccoons come at night now and feast on them. I hear them from my bed. Go in. There are no more animals inside as there used to be, though you seldom mentioned them."

"I didn't? I'm sorry."

When we got into the house, I looked at the telephone wishing it would ring; but even if it did, it wouldn't be Truman. He never called late.

"Let me give you a cup of tea, Father. Did you drive from Brooklyn? Or did you have business on the North Shore?"

"I drove from Brooklyn."

He looked to me as if he had come to say good-bye. His good-byes had occurred so frequently in the past that I had come to disbelieve in their reality. Unless this time he meant it. He sat down in Truman's chair by the window. Maybe the telephone would ring again and it would be Truman, even if it was late, and cut Father Synge's good-bye short if it was good-bye. I wanted the "echo" of old times with Truman back again, when I felt protected, safe, cared for, listened to, loved, wanted, praised, embowered, tunneled, secure. I gave Father Synge his tea. He drank it, put down the cup on the little yellow table alongside Truman's chair that I had bought for him when we first came to Sagaponack.

"I got that table for you, Truman."

"I know you did."

I don't know why I remembered that as Father Synge was leaving without telling me why he had come to see me in the first place. I did, though, and it speared me, a little, innocuous thing like that. Father Synge was leaving for good. Why? Why had he wanted to know if I had a radio? Why was he acting as if he knew something that I didn't know? Well, he had always been like that. It's a priestly failing, I guess.

Because of the "echo" I felt happy, I felt hilarious. Nothing in Father Synge's air of righteousness nudged me to be wary. He was acting like a subordinate actor taking his bow at the end of a play, careful not to push himself forward, aware that he had not been the whole cheese.

Our way had never been to be cautious. The "echo" had made me proud, vainglorious. I guessed what Father Synge could not bring himself to tell me, but I wasn't afraid. I wasn't afraid, and I was not wary, but I was grieving. I was grieving the way the earth seems to grieve for spring in the dead of winter, but I wasn't afraid, because nothing, I told myself, can take our halcyon days away. Kelly, his coat sunrusted, regarded me from the old rowboat as I gave the oars to Truman and took my turn snorkling in the blue water in the shadow of the green Sicilian rocks. Splash! and my heart broke. Splash! it broke again. It broke as I followed Father Synge out of the house. Breaking breaking breaking. The grapes had no scent. Crickets stopped singing. It was only still. Nor could our sea be heard. My feelings of deprivation mounted to where I felt I had no heart left me, but I wasn't afraid. The dirty north wind brought the smell of other people, no wildness in the air. The taillights of Father Synge's car turned out of the drive. I was enclosed in darkness.

5 July '72

Darling Jack—

I finished the Hazlitt book,
and fell asleep, and woke up with
such a feeling of warmth and gratitude
and love for you. You are the only
good thing that ever happened to me.
I admire and respect you so. I think
that is more important perhaps than loving
you. You ~~can~~ can love for such
shallow and wrong reasons. I love you
for the right ones.

T.

P.S. This isn't your birthday present. I just want you
to have it now.

Index